BLACK BOY

By Richard Wright

UNCLE TOM'S CHILDREN (available in a Perennial edition)

NATIVE SON (available in a Perennial edition)

BRIGHT AND MORNING STAR

TWELVE MILLION BLACK VOICES

BLACK BOY

BLACK BOY (essay in *The God That Failed*)

THE OUTSIDER (available in a Perennial edition)

BLACK POWER

SAVAGE HOLIDAY

THE COLOR CURTAIN: A REPORT ON THE BANDUNG CONFERENCE

PAGAN SPAIN

WHITE MAN, LISTEN!

THE LONG DREAM

EIGHT MEN

LAWD TODAY

BLACK BOY

A Record of Childhood and Youth

by Richard Wright

A Perennial Classic
Harper & Row, Publishers
New York, Hagerstown
San Francisco, London

80 81 82 30 29 28 27 26 25 24 23

For ELLEN *and* JULIA
who live always in my heart

They meet with darkness in the daytime
And they grope at noonday as in the night . . .

—JOB

Introductory Note

More than eighty-five years ago, Oliver Wendell Holmes nobly said: "It is so much easier to consign a soul to perdition or to say prayers to save it, than to take the blame on ourselves for letting it grow up in neglect and run to ruin. The English law began, only in the late eighteenth century, to get hold of the idea that crime is not necessarily a sin. The limitations of human responsibility have never been properly studied."

If Dr. Holmes were alive now, he would be proud, as I am proud, of the chance to help bring to the thoughtful attention of intelligent, morally responsible Americans, the honest, dreadful, heart-breaking story of a Negro childhood and youth, as set down by that rarely gifted American author, Richard Wright.

DOROTHY CANFIELD FISHER

Arlington, Vermont

Chapter One

ONE winter morning in the long-ago, four-year-old days of my life I found myself standing before a fireplace, warming my hands over a mound of glowing coals, listening to the wind whistle past the house outside. All morning my mother had been scolding me, telling me to keep still, warning me that I must make no noise. And I was angry, fretful, and impatient. In the next room Granny lay ill and under the day and night care of a doctor and I knew that I would be punished if I did not obey. I crossed restlessly to the window and pushed back the long fluffy white curtains—which I had been forbidden to touch—and looked yearningly out into the empty street. I was dreaming of running and playing and shouting, but the vivid image of Granny's old, white, wrinkled, grim face, framed by a halo of tumbling black hair, lying upon a huge feather pillow, made me afraid

The house was quiet. Behind me my brother— a year younger than I— was playing placidly upon the floor with a toy. A bird wheeled past the window and I greeted it with a glad shout.

"You better hush," my brother said.

"You shut up," I said.

My mother stepped briskly into the room and closed the door behind her. She came to me and shook her finger in my face.

"You stop that yelling, you hear?" she whispered. "You know Granny's sick and you better keep quiet!"

I hung my head and sulked. She left and I ached with boredom.

"I told you so," my brother gloated.

"You shut up," I told him again.

I wandered listlessly about the room, trying to think of something to do, dreading the return of my mother, resentful of being neglected. The room held nothing of interest except the fire and finally I stood before the shimmering embers, fascinated by the quivering coals. An idea of a new kind of game grew and took root in my mind. Why not throw something into the fire and watch it burn? I looked about. There was only my picture book and my mother would beat me if I burned that. Then what? I hunted around until I saw the broom leaning in a closet. That's it . . . Who would bother about a few straws if I burned them? I pulled out the broom and tore out a batch of straws and tossed them into the fire and watched them smoke, turn black, blaze, and finally become white wisps of ghosts that vanished. Burning straws was a teasing kind of fun and I took more of them from the broom and cast them into the fire. My brother came to my side, his eyes drawn by the blazing straws.

"Don't do that," he said.

"How come?" I asked.

"You'll burn the whole broom," he said.

"You hush," I said.

"I'll tell," he said.

"And I'll hit you," I said.

My idea was growing, blooming. Now I was wondering just how the long fluffy white curtains would look if I lit a bunch of straws and held it under them. Would I try it? Sure. I pulled several straws from the broom and held them to the fire until they blazed; I rushed to the window and brought the flame in touch with the hems of the curtains. My brother shook his head.

"Naw," he said.

He spoke too late. Red circles were eating into the white cloth; then a flare of flames shot out. Startled,

I backed away. The fire soared to the ceiling and I trembled with fright. Soon a sheet of yellow lit the room. I was terrified; I wanted to scream but was afraid. I looked around for my brother; he was gone. One half of the room was now ablaze. Smoke was choking me and the fire was licking at my face, making me gasp.

I made for the kitchen; smoke was surging there too. Soon my mother would smell that smoke and see the fire and come and beat me. I had done something wrong, something which I could not hide or deny. Yes, I would run away and never come back. I ran out of the kitchen and into the back yard. Where could I go? Yes, under the house! Nobody would find me there. I crawled under the house and crept into a dark hollow of a brick chimney and balled myself into a tight knot. My mother must not find me and whip me for what I had done. Anyway, it was all an accident; I had not really intended to set the house afire. I had just wanted to see how the curtains would look when they burned. And neither did it occur to me that I was hiding under a burning house.

Presently footsteps pounded on the floor above me. Then I heard screams. Later the gongs of fire wagons and the clopping hoofs of horses came from the direction of the street. Yes, there was really a fire, a fire like the one I had seen one day burn a house down to the ground, leaving only a chimney standing black. I was stiff with terror. The thunder of sound above me shook the chimney to which I clung. The screams came louder. I saw the image of my grandmother lying helplessly upon her bed and there were yellow flames in her black hair. Was my mother afire? Would my brother burn? Perhaps everybody in the house would burn! Why had I not thought of those things before I fired the curtains? I yearned to become invisible, to stop living. The commotion above me increased and I began to cry. It seemed that I had been hiding for ages, and when the stomping and screaming died down

I felt lonely, cast forever out of life. Voices sounded near-by and I shivered.

"Richard!" my mother was calling frantically.

I saw her legs and the hem of her dress moving swiftly about the back yard. Her wails were full of an agony whose intensity told me that my punishment would be measured by its depth. Then I saw her taut face peering under the edge of the house. She had found me! I held my breath and waited to hear her command me to come to her. Her face went away; no, she had not seen me huddled in the dark nook of the chimney. I tucked my head into my arms and my teeth chattered.

"Richard!"

The distress I sensed in her voice was as sharp and painful as the lash of a whip on my flesh.

"Richard! The house is on fire. Oh, find my child!"

Yes, the house was afire, but I was determined not to leave my place of safety. Finally I saw another face peering under the edge of the house; it was my father's. His eyes must have become accustomed to the shadows, for he was now pointing at me.

"There he is!"

"Naw!" I screamed.

"Come here, boy!"

"Naw!"

"The house is on fire!"

"Leave me 'lone!"

He crawled to me and caught hold of one of my legs. I hugged the edge of the brick chimney with all of my strength. My father yanked my leg and I clawed at the chimney harder.

"Come outta there, you little fool!"

"Turn me loose!"

I could not withstand the tugging at my leg and my fingers relaxed. It was over. I would be beaten. I did not care any more. I knew what was coming. He dragged me into the back yard and the instant his hand left me I jumped to my feet and broke into a wild run, trying to elude the people who surrounded me, heading for the street. I was caught before I had gone ten paces.

From that moment on things became tangled for me. Out of the weeping and the shouting and the wild talk, I learned that no one had died in the fire. My brother, it seemed, had finally overcome enough of his panic to warn my mother, but not before more than half the house had been destroyed. Using the mattress as a stretcher, Grandpa and an uncle had lifted Granny from her bed and had rushed her to the safety of a neighbor's house. My long absence and silence had made everyone think, for a while, that I had perished in the blaze.

"You almost scared us to death," my mother muttered as she stripped the leaves from a tree limb to prepare it for my back.

I was lashed so hard and long that I lost consciousness. I was beaten out of my senses and later I found myself in bed, screaming, determined to run away, tussling with my mother and father who were trying to keep me still. I was lost in a fog of fear. A doctor was called—I was afterwards told—and he ordered that I be kept abed, that I be kept quiet, that my very life depended upon it. My body seemed on fire and I could not sleep. Packs of ice were put on my forehead to keep down the fever. Whenever I tried to sleep I would see huge wobbly white bags, like the full udders of cows, suspended from the ceiling above me. Later, as I grew worse, I could see the bags in the daytime with my eyes open and I was gripped by the fear that they were going to fall and drench me with some horrible liquid. Day and night I begged my mother and father to take the bags away, pointing to them, shaking with terror because no one saw them but me. Exhaustion would make me drift toward sleep and then I would scream until I was wide awake again; I was afraid to sleep. Time finally bore me away from the dangerous bags and I got well. But for a long time I was chastened whenever I remembered that my mother had come close to killing me.

Each event spoke with a cryptic tongue. And the moments of living slowly revealed their coded meanings. There was the wonder I felt when I first saw a brace of mountainlike, spotted, black-and-white horses clopping down a dusty road through clouds of powdered clay.

There was the delight I caught in seeing long straight rows of red and green vegetables stretching away in the sun to the bright horizon.

There was the faint, cool kiss of sensuality when dew came on to my cheeks and shins as I ran down the wet green garden paths in the early morning.

There was the vague sense of the infinite as I looked down upon the yellow, dreaming waters of the Mississippi River from the verdant bluffs of Natchez.

There were the echoes of nostalgia I heard in the crying strings of wild geese winging south against a bleak, autumn sky.

There was the tantalizing melancholy in the tingling scent of burning hickory wood.

There was the teasing and impossible desire to imitate the petty pride of sparrows wallowing and flouncing in the red dust of country roads.

There was the yearning for identification loosed in me by the sight of a solitary ant carrying a burden upon a mysterious journey.

There was the disdain that filled me as I tortured a delicate, blue-pink crawfish that huddled fearfully in the mudsill of a rusty tin can.

There was the aching glory in masses of clouds burning gold and purple from an invisible sun.

There was the liquid alarm I saw in the blood-red glare of the sun's afterglow mirrored in the squared panes of whitewashed frame houses.

There was the languor I felt when I heard green leaves rustling with a rainlike sound.

There was the incomprehensible secret embodied in a whitish toadstool hiding in the dark shade of a rotting log.

There was the experience of feeling death without

dying that came from watching a chicken leap about blindly after its neck had been snapped by a quick twist of my father's wrist.

There was the great joke that I felt God had played on cats and dogs by making them lap their milk and water with their tongues.

There was the thirst I had when I watched clear, sweet juice trickle from sugar cane being crushed.

There was the hot panic that welled up in my throat and swept through my blood when I first saw the lazy, limp coils of a blue-skinned snake sleeping in the sun.

There was the speechless astonishment of seeing a hog stabbed through the heart, dipped into boiling water, scraped, split open, gutted, and strung up gaping and bloody.

There was the love I had for the mute regality of tall, moss-clad oaks.

There was the hint of cosmic cruelty that I felt when I saw the curved timbers of a wooden shack that had been warped in the summer sun.

There was the saliva that formed in my mouth whenever I smelt clay dust potted with fresh rain.

There was the cloudy notion of hunger when I breathed the odor of new-cut, bleeding grass.

And there was the quiet terror that suffused my senses when vast hazes of gold washed earthward from star-heavy skies on silent nights . . .

One day my mother told me that we were going to Memphis on a boat, the *Kate Adams*, and my eagerness thereafter made the days seem endless. Each night I went to bed hoping that the next morning would be the day of departure.

"How big is the boat?" I asked my mother.

"As big as a mountain," she said.

"Has it got a whistle?"

"Yes."

"Does the whistle blow?"

"Yes."

"When?"

"When the captain wants it to blow."

"Why do they call it the *Kate Adams*?"

"Because that's the boat's name."

"What color is the boat?"

"White."

"How long will we be on the boat?"

"All day and all night."

"Will we sleep on the boat?"

"Yes, when we get sleepy, we'll sleep. Now, hush."

For days I had dreamed about a huge white boat floating on a vast body of water, but when my mother took me down to the levee on the day of leaving, I saw a tiny, dirty boat that was not at all like the boat I had imagined. I was disappointed and when time came to go on board I cried and my mother thought that I did not want to go with her to Memphis, and I could not tell her what the trouble was. Solace came when I wandered about the boat and gazed at Negroes throwing dice, drinking whisky, playing cards, lolling on boxes, eating, talking, and singing. My father took me down into the engine room and the throbbing machines enthralled me for hours.

In Memphis we lived in a one-story brick tenement. The stone buildings and the concrete pavements looked bleak and hostile to me. The absence of green, growing things made the city seem dead. Living space for the four of us—my mother, my brother, my father, and me—was a kitchen and a bedroom. In the front and rear were paved areas in which my brother and I could play, but for days I was afraid to go into the strange city streets alone.

It was in this tenement that the personality of my father first came fully into the orbit of my concern. He worked as a night porter in a Beale Street drugstore and he became important and forbidding to me only when I learned that I could not make noise when he was asleep in the daytime. He was the lawgiver in our family and I never laughed in his presence. I used to lurk timidly in the kitchen doorway and watch his huge body sitting slumped at the table. I stared at him with awe as he gulped his beer from a tin bucket, as he ate long and heavily, sighed, belched, closed his eyes to nod on a stuffed belly. He was quite fat and his bloated stomach always lapped over his belt. He was always a stranger to me, always somehow alien and remote.

One morning my brother and I, while playing in the rear of our flat, found a stray kitten that set up a loud, persistent meowing. We fed it some scraps of food and gave it water, but it still meowed. My father, clad in his underwear, stumbled sleepily to the back door and demanded that we keep quiet. We told him that it was the kitten that was making the noise and he ordered us to drive it away. We tried to make the kitten leave, but it would not budge. My father took a hand.

"Scat!" he shouted.

The scrawny kitten lingered, brushing itself against our legs, and meowing plaintively.

"Kill that damn thing!" my father exploded. "Do anything, but get it away from here!"

He went inside, grumbling. I resented his shouting and it irked me that I could never make him feel my resentment. How could I hit back at him? Oh, yes . . . He had said to kill the kitten and I would kill it! I knew that he had not really meant for me to kill the kitten, but my deep hate of him urged me toward a literal acceptance of his word.

"He said for us to kill the kitten," I told my brother.

"He didn't mean it," my brother said.

"He did, and I'm going to kill 'im."

"Then he *will* howl," my brother said.

"He can't howl if he's dead," I said.

"He didn't really say kill 'im," my brother protested.

"He did!" I said. "And you heard him!"

My brother ran away in fright. I found a piece of rope, made a noose, slipped it about the kitten's neck, pulled it over a nail, then jerked the animal clear of the ground. It gasped, slobbered, spun, doubled, clawed the air frantically; finally its mouth gaped and its pink-white tongue shot out stiffly. I tied the rope to a nail and went to find my brother. He was crouching behind a corner of the building.

"I killed 'im," I whispered.

"You did bad," my brother said.

"Now Papa can sleep," I said, deeply satisfied.

"He didn't mean for you to kill 'im," my brother said.

"Then why did he *tell* me to do it?" I demanded.

My brother could not answer; he stared fearfully at the dangling kitten.

"That kitten's going to get you," he warned me.

"That kitten can't even breathe now," I said.

"I'm going to tell," my brother said, running into the house.

I waited, resolving to defend myself with my father's rash words, anticipating my enjoyment in repeating them to him even though I knew that he had spoken them in anger. My mother hurried toward me, drying her hands upon her apron. She stopped and paled when she saw the kitten suspended from the rope.

"What in God's name have you done?" she asked.

"The kitten was making noise and Papa said to kill it," I explained.

"You little fool!" she said. "Your father's going to beat you for this!"

"But he told me to kill it," I said.

"You shut your mouth!"

She grabbed my hand and dragged me to my father's bedside and told him what I had done.

"You know better than that!" my father stormed.

"You told me to kill 'im," I said.

"I told you to drive him away," he said.

"You told me to kill 'im," I countered positively.

"You get out of my eyes before I smack you down!" my father bellowed in disgust, then turned over in bed.

I had had my first triumph over my father. I had made him believe that I had taken his words literally.

He could not punish me now without risking his authority. I was happy because I had at last found a way to throw my criticism of him into his face. I had made him feel that, if he whipped me for killing the kitten, I would never give serious weight to his words again. I had made him know that I felt he was cruel and I had done it without his punishing me.

But my mother, being more imaginative, retaliated with an assault upon my sensibilities that crushed me with the moral horror involved in taking a life. All that afternoon she directed toward me calculated words that spawned in my mind a horde of invisible demons bent upon exacting vengeance for what I had done. As evening drew near, anxiety filled me and I was afraid to go into an empty room alone.

"You owe a debt you can never pay," my mother said.

"I'm sorry," I mumbled.

"Being sorry can't make that kitten live again," she said.

Then, just before I was to go to bed, she uttered a paralyzing injunction: she ordered me to go out into the dark, dig a grave, and bury the kitten.

"No!" I screamed, feeling that if I went out of doors some evil spirit would whisk me away.

"Get out there and bury that poor kitten," she ordered.

"I'm scared!"

"And wasn't that kitten scared when you put that rope around its neck?" she asked.

"But it was only a kitten," I explained.

"But it was alive," she said. "Can you make it live again?"

"But Papa said to kill it," I said, trying to shift the moral blame upon my father.

My mother whacked me across my mouth with the flat palm of her hand.

"You stop that lying! You knew what he meant!"

"I didn't!" I bawled.

She shoved a tiny spade into my hands.

"Go out there and dig a hole and bury that kitten!"

I stumbled out into the black night, sobbing, my legs wobbly from fear. Though I knew that I had killed the kitten, my mother's words had made it live again in my mind. What would that kitten do to me when I touched it? Would it claw at my eyes? As I groped toward the dead kitten, my mother lingered behind me, unseen in the dark, her disembodied voice egging me on.

"Mama, come and stand by me," I begged.

"You didn't stand by that kitten, so why should I stand by you?" she asked tauntingly from the menacing darkness.

"I can't touch it," I whimpered, feeling that the kitten was staring at me with reproachful eyes.

"Untie it!" she ordered.

Shuddering, I fumbled at the rope and the kitten dropped to the pavement with a thud that echoed in my mind for many days and nights. Then, obeying my mother's floating voice, I hunted for a spot of earth, dug a shallow hole, and buried the stiff kitten; as I handled its cold body my skin prickled. When I had completed the burial, I sighed and started back to the flat, but my mother caught hold of my hand and led me again to the kitten's grave.

"Shut your eyes and repeat after me," she said.

I closed my eyes tightly, my hand clinging to hers.

"Dear God, our Father, forgive me, for I knew not what I was doing . . ."

"Dear God, our Father, forgive me, for I knew not what I was doing," I repeated.

"And spare my poor life, even though I did not spare the life of the kitten . . ."

"And spare my poor life, even though I did not spare the life of the kitten," I repeated.

"And while I sleep tonight, do not snatch the breath of life from me . . ."

I opened my mouth but no words came. My mind was frozen with horror. I pictured myself gasping for breath and dying in my sleep. I broke away from my mother and ran into the night, crying, shaking with dread.

"No," I sobbed.

My mother called to me many times, but I would not go to her.

"Well, I suppose you've learned your lesson," she said at last.

Contrite, I went to bed, hoping that I would never see another kitten.

Hunger stole upon me so slowly that at first I was not aware of what hunger really meant. Hunger had always been more or less at my elbow when I played, but now I began to wake up at night to find hunger standing at my bedside, staring at me gauntly. The hunger I had known before this had been no grim, hostile stranger; it had been a normal hunger that had made me beg constantly for bread, and when I ate a crust or two I was satisfied. But this new hunger baffled me, scared me, made me angry and insistent. Whenever I begged for food now my mother would pour me a cup of tea which would still the clamor in my stomach for a moment or two; but a little later I would feel hunger nudging my ribs, twisting my empty guts until they ached. I would grow dizzy and my vision would dim. I became less active in my play, and for the first time in my life I had to pause and think of what was happening to me.

"Mama, I'm hungry," I complained one afternoon.

"Jump up and catch a kungry," she said, trying to make me laugh and forget.

"What's a *kungry?*"

"It's what little boys eat when they get hungry," she said.

"What does it taste like?"

"I don't know."

"Then why do you tell me to catch one?"

"Because you said that you were hungry," she said, smiling.

I sensed that she was teasing me and it made me angry.

"But I'm hungry. I want to eat."

"You'll have to wait."

"But I want to eat now."

"But there's nothing to eat," she told me.

"Why?"

"Just because there's none," she explained.

"But I want to eat," I said, beginning to cry.

"You'll just have to wait," she said again.

"But why?"

"For God to send some food."

"When is He going to send it?"

"I don't know."

"But I'm hungry!"

She was ironing and she paused and looked at me with tears in her eyes.

"Where's your father?" she asked me.

I stared in bewilderment. Yes, it was true that my father had not come home to sleep for many days now and I could make as much noise as I wanted. Though I had not known why he was absent, I had been glad that he was not there to shout his restrictions at me. But it had never occurred to me that his absence would mean that there would be no food.

"I don't know," I said.

"Who brings food into the house?" my mother asked me.

"Papa," I said. "He always brought food."

"Well, your father isn't here now," she said.

"Where is he?"

"I don't know," she said.

"But I'm hungry," I whimpered, stomping my feet.

"You'll have to wait until I get a job and buy food," she said.

As the days slid past the image of my father became associated with my pangs of hunger, and whenever I felt hunger I thought of him with a deep biological bitterness.

My mother finally went to work as a cook and

left me and my brother alone in the flat each day with a loaf of bread and a pot of tea. When she returned at evening she would be tired and dispirited and would cry a lot. Sometimes, when she was in despair, she would call us to her and talk to us for hours, telling us that we now had no father, that our lives would be different from those of other children, that we must learn as soon as possible to take care of ourselves, to dress ourselves, to prepare our own food; that we must take upon ourselves the responsibility of the flat while she worked. Half frightened, we would promise solemnly. We did not understand what had happened between our father and our mother and the most that these long talks did to us was to make us feel a vague dread. Whenever we asked why father had left, she would tell us that we were too young to know.

One evening my mother told me that thereafter I would have to do the shopping for food. She took me to the corner store to show me the way. I was proud; I felt like a grownup. The next afternoon I looped the basket over my arm and went down the pavement toward the store. When I reached the corner, a gang of boys grabbed me, knocked me down, snatched the basket, took the money, and sent me running home in panic. That evening I told my mother what had happened, but she made no comment; she sat down at once, wrote another note, gave me more money, and sent me out to the grocery again. I crept down the steps and saw the same gang of boys playing down the street. I ran back into the house.

"What's the matter?" my mother asked.

"It's those same boys," I said. "They'll beat me."

"You've got to get over that," she said. "Now, go on."

"I'm scared," I said.

"Go on and don't pay any attention to them," she said.

I went out of the door and walked briskly down the sidewalk, praying that the gang would not molest me. But when I came abreast of them someone shouted.

"There he is!"

They came toward me and I broke into a wild run toward home. They overtook me and flung me to the pavement. I yelled, pleaded, kicked, but they wrenched the money out of my hand. They yanked me to my feet, gave me a few slaps, and sent me home sobbing. My mother met me at the door.

"They b-beat m-me," I gasped. "They t-t-took the m-money."

I started up the steps, seeking the shelter of the house.

"Don't you come in here," my mother warned me.

I froze in my tracks and stared at her.

"But they're coming after me," I said.

"You just stay right where you are," she said in a deadly tone. "I'm going to teach you this night to stand up and fight for yourself."

She went into the house and I waited, terrified, wondering what she was about. Presently she returned with more money and another note; she also had a long heavy stick.

"Take this money, this note, and this stick," she said. "Go to the store and buy those groceries. If those boys bother you, then fight."

I was baffled. My mother was telling me to fight, a thing that she had never done before.

"But I'm scared," I said.

"Don't you come into this house until you've gotten those groceries," she said.

"They'll beat me; they'll beat me," I said.

"Then stay in the streets; don't come back here!"

I ran up the steps and tried to force my way past her into the house. A stinging slap came on my jaw. I stood on the sidewalk, crying.

"Please, let me wait until tomorrow," I begged.

"No," she said. "Go now! If you come back into this house without those groceries, I'll whip you!"

She slammed the door and I heard the key turn in the lock. I shook with fright. I was alone upon the dark, hostile streets and gangs were after me. I had the choice of being beaten at home or away from home. I clutched the stick, crying, trying to reason. If I were beaten at home, there was absolutely nothing that I could do about it; but if I were beaten in the streets, I had a chance to fight and defend myself. I walked slowly down the sidewalk, coming closer to the gang of boys, holding the stick tightly. I was so full of fear that I could scarcely breathe. I was almost upon them now.

"There he is again!" the cry went up.

They surrounded me quickly and began to grab for my hand.

"I'll kill you!" I threatened.

They closed in. In blind fear I let the stick fly, feeling it crack against a boy's skull. I swung again, lamming another skull, then another. Realizing that they would retaliate if I let up for but a second, I fought to lay them low, to knock them cold, to kill them so that they could not strike back at me. I flayed with tears in my eyes, teeth clenched, stark fear making me throw every ounce of my strength behind each blow. I hit again and again, dropping the money and the grocery list. The boys scattered, yelling, nursing their heads, staring at me in utter disbelief. They had never seen such frenzy. I stood panting, egging them on, taunting them to come on and fight. When they refused, I ran after them and they tore out for their homes, screaming. The parents of the boys rushed into the streets and threatened me, and for the first time in my life I shouted at grownups, telling them that I would give them the same if they bothered me. I finally found my grocery list and the money and went to the store. On my way back I kept my stick poised for instant use, but there was not a single boy in sight. That night I won the right to the streets of Memphis.

Of a summer morning, when my mother had gone to work, I would follow a crowd of black children—abandoned for the day by their working parents—to the bottom of a sloping hill whose top held a long row of ramshackle, wooden outdoor privies whose opened rear ends provided a raw and startling view. We would crouch at the foot of the slope and look up—a distance of twenty-five feet or more—at the secret and fantastic anatomies of black, brown, yellow, and ivory men and women. For hours we would laugh, point, whisper, joke, and identify our neighbors by the signs of their physiological oddities, commenting upon the difficulty or projectile force of their excretions. Finally some grownup would see us and drive us away with disgusted shouts. Occasionally children of two and three years of age would emerge from behind the hill with their faces smeared and their breath reeking. At last a white policeman was stationed behind the privies to keep the children away and our course in human anatomy was postponed.

To keep us out of mischief, my mother often took my brother and me with her to her cooking job. Standing hungrily and silently in a corner of the kitchen, we would watch her go from the stove to the sink, from the cabinet to the table. I always loved to stand in the white folks' kitchen when my mother cooked, for it meant that I got occasional scraps of bread and meat; but many times I regretted having come, for my nostrils would be assailed with the scent of food that did not belong to me and which I was forbidden to eat. Toward evening my mother would take the hot dishes into the dining room where the white people were seated, and I would stand as near the dining-room door as possible to get a quick glimpse of the white faces gathered around the loaded table, eating, laughing, talking. If the white people left anything, my brother and I would eat well; but if they did not, we would have our usual bread and tea.

Watching the white people eat would make my empty stomach churn and I would grow vaguely angry. Why could I not eat when I was hungry? Why did I always have to wait until others were through? I could not understand why some people had enough food and others did not.

I now found it irresistible to roam during the day

while my mother was cooking in the kitchens of the white folks. A block away from our flat was a saloon in front of which I used to loiter all day long. Its interior was an enchanting place that both lured and frightened me. I would beg for pennies, then peer under the swinging doors to watch the men and women drink. When some neighbor would chase me away from the door, I would follow the drunks about the streets, trying to understand their mysterious mumblings, pointing at them, teasing them, laughing at them, imitating them, jeering, mocking, and taunting them about their lurching antics. For me the most amusing spectacle was a drunken woman stumbling and urinating, the dampness seeping down her stockinged legs. Or I would stare in horror at a man retching. Somebody informed my mother about my fondness for the saloon and she beat me, but it did not keep me from peering under the swinging doors and listening to the wild talk of drunks when she was at work.

One summer afternoon—in my sixth year—while peering under the swinging doors of the neighborhood saloon, a black man caught hold of my arm and dragged me into its smoky and noisy depths. The odor of alcohol stung my nostrils. I yelled and struggled, trying to break free of him, afraid of the staring crowd of men and women, but he would not let me go. He lifted me and sat me upon the counter, put his hat upon my head and ordered a drink for me. The tipsy men and women yelled with delight. Somebody tried to jam a cigar into my mouth, but I twisted out of the way.

"How do you feel, setting there like a man, boy?" a man asked.

"Make 'im drunk and he'll stop peeping in here," somebody said.

"Let's buy 'im drinks," somebody said.

Some of my fright left as I stared about. Whisky was set before me.

"Drink it, boy," somebody said.

I shook my head. The man who had dragged me in

urged me to drink it, telling me that it would not hurt me. I refused.

"Drink it; it'll make you feel good," he said.

I took a sip and coughed. The men and women laughed. The entire crowd in the saloon gathered about me now, urging me to drink. I took another sip. Then another. My head spun and I laughed. I was put on the floor and I ran giggling and shouting among the yelling crowd. As I would pass each man, I would take a sip from an offered glass. Soon I was drunk.

A man called me to him and whispered some words into my ear and told me that he would give me a nickel if I went to a woman and repeated them to her. I told him that I would say them; he gave me the nickel and I ran to the woman and shouted the words. A gale of laughter went up in the saloon.

"Don't teach that boy that," someone said.

"He doesn't know what it is," another said.

From then on, for a penny or a nickel, I would repeat to anyone whatever was whispered to me. In my foggy, tipsy state the reaction of the men and women to my mysterious words enthralled me. I ran from person to person, laughing, hiccoughing, spewing out filth that made them bend double with glee.

"Let that boy alone now," someone said.

"It ain't going to hurt 'im," another said.

"It's a shame," a woman said, giggling.

"Go home, boy," somebody yelled at me.

Toward early evening they let me go. I staggered along the pavements, drunk, repeating obscenities to the horror of the women I passed and to the amusement of the men en route to their homes from work.

To beg drinks in the saloon became an obsession. Many evenings my mother would find me wandering in a daze and take me home and beat me; but the next morning, no sooner had she gone to her job than I would run to the saloon and wait for someone to take me in and buy me a drink. My mother protested tearfully to the proprietor of the saloon, who ordered me to keep out of his place. But the men—reluctant to surrender their sport—would buy me drinks anyway, letting me drink out of their flasks on the streets, urging me to repeat obscenities.

I was a drunkard in my sixth year, before I had begun school. With a gang of children, I roamed the streets, begging pennies from passers-by, haunting the doors of saloons, wandering farther and farther away from home each day. I saw more than I could understand and heard more than I could remember. The point of life became for me the times when I could beg drinks. My mother was in despair. She beat me; then she prayed and wept over me, imploring me to be good, telling me that she had to work, all of which carried no weight to my wayward mind. Finally she placed me and my brother in the keeping of an old black woman who watched me every moment to keep me from running to the doors of the saloons to beg for whisky. The craving for alcohol finally left me and I forgot the taste of it.

In the immediate neighborhood there were many school children who, in the afternoons, would stop and play en route to their homes; they would leave their books upon the sidewalk and I would thumb through the pages and question them about the baffling black print. When I had learned to recognize certain words, I told my mother that I wanted to learn to read and she encouraged me. Soon I was able to pick my way through most of the children's books I ran across. There grew in me a consuming curiosity about what was happening around me and, when my mother came home from a hard day's work, I would question her so relentlessly about what I had heard in the streets that she refused to talk to me.

One cold morning my mother awakened me and told me that, because there was no coal in the house, she was taking my brother to the job with her and that I must remain in bed until the coal she had ordered was delivered. For the payment of the coal, she left a note together with some money under the dresser scarf.

I went back to sleep and was awakened by the ringing of the doorbell. I opened the door, let in the coal man, and gave him the money and the note. He brought in a few bushels of coal, then lingered, asking me if I were cold.

"Yes," I said, shivering.

He made a fire, then sat and smoked.

"How much change do I owe you?" he asked me.

"I don't know," I said.

"Shame on you," he said. "Don't you know how to count?"

"No, sir," I said.

"Listen and repeat after me," he said.

He counted to ten and I listened carefully; then he asked me to count alone and I did. He then made me memorize the words twenty, thirty, forty, etc., then told me to add one, two, three, and so on. In about an hour's time I had learned to count to a hundred and I was overjoyed. Long after the coal man had gone I danced up and down on the bed in my nightclothes, counting again and again to a hundred, afraid that if I did not keep repeating the numbers I would forget them. When my mother returned from her job that night I insisted that she stand still and listen while I counted to one hundred. She was dumfounded. After that she taught me to read, told me stories. On Sundays I would read the newspapers with my mother guiding me and spelling out the words.

I soon made myself a nuisance by asking far too many questions of everybody. Every happening in the neighborhood, no matter how trivial, became my business. It was in this manner that I first stumbled upon the relations between whites and blacks, and what I learned frightened me. Though I had long known that there were people called "white" people, it had never meant anything to me emotionally. I had seen white men and women upon the streets a thousand times, but they had never looked particularly "white." To me they were merely people like other people, yet somehow strangely different because I had never come in close touch with any of them. For the most part I never thought of them; they simply existed somewhere in the background of the city as a whole. It might have been that my tardiness in learning to sense white people as "white" people came from the fact that many of my relatives were "white"-looking people. My grandmother, who was white as any "white" person, had never looked "white" to me. And when word circulated among the black people of the neighborhood that a "black" boy had been severely beaten by a "white" man, I felt that the "white" man had had a right to beat the "black" boy, for I naïvely assumed that the "white" man must have been the "black" boy's father. And did not all fathers, like my father, have the right to beat their children? A paternal right was the only right, to my understanding, that a man had to beat a child. But when my mother told me that the "white" man was not the father of the "black" boy, was no kin to him at all, I was puzzled.

"Then why did the 'white' man whip the 'black' boy?" I asked my mother.

"The 'white' man did not *whip* the 'black' boy," my mother told me. "He *beat* the 'black' boy."

"But why?"

"You're too young to understand."

"I'm not going to let anybody beat me," I said stoutly.

"Then stop running wild in the streets," my mother said.

I brooded for a long time about the seemingly causeless beating of the "black" boy by the "white" man and the more questions I asked the more bewildering it all became. Whenever I saw "white" people now I stared at them, wondering what they were really like.

I began school at Howard Institute at a later age than was usual; my mother had not been able to buy me the necessary clothes to make me presentable. The boys of the neighborhood took me to school the first day and when I reached the edge of the school grounds I became terrified, wanted to return home, wanted to put it off. But the boys simply took my hand and pulled me inside the building. I was frightened speechless and the other children had to identify me, tell the teacher my name and address. I sat listening to pupils recite, knowing and understanding what was being said and done, but utterly incapable of opening my mouth when called upon. The students around me seemed so sure of themselves that I despaired of ever being able to conduct myself as they did.

On the playground at noon I attached myself to a group of older boys and followed them about, listening to their talk, asking countless questions. During that noon hour I learned all the four-letter words describing physiological and sex functions, and discovered that I had known them before—had spoken them in the saloon—although I had not known what they meant. A tall black boy recited a long, funny piece of doggerel, replete with filth, describing the physiological relations between men and women, and I memorized it word for word after having heard it but once. Yet, despite my retentive memory, I found it impossible to recite when I went back into the classroom. The teacher called upon me and I rose, holding my book before my eyes, but I could make no words come from me. I could feel the presence of the strange boys and girls behind me, waiting to hear me read, and fear paralyzed me.

Yet when school let out that first day I ran joyously home with a brain burdened with racy and daring knowledge, but not a single idea from books. I gobbled my cold food that had been left covered on the table, seized a piece of soap and rushed into the streets, eager to display all I had learned in school since morning. I went from window to window and printed in huge soap-letters all my newly acquired four-letter words. I had written on nearly all the windows in the neighborhood when a woman stopped me and drove me home. That night the woman visited my mother and informed her of what I had done, taking her from window to window and pointing out my inspirational scribblings.

My mother was horrified. She demanded that I tell her where I had learned the words and she refused to believe me when I told her that I had learned them at school. My mother got a pail of water and a towel and took me by the hand and led me to a smeared window.

"Now, scrub until that word's gone," she ordered.

Neighbors gathered, giggling, muttering words of pity and astonishment, asking my mother how on earth I could have learned so much so quickly. I scrubbed at the four-letter soap-words and grew blind with anger. I sobbed, begging my mother to let me go, telling her that I would never write such words again; but she did not relent until the last soap-word had been cleaned away. Never again did I write words like that; I kept them to myself.

After my father's desertion, my mother's ardently religious disposition dominated the household and I was often taken to Sunday school where I met God's representative in the guise of a tall, black preacher. One Sunday my mother invited the tall, black preacher to a dinner of fried chicken. I was happy, not because the preacher was coming but because of the chicken. One or two neighbors also were invited. But no sooner had the preacher arrived than I began to resent him, for I learned at once that he, like my father, was used to having his own way. The hour for dinner came and I was wedged at the table between talking and laughing adults. In the center of the table was a huge platter of golden-brown fried chicken. I compared the bowl of soup that sat before me with the crispy chicken and decided in favor of the chicken. The others began to eat their soup, but I could not touch mine.

"Eat your soup," my mother said.

"I don't want any," I said.

"You won't get anything else until you've eaten your soup," she said.

The preacher had finished his soup and had asked that the platter of chicken be passed to him. It galled me. He smiled, cocked his head this way and that, picking out choice pieces. I forced a spoonful of soup down my throat and looked to see if my speed matched that of the preacher. It did not. There were already bare chicken bones on his plate, and he was reaching for more. I tried eating my soup faster, but it was no use; the other people were now serving themselves chicken and the platter was more than half empty. I gave up and sat staring in despair at the vanishing pieces of fried chicken.

"Eat your soup or you won't get anything," my mother warned.

I looked at her appealingly and could not answer. As piece after piece of chicken was eaten, I was unable to eat my soup at all. I grew hot with anger. The preacher was laughing and joking and the grownups were hanging on his words. My growing hate of the preacher finally became more important than God or religion and I could no longer contain myself. I leaped up from the table, knowing that I should be ashamed of what I was doing, but unable to stop, and screamed, running blindly from the room.

"That preacher's going to eat *all* the chicken!" I bawled.

The preacher tossed back his head and roared with laughter, but my mother was angry and told me that I was to have no dinner because of my bad manners.

When I awakened one morning my mother told me that we were going to see a judge who would make my father support me and my brother. An hour later all three of us were sitting in a huge crowded room. I was overwhelmed by the many faces and the voices which I could not understand. High above me was a white face which my mother told me was the face of the judge. Across the huge room sat my father, smiling confidently, looking at us. My mother warned me not to be fooled by my father's friendly manner; she told me that the judge might ask me questions, and if he did I must tell him the truth. I agreed, yet I hoped that the judge would not ask me anything.

For some reason the entire thing struck me as being useless; I felt that if my father were going to feed me, then he would have done so regardless of what a judge said to him. And I did not want my father to feed me; I was hungry, but my thoughts of food did not now center about him. I waited, growing restless, hungry. My mother gave me a dry sandwich and I munched and stared, longing to go home. Finally I heard my mother's name called; she rose and began weeping so copiously that she could not talk for a few moments; at last she managed to say that her husband had deserted her and two children, that her children were hungry, that they stayed hungry, that she worked, that she was trying to raise them alone. Then my father was called; he came forward jauntily, smiling. He tried to kiss my mother, but she turned away from him. I only heard one sentence of what he said.

"I'm doing all I can, Your Honor," he mumbled, grinning.

It had been painful to sit and watch my mother crying and my father laughing and I was glad when we were outside in the sunny streets. Back at home my mother wept again and talked complainingly about the unfairness of the judge who had accepted my father's word. After the court scene, I tried to forget my father; I did not hate him; I simply did not want to think of him. Often when we were hungry my mother would beg me to go to my father's job and ask him for a dollar, a dime, a nickel . . . But I would never consent to go. I did not want to see him.

My mother fell ill and the problem of food became an acute, daily agony. Hunger was with us always. Sometimes the neighbors would feed us or a dollar bill would come in the mail from my grandmother. It was winter and I would buy a dime's worth of coal each morning from the corner coalyard and lug it home in paper bags. For a time I remained out of school to wait upon my mother, then Granny came to visit us and I returned to school.

At night there were long, halting discussions about our going to live with Granny, but nothing came of it. Perhaps there was not enough money for railroad fare. Angered by having been hauled into court, my father now spurned us completely. I heard long, angrily whispered conversations between my mother and grandmother to the effect that "that woman ought to be killed for breaking up a home." What irked me was the ceaseless talk and no action. If someone had suggested that my father be killed, I would perhaps have become interested; if someone had suggested that his name never be mentioned, I would no doubt have agreed; if someone had suggested that we move to another city, I would have been glad. But there was only endless talk that led nowhere and I began to keep away from home as much as possible, preferring the simplicity of the streets to the worried, futile talk at home.

Finally we could no longer pay the rent for our dingy flat; the few dollars that Granny had left us before she went home were gone. Half sick and in despair, my mother made the rounds of the charitable institutions, seeking help. She found an orphan home that agreed to assume the guidance of me and my brother provided my mother worked and made small payments. My mother hated to be separated from us, but she had no choice.

The orphan home was a two-story frame building set amid trees in a wide, green field. My mother ushered me and my brother one morning into the building and into the presence of a tall, gaunt, mulatto woman who called herself Miss Simon. At once she took a fancy to me and I was frightened speechless; I was afraid of her the moment I saw her and my fear lasted during my entire stay in the home.

The house was crowded with children and there was always a storm of noise. The daily routine was blurred to me and I never quite grasped it. The most abiding feeling I had each day was hunger and fear. The meals were skimpy and there were only two of them. Just before we went to bed each night we were given a slice of bread smeared with molasses. The children were silent, hostile, vindictive, continuously complaining of hunger. There was an over-all atmosphere of nervousness and intrigue, of children telling tales upon others, of children being deprived of food to punish them.

The home did not have the money to check the growth of the wide stretches of grass by having it mown, so it had to be pulled by hand. Each morning after we had eaten a breakfast that seemed like no breakfast at all, an older child would lead a herd of us to the vast lawn and we would get to our knees and wrench the grass loose from the dirt with our fingers. At intervals Miss Simon would make a tour of inspection, examining the pile of pulled grass beside each child, scolding or praising according to the size of the pile. Many mornings I was too weak from hunger to pull the grass; I would grow dizzy and my mind would become blank and I would find myself, after an interval of unconsciousness, upon my hands and knees, my head whirling, my eyes staring in bleak astonishment at the green grass, wondering where I was, feeling that I was emerging from a dream . . .

During the first days my mother came each night to visit me and my brother, then her visits stopped. I began to wonder if she, too, like my father, had disappeared into the unknown. I was rapidly learning to distrust everything and everybody. When my mother did come, I asked her why had she remained away so long and she told me that Miss Simon had forbidden her to visit us, that Miss Simon had said that she was spoiling us with too much attention. I begged my mother to take me away; she wept and told me to wait, that soon she would take us to Arkansas. She left and my heart sank.

Miss Simon tried to win my confidence; she asked me if I would like to be adopted by her if my mother consented and I said no. She would take me into her apartment and talk to me, but her words had no effect. Dread and distrust had already become a daily part of my being and my memory grew sharp, my senses more impressionable; I began to be aware of myself as a distinct personality striving against others. I held myself in, afraid to act or speak until I was sure of my surroundings, feeling most of the time that I was suspended over a void. My imagination soared; I dreamed of running away. Each morning I vowed that I would leave the next morning, but the next morning always found me afraid.

One day Miss Simon told me that thereafter I was to help her in the office. I ate lunch with her and, strangely, when I sat facing her at the table, my hunger vanished. The woman killed something in me. Next she called me to her desk where she sat addressing envelopes.

"Step up close to the desk," she said. "Don't be afraid."

I went and stood at her elbow. There was a wart on her chin and I stared at it.

"Now, take a blotter from over there and blot each envelope after I'm through writing on it," she instructed me, pointing to a blotter that stood about a foot from my hand.

I stared and did not move or answer.

"Take the blotter," she said.

I wanted to reach for the blotter and succeeded only in twitching my arm.

"Here," she said sharply, reaching for the blotter and shoving it into my fingers.

She wrote in ink on an envelope and pushed it toward me. Holding the blotter in my hand, I stared at the envelope and could not move.

"Blot it," she said.

I could not lift my hand. I knew what she had said; I knew what she wanted me to do; and I had heard her correctly. I wanted to look at her and say something, tell her why I could not move; but my eyes were fixed upon the floor. I could not summon enough courage while she sat there looking at me to reach over the yawning space of twelve inches and blot the wet ink on the envelope.

"Blot it!" she spoke sharply.

Still I could not move or answer.

"Look at me!"

I could not lift my eyes. She reached her hand to my face and I twisted away.

"What's wrong with you?" she demanded.

I began to cry and she drove me from the room. I decided that as soon as night came I would run away. The dinner bell rang and I did not go to the table, but hid in a corner of the hallway. When I heard the dishes rattling at the table, I opened the door and ran down the walk to the street. Dusk was falling. Doubt made me stop. Ought I go back? No; hunger was back there, and fear. I went on, coming to concrete sidewalks. People passed me. Where was I going? I did not know. The farther I walked the more frantic I became. In a confused and vague way I knew that I was doing more running *away* from than running *toward* something. I stopped. The streets seemed dangerous. The buildings were massive and dark. The moon shone and the trees loomed frighteningly. No, I could not go on. I would go back. But i had walked so far and had turned too many corners and had not kept track of the direction. Which way led back to the orphan home? I did not know. I was lost.

I stood in the middle of the sidewalk and cried. A "white" policeman came to me and I wondered if he was going to beat me. He asked me what was the matter and I told him that I was trying to find my mother. His "white" face created a new fear in me. I was remembering the tale of the "white" man who had beaten the "black" boy. A crowd gathered and I was urged to tell where I lived. Curiously, I was too full of fear to cry now. I wanted to tell the "white" face that I had run off from an orphan home and that Miss Simon ran it, but I was afraid. Finally I was taken to the police station where I was fed. I felt better. I sat in a big chair where I was surrounded by "white" policemen, but they seemed to ignore me. Through the window I could see that night had completely fallen and that lights now gleamed in the streets. I grew sleepy and dozed. My shoulder was shaken gently and I opened my eyes and looked into a "white" face of another policeman who was sitting beside me. He asked me questions in a quiet, confidential tone, and quite before I knew it he was not "white" any more. I told him that I had run away from an orphan home and that Miss Simon ran it.

It was but a matter of minutes before I was walking alongside a policeman, heading toward the home. The policeman led me to the front gate and I saw Miss Simon waiting for me on the steps. She identified me and I was left in her charge. I begged her not to beat me, but she yanked me upstairs into an empty room and lashed me thoroughly. Sobbing, I slunk off to bed, resolved to run away again. But I was watched closely after that.

My mother was informed upon her next visit that I had tried to run away and she was terribly upset.

"Why did you do it?" she asked.

"I don't want to stay here," I told her.

"But you must," she said. "How can I work if I'm to worry about you? You must remember that you have no father. I'm doing all I can."

"I don't want to stay here," I repeated.

"Then, if I take you to your father . . ."

"I don't want to stay with him either," I said.

"But I want you to ask him for enough money for us to go to my sister's in Arkansas," she said.

Again I was faced with choices I did not like, but I finally agreed. After all, my hate for my father was not so great and urgent as my hate for the orphan home. My mother held to her idea and one night a week or so later I found myself standing in a room in a frame house. My father and a strange woman were sitting before a bright fire that blazed in a grate. My mother and I were standing about six feet away, as though we were afraid to approach them any closer.

"It's not for me," my mother was saying. "It's for your children that I'm asking you for money."

"I ain't got nothing," my father said, laughing.

"Come here, boy," the strange woman called to me. I looked at her and did not move.

"Give him a nickel," the woman said. "He's cute."

"Come here, Richard," my father said, stretching out his hand.

I backed away, shaking my head, keeping my eyes on the fire.

"He is a cute child," the strange woman said.

"You ought to be ashamed," my mother said to the strange woman. "You're starving my children."

"Now, don't you-all fight," my father said, laughing.

"I'll take that poker and hit you!" I blurted at my father.

He looked at my mother and laughed louder.

"You told him to say that," he said.

"Don't say such things, Richard," my mother said.

"You ought to be dead," I said to the strange woman.

The woman laughed and threw her arms about my father's neck. I grew ashamed and wanted to leave.

"How can you starve your children?" my mother asked.

"Let Richard stay with me," my father said.

"Do you want to stay with your father, Richard?" my mother asked.

"No," I said.

"You'll get plenty to eat," he said.

"I'm hungry now," I told him. "But I won't stay with you."

"Aw, give the boy a nickel," the woman said.

My father ran his hand into his pocket and pulled out a nickel.

"Here, Richard," he said.

"Don't take it," my mother said.

· "Don't teach him to be a fool," my father said. "Here, Richard, take it."

I looked at my mother, at the strange woman, at my father, then into the fire. I wanted to take the nickel, but I did not want to take it from my father.

"You ought to be ashamed," my mother said, weeping. "Giving your son a nickel when he's hungry. If there's a God, He'll pay you back."

"That's all I got," my father said, laughing again and returning the nickel to his pocket.

We left. I had the feeling that I had had to do with something unclean. Many times in the years after that the image of my father and the strange woman, their faces lit by the dancing flames, would surge up in my imagination so vivid and strong that I felt I could reach out and touch it; I would stare at it, feeling that it possessed some vital meaning which always eluded me.

A quarter of a century was to elapse between the time when I saw my father sitting with the strange woman and the time when I was to see him again, standing alone upon the red clay of a Mississippi plantation, a sharecropper, clad in ragged overalls, holding a muddy hoe in his gnarled, veined hands—a quarter of a century during which my mind and consciousness had become so greatly and violently altered that when I tried to talk to him I realized that, though ties of blood made us kin, though I could see a shadow of my face in his face, though there was an echo of my voice in his voice, we were forever strangers, speaking a different language, living on vastly distant planes of reality. That day a quarter of a century later when I visited him on the plantation—he was standing against the sky, smiling toothlessly, his hair whitened, his body bent, his eyes glazed with dim recollection, his fearsome aspect of twenty-five years ago gone forever from him—I was overwhelmed to realize that he could never understand me or the scalding experiences that had swept me beyond his life and into an area of living that he could never know. I stood before him, poised, my mind aching as it embraced the simple nakedness of his life, feeling how completely his soul was imprisoned by the slow flow of the seasons, by wind and rain and sun, how fastened were his memories to a crude and raw past, how chained were his actions and emotions to the direct, animalistic impulses of his withering body . . .

From the white landowners above him there had not been handed to him a chance to learn the meaning of loyalty, of sentiment, of tradition. Joy was as unknown to him as was despair. As a creature of the earth, he endured, hearty, whole, seemingly indestructible, with no regrets and no hope. He asked easy, drawling questions about me, his other son, his wife, and he laughed, amused, when I informed him of their destinies. I forgave him and pitied him as my eyes looked past him to the unpainted wooden shack. From far beyond the horizons that bound this bleak plantation there had come to me through my living the knowledge that my father was a black peasant who had gone to the city seeking life, but who had failed in the city; a black peasant whose life had been hopelessly snarled in the city, and who had at last fled the city—that same city which had lifted me in its burning arms and borne me toward alien and undreamed-of shores of knowing.

Chapter Two

THE glad days that dawned gave me liberty for the free play of impulse and, from anxiety and restraint, I leaped to license and thoughtless action. My mother arrived one afternoon with the news that we were going to live with her sister in Elaine, Arkansas, and that en route we would visit Granny, who had moved from Natchez to Jackson, Mississippi. As the words fell from my mother's lips, a long and heavy anxiety lifted from me. Excited, I rushed about and gathered my ragged clothes. I was leaving the hated home, hunger, fear, leaving days that had been as dark and lonely as death.

While I was packing, a playmate came to tell me that one of my shirts was hanging damp upon the clothesline. Filled more with the sense of coming freedom than with generosity, I told him that he could have it. What was a shirt to me now? The children stood about and watched me with envious eyes as I crammed my things into a suitcase, but I did not notice them. The moment I had learned that I was to leave, my feelings had recoiled so sharply and quickly from the home that the children simply did not exist for me any more. Their faces possessed the power of evoking in me a million memories that I longed to forget, and instead of my leaving drawing me to them in communion, it had flung me forever beyond them.

I was so eager to be gone that when I stood in the front hallway, packed and ready, I did not even think of saying good-bye to the boys and girls with whom I had eaten and slept and lived for so many weeks. My mother scolded me for my thoughtlessness and bade me say good-bye to them. Reluctantly I obeyed her, wishing that I did not have to do so. As I shook the dingy palms extended to me I kept my eyes averted, not wanting to look again into faces that hurt me because they had become so thoroughly associated in my feelings with hunger and fear. In shaking hands I was doing something that I was to do countless times in the years to come: acting in conformity with what others expected of me even though, by the very nature and form of my life, I did not and could not share their spirit.

(After I had outlived the shocks of childhood, after the habit of reflection had been born in me, I used to mull over the strange absence of real kindness in Negroes, how unstable was our tenderness, how lacking in genuine passion we were, how void of great hope, how timid our joy, how bare our traditions, how hollow our memories, how lacking we were in those intangible sentiments that bind man to man, and how shallow was even our despair. After I had learned other ways of life I used to brood upon the unconscious irony of those who felt that Negroes led so passional an existence! I saw that what had been taken for our emotional strength was our negative confusions, our flights, our fears, our frenzy under pressure.

(Whenever I thought of the essential bleakness of black life in America, I knew that Negroes had never been allowed to catch the full spirit of Western civilization, that they lived somehow in it but not of it. And when I brooded upon the cultural barrenness of black life, I wondered if clean, positive tenderness, love, honor, loyalty, and the capacity to remember were native with man. I asked myself if these human qualities were not fostered, won, struggled and suffered for, preserved in ritual from one generation to another.)

Granny's home in Jackson was an enchanting place

to explore. It was a two-story frame structure of seven rooms. My brother and I used to play hide and seek in the long, narrow hallways, and on and under the stairs. Granny's son, Uncle Clark, had bought her this home, and its white plastered walls, its front and back porches, its round columns and banisters, made me feel that surely there was no finer house in all the round world.

There were wide green fields in which my brother and I roamed and played and shouted. And there were the timid children of the neighbors, boys and girls to whom my brother and I felt superior in worldly knowledge. We took pride in telling them what it was like to ride on a train, what the yellow, sleepy Mississippi River looked like, how it felt to sail on the *Kate Adams*, what Memphis looked like, and how I had run off from the orphan home. And we would hint that we were pausing for but a few days and then would be off to even more fabulous places and marvelous experiences.

To help support the household my grandmother boarded a colored schoolteacher, Ella, a young woman with so remote and dreamy and silent a manner that I was as much afraid of her as I was attracted to her. I had long wanted to ask her to tell me about the books that she was always reading, but I could never quite summon enough courage to do so. One afternoon I found her sitting alone upon the front porch, reading.

"Ella," I begged, "please tell me what you are reading."

"It's just a book," she said evasively, looking about with apprehension.

"But what's it about?" I asked.

"Your grandmother wouldn't like it if I talked to you about novels," she told me.

I detected a note of sympathy in her voice.

"I don't care," I said loudly and bravely.

"Shhh— You mustn't say things like that," she said.

"But I want to know."

"When you grow up, you'll read books and know what's in them," she explained.

"But I want to know now."

She thought a while, then closed the book.

"Come here," she said.

I sat at her feet and lifted my face to hers.

"Once upon a time there was an old, old man named Bluebeard," she began in a low voice.

She whispered to me the story of *Bluebeard and His Seven Wives* and I ceased to see the porch, the sunshine, her face, everything. As her words fell upon my new ears, I endowed them with a reality that welled up from somewhere within me. She told how Bluebeard had duped and married his seven wives, how he had loved and slain them, how he had hanged them up by their hair in a dark closet. The tale made the world around me be, throb, live. As she spoke, reality changed, the look of things altered, and the world became peopled with magical presences. My sense of life deepened and the feel of things was different, somehow. Enchanted and enthralled, I stopped her constantly to ask for details. My imagination blazed. The sensations the story aroused in me were never to leave me. When she was about to finish, when my interest was keenest, when I was lost to the world around me, Granny stepped briskly onto the porch.

"You stop that, you evil gal!" she shouted. "I want none of that Devil stuff in my house!"

Her voice jarred me so that I gasped. For a moment I did not know what was happening.

"I'm sorry, Mrs. Wilson," Ella stammered, rising. "But he asked me—"

"He's just a foolish child and you know it!" Granny blazed.

Ella bowed her head and went into the house.

"But, Granny, she didn't finish," I protested, knowing that I should have kept quiet.

She bared her teeth and slapped me across my mouth with the back of her hand.

"You shut your mouth," she hissed. "You don't know what you're talking about!"

"But I want to hear what happened!" I wailed, dodging another blow that I thought was coming.

"That's the Devil's work!" she shouted.

My grandmother was as nearly white as a Negro can get without being white, which means that she was white. The sagging flesh of her face quivered; her eyes, large, dark, deep-set, wide apart, glared at me. Her lips narrowed to a line. Her high forehead wrinkled. When she was angry her eyelids drooped halfway down over her pupils, giving her a baleful aspect.

"But I liked the story," I told her.

"You're going to burn in hell," she said with such furious conviction that for a moment I believed her.

Not to know the end of the tale filled me with a sense of emptiness, loss. I hungered for the sharp, frightening, breath-taking, almost painful excitement that the story had given me, and I vowed that as soon as I was old enough I would buy all the novels there were and read them to feed that thirst for violence that was in me, for intrigue, for plotting, for secrecy, for bloody murders. So profoundly responsive a chord had the tale struck in me that the threats of my mother and grandmother had no effect whatsoever. They read my insistence as mere obstinacy, as foolishness, something that would quickly pass; and they had no notion how desperately serious the tale had made me. They could not have known that Ella's whispered story of deception and murder had been the first experience in my life that had elicited from me a total emotional response. No words or punishment could have possibly made me doubt. I had tasted what to me was life, and I would have more of it, somehow, someway. I realized that they could not understand what I was feeling and I kept quiet. But when no one was looking I would slip into Ella's room and steal a book and take it back of the barn and try to read it. Usually I could not decipher enough words to make the story have meaning. I burned to learn to read novels and I tortured my mother into telling me the meaning of every strange word I saw, not because the word itself had any value, but because it was the gateway to a forbidden and enchanting land.

One afternoon my mother became so ill that she had to go to bed. When night fell Granny assumed the task of seeing that my brother and I bathed. She set two tubs of water in our room and ordered us to pull off our clothes, which we did. She sat at one end of the room, knitting, lifting her eyes now and then from the wool to watch us and direct us. My brother and I splashed in the water, playing, laughing, trying our utmost to fling suds into each other's eyes. The floor was getting so sloppy that Granny scolded us.

"Stop that foolishness and wash yourselves!"

"Yes, ma'am," we answered automatically and proceeded with our playing.

I scooped up a double handful of suds and called to my brother. He looked and I flung the suds, but he ducked and the white foam spattered on to the floor.

"Richard, stop that playing and bathe!"

"Yes, ma'am," I said, watching my brother to catch him unawares so that I could fling more suds at him.

"Come here, you Richard!" Granny said, putting her knitting aside.

I went to her, walking sheepishly and nakedly across the floor. She snatched the towel from my hand and began to scrub my ears, my face, my neck.

"Bend over," she ordered.

I stooped and she scrubbed my anus. My mind was in a sort of daze, midway between daydreaming and thinking. Then, before I knew it, words—words whose meaning I did not fully know—had slipped out of my mouth.

"When you get through, kiss back there," I said, the words rolling softly but unpremeditatedly.

My first indication that something was wrong was that Granny became terribly still, then she pushed me violently from her. I turned around and saw that her white face was frozen, that her black, deep-set eyes were blazing at me unblinkingly. Taking my cue from her queer expression, I knew that I had said something awful, but I had no notion at that moment just how awful it was. Granny rose slowly and lifted the wet towel high above her head and brought it down across my naked back with all the outraged fury of her sixty-odd-year-old body, leaving an aching streak of fire burning and quivering on my skin. I gasped and held my breath, fighting against the pain; then I howled and cringed. I had not realized the meaning of what I had said; its moral horror was unfelt by me, and her attack seemed without cause. She lifted the wet towel and struck me again with such force that I dropped to my knees. I knew that if I did not get out of her reach she would kill me. Naked, I rose and ran out of the room, screaming. My mother hurried from her bed.

"What's the matter, mama?" she asked Granny.

I lingered in the hallway, trembling, looking at Granny, trying to speak but only moving my lips. Granny seemed to have gone out of her mind, for she stood like stone, her eyes dead upon me, not saying a word.

"Richard, what have you done?" my mother asked.

Poised to run again, I shook my head.

"What's the matter, for God's sake?" my mother asked of me, of Granny, of my brother, turning her face from one to another.

Granny wilted, half turned, flung the towel to the floor, then burst into tears.

"He . . . I was trying to wash him," Granny whimpered, "here," she continued, pointing, "and . . . that black little Devil . . ." Her body was shaking with insult and rage. "He told me to kiss him there when I was through."

Now my mother stared without speaking.

"No!" my mother exclaimed.

"He did," Granny whimpered.

"He didn't say *that*," my mother protested.

"He did," Granny sighed.

I listened, vaguely knowing now that I had committed some awful wrong that I could not undo, that I had uttered words I could not recall even though I ached to nullify them, kill them, turn back time to the moment before I had talked so that I could have another chance to save myself. My mother picked up the wet towel and came toward me. I ran into the kitchen, naked, yelling. She came hard upon my heels and I scuttled into the back yard, running blindly in the dark, butting my head against the fence, the tree, bruising my toes on sticks of wood, still screaming. I had no way of measuring the gravity of my wrong and I assumed that I had done something for which I would never be forgiven. Had I known just how my words had struck them, I would have remained still and taken my punishment, but it was the feeling that anything could or would happen to me that made me wild with fear.

"Come here, you little filthy fool!" my mother called.

I dodged her and ran back into the house, then again into the hallway, my naked body flashing frantically through the air. I crouched in a dark corner. My mother rushed upon me, breathing hard. I ducked, crawled, stood, and ran again.

"You may as well stand still," my mother said. "I'm going to beat you tonight if it is the last thing I do on this earth!"

Again she charged me and I dodged, just missing the stinging swish of the wet towel, and scooted into the room where my brother stood.

"What's the matter?" he asked, for he had not heard what I had said.

A blow fell on my mouth. I whirled. Granny was upon me. She struck me another blow on my head with the back of her hand. Then my mother came into the room. I fell to the floor and crawled under the bed.

"You come out of there," my mother called.

"Naw," I cried.

"Come out or I'll beat you to within an inch of your life," she said.

"Naw," I said.

"Call Papa," Granny said.

I trembled. Granny was sending my brother to fetch Grandpa, of whom I was mortally afraid. He was a tall, skinny, silent, grim, black man who had fought in the Civil War with the Union Army. When he was angry he gritted his teeth with a terrifying, grating sound. He kept his army gun in his room, standing in a corner, loaded. He was under the delusion that the war between the states would be resumed. I heard my brother rush out of the room and I knew it was but a matter of minutes before Grandpa would come. I balled myself into a knot and moaned:

"Naw, naw, naw . . ."

Grandpa came and ordered me from under the bed. I refused to move.

"Come out of there, little man," he said.

"Naw."

"Do you want me to get my gun?"

"Naw, sir. Please don't shoot me!" I cried.

"Then come out!"

I remained still. Grandpa took hold of the bed and pulled it. I clung to a bedpost and was dragged over the floor. Grandpa ran at me and tried to grab my leg, but I crawled out of reach. I rested on all fours and kept in the center of the bed and each time the bed moved, I moved, following it.

"Come out and get your whipping!" my mother called.

I remained still. The bed moved and I moved. I did not think; I did not plan; I did not plot. Instinct told me what to do. There was painful danger and I had to avoid it. Grandpa finally gave up and went back to his room.

"When you come out, you'll get your whipping," my mother said. "No matter how long you stay under there, you're going to get it. And no food for you tonight."

"What did he do?" my brother asked.

"Something he ought to be killed for," Granny said.

"But what?" my brother asked.

"Shut you up and get to bed," my mother said.

I stayed under the bed far into the night. The household went to sleep. Finally hunger and thirst drove me out; when I stood up I found my mother lurking in the doorway, waiting for me.

"Come into the kitchen," she said.

I followed her and she beat me, but she did not use the wet towel; Grandpa had forbade that. Between strokes of the switch she would ask me where had I learned the dirty words and I could not tell her; and my inability to tell her made her furious.

"I'm going to beat you until you tell me," she declared.

And I could not tell her because I did not know. None of the obscene words I had learned at school in Memphis had dealt with perversions of any sort, although I might have learned the words while loitering drunkenly in saloons. The next day Granny said emphatically that she knew who had ruined me, that she knew I had learned about "foul practices" from reading Ella's books, and when I asked what "foul practices" were, my mother beat me afresh. No matter how hard I tried to convince them that I had not read the words in a book or that I could not remember having heard anyone say them, they would not believe me. Granny finally charged Ella with telling me things that I should not know and Ella, weeping and distraught, packed her things and moved. The tremendous upheaval that my words had caused made me know that there lay back of them much more than I could figure out, and I resolved that in the future I would learn the meaning of why they had beat and denounced me.

The days and hours began to speak now with a clearer tongue. Each experience had a sharp meaning of its own.

There was the breathlessly anxious fun of chasing and catching flitting fireflies on drowsy summer nights.

There was the drenching hospitality in the pervading smell of sweet magnolias.

There was the aura of limitless freedom distilled from the rolling sweep of tall green grass swaying and glinting in the wind and sun.

There was the feeling of impersonal plenty when I saw a boll of cotton whose cup had spilt over and straggled its white fleece toward the earth.

There was the pitying chuckle that bubbled in my throat when I watched a fat duck waddle across the back yard.

There was the suspense I felt when I heard the taut, sharp song of a yellow-black bee hovering nervously but patiently above a white rose.

There was the drugged, sleepy feeling that came from sipping glasses of milk, drinking them slowly so that they would last a long time, and drinking enough for the first time in my life.

There was the bitter amusement of going into town with Granny and watching the baffled stares of white folks who saw an old white woman leading two undeniably Negro boys in and out of stores on Capitol Strect.

There was the slow, fresh, saliva-stimulating smell of cooking cotton seeds.

There was the excitement of fishing in muddy country creeks with my grandpa on cloudy days.

There was the fear and awe I felt when Grandpa took me to a sawmill to watch the giant whirring steel blades whine and scream as they bit into wet green logs.

There was the puckery taste that almost made me cry when I ate my first half-ripe persimmon.

There was the greedy joy in the tangy taste of wild hickory nuts.

There was the dry hot summer morning when I scratched my bare arms on briers while picking blackberries and came home with my fingers and lips stained black with sweet berry juice.

There was the relish of eating my first fried fish

sandwich, nibbling at it slowly and hoping that I would never eat it up.

There was the all-night ache in my stomach after I had climbed a neighbor's tree and eaten stolen, unripe peaches.

There was the morning when I thought I would fall dead from fear after I had stepped with my bare feet upon a bright little green garden snake.

And there were the long, slow, drowsy days and nights of drizzling rain . . .

At last we were at the railroad station with our bags, waiting for the train that would take us to Arkansas; and for the first time I noticed that there were two lines of people at the ticket window, a "white" line and a "black" line. During my visit at Granny's a sense of the two races had been born in me with a sharp concreteness that would never die until I died. When I boarded the train I was aware that we Negroes were in one part of the train and that the whites were in another. Naïvely I wanted to go and see how the whites looked while sitting in their part of the train.

"Can I go and peep at the white folks?" I asked my mother.

"You keep quiet," she said.

"But that wouldn't be wrong, would it?"

"Will you keep still?"

"But why can't I?"

"Quit talking foolishness!"

I had begun to notice that my mother became irritated when I questioned her about whites and blacks, and I could not quite understand it. I wanted to understand these two sets of people who lived side by side and never touched, it seemed, except in violence. Now, there was my grandmother . . . Was she white? Just how white was she? What did the whites think of her whiteness?

"Mama, is Granny white?" I asked as the train rolled through the darkness.

"If you've got eyes, you can see what color she is," my mother said.

"I mean, do the white folks think she's white?"

"Why don't you ask the white folks that?" she countered.

"But you know," I insisted.

"Why should I know?" she asked. "I'm not white."

"Granny looks white," I said, hoping to establish one fact, at least. "Then why is she living with us colored folks?"

"Don't you want Granny to live with us?" she asked, blunting my question.

"Yes."

"Then why are you asking?"

"I want to *know*."

"Doesn't Granny live with us?"

"Yes."

"Isn't that enough?"

"But does she *want* to live with us?"

"Why didn't you ask Granny that?" my mother evaded me again in a taunting voice.

"Did Granny become colored when she married Grandpa?"

"Will you stop asking silly questions!"

"But did she?"

"Granny didn't *become* colored," my mother said angrily. "She was *born* the color she is now."

Again I was being shut out of the secret, the thing, the reality I felt somewhere beneath all the words and silences.

"Why didn't Granny marry a white man?" I asked.

"Because she didn't want to," my mother said peevishly.

"Why don't you want to talk to me?" I asked.

She slapped me and I cried. Later, grudgingly, she told me that Granny came of Irish, Scotch, and French stock in which Negro blood had somewhere and somehow been infused. She explained it all in a matter-of-fact, offhand, neutral way; her emotions were not involved at all.

"What was Granny's name before she married Grandpa?"

"Bolden."

"Who gave her that name?"

"The white man who owned her."

"She was a slave?"

"Yes."

"And Bolden was the name of Granny's father?"

"Granny doesn't know who her father was."

"So they just gave her any name?"

"They gave her a name; that's all I know."

"Couldn't Granny find out who her father was?"

"For what, silly?"

"So she could know."

"Know for what?"

"Just to know."

"But for *what*?"

I could not say. I could not get anywhere.

"Mama, where did Father get his name?"

"From his father."

"And where did the father of my father get his name?"

"Like Granny got hers. From a white man."

"Do they know who he is?"

"I don't know."

"Why don't they find out?"

"For what?" my mother demanded harshly.

And I could think of no rational or practical reason why my father should try to find out who his father's father was.

"What has Papa got in him?" I asked.

"Some white and some red and some black," she said.

"Indian, white, and Negro?"

"Yes."

"Then what am I?"

"They'll call you a colored man when you grow up," she said. Then she turned to me and smiled mockingly and asked: "Do you mind, Mr. Wright?"

I was angry and I did not answer. I did not object

to being called colored, but I knew that there was something my mother was holding back. She was not concealing facts, but feelings, attitudes, convictions which she did not want me to know; and she became angry when I prodded her. All right, I would find out someday. Just wait. All right, I was colored. It was fine. I did not know enough to be afraid or to anticipate in a concrete manner. True, I had heard that colored people were killed and beaten, but so far it all had seemed remote. There was, of course, a vague uneasiness about it all, but I would be able to handle that when I came to it. It would be simple. If anybody tried to kill me, then I would kill them first.

When we arrived in Elaine I saw that Aunt Maggie lived in a bungalow that had a fence around it. It looked like home and I was glad. I had no suspicion that I was to live here for but a short time and that the manner of my leaving would be my first baptism of racial emotion.

A wide dusty road ran past the house and on each side of the road wild flowers grew. It was summer and the smell of clay dust was everywhere, day and night. I would get up early every morning to wade with my bare feet through the dust of the road, reveling in the strange mixture of the cold dew-wet crust on top of the road and the warm, sun-baked dust beneath.

After sunrise the bees would come out and I discovered that by slapping my two palms together smartly I could kill a bee. My mother warned me to stop, telling me that bees made honey, that it was not good to kill things that made food, that I would eventually be stung. But I felt confident of outwitting any bee. One morning I slapped an enormous bee between my hands just as it had lit upon a flower and it stung me in the tender center of my left palm. I ran home screaming.

"Good enough for you," my mother commented dryly.

I never crushed any more bees.

Aunt Maggie's husband, Uncle Hoskins, owned a saloon that catered to the hundreds of Negroes who worked in the surrounding sawmills. Remembering the saloon of my Memphis days, I begged Uncle Hoskins to take me to see it and he promised; but my mother said no; she was afraid that I would grow up to be a drunkard if I went inside of a saloon again while still a child. Well, if I could not see the saloon, at least I could eat. And at mealtime Aunt Maggie's table was so loaded with food that I could scarcely believe it was real. It took me some time to get used to the idea of there being enough to eat; I felt that if I ate enough there would not be anything left for another time. When I first sat down at Aunt Maggie's table, I could not eat until I had asked:

"Can I eat all I want?"

"Eat as much as you like," Uncle Hoskins said.

I did not believe him. I ate until my stomach hurt, but even then I did not want to get up from the table.

"Your eyes are bigger than your stomach," my mother said.

"Let him eat all he wants to and get used to food," Uncle Hoskins said.

When supper was over I saw that there were many biscuits piled high upon the bread platter, an astonishing and unbelievable sight to me. Though the biscuits were right before my eyes, and though there was more flour in the kitchen, I was apprehensive lest there be no bread for breakfast in the morning. I was afraid that somehow the biscuits might disappear during the night, while I was sleeping. I did not want to wake up in the morning, as I had so often in the past, feeling hungry and knowing that there was no food in the house. So, surreptitiously, I took some of the biscuits from the platter and slipped them into my pocket, not to eat, but to keep as a bulwark against any possible attack of hunger. Even after I had got used to seeing the table loaded with food at each meal, I still stole bread and put it into my pockets. In washing my clothes my mother found the gummy wads and scolded me to break me of the habit; I stopped hiding the bread

in my pockets and hid it about the house, in corners, behind dressers. I did not break the habit of stealing and
hoarding bread until my faith that food would be
forthcoming at each meal had been somewhat estab-
lished.

Uncle Hoskins had a horse and buggy and sometimes he used to take me with him to Helena, where he
traded. One day when I was riding with him he said:

"Richard, would you like to see this horse drink
water out of the middle of the river?"

"Yes," I said, laughing. "But this horse can't do that."

"Yes, he can," Uncle Hoskins said. "Just wait and
see."

He lashed the horse and headed the buggy straight
for the Mississippi River.

"Where're you going?" I asked, alarm mounting in
me.

"We're going to the middle of the river so the horse
can drink," he said.

He drove over the levee and down the long slope of
cobblestones to the river's edge and the horse plunged
wildly in. I looked at the mile stretch of water that lay
ahead and leaped up in terror.

"Naw!" I screamed.

"This horse has to drink," Uncle Hoskins said grimly.

"The river's deep!" I shouted.

"The horse can't drink here," Uncle Hoskins said,
lashing the back of the struggling animal.

The buggy went farther. The horse slowed a little and
tossed his head above the current. I grabbed the sides
of the buggy, ready to jump, even though I could not
swim.

"Sit down or you'll fall out!" Uncle Hoskins shouted.

"Let me out!" I screamed.

The water now came up to the hubs of the wheels of
the buggy. I tried to leap into the river and he caught
hold of my leg. We were now surrounded by water.

"Let me out!" I screamed.

The buggy rolled on and the water rose higher. The
horse wagged his head, arched his neck, flung his tail

about, walled his eyes, and snorted. I gripped the sides of the buggy with all the strength I had, ready to wrench free and leap if the buggy slipped deeper into the river. Uncle Hoskins and I tussled.

"Whoa!" he yelled at last to the horse.

The horse stopped and neighed. The swirling yellow water was so close that I could have touched the surface of the river. Uncle Hoskins looked at me and laughed.

"Did you really think that I was going to drive this buggy into the middle of the river?" he asked.

I was too scared to answer; my muscles were so taut that they ached.

"It's all right," he said soothingly.

He turned the buggy around and started back toward the levee. I was still clutching the sides of the buggy so tightly that I could not turn them loose.

"We're safe now," he said.

The buggy rolled onto dry land and, as my fear ebbed, I felt that I was dropping from a great height. It seemed that I could smell a sharp, fresh odor. My forehead was damp and my heart thumped heavily.

"I want to get out," I said.

"What's the matter?" he asked.

"I want to get out!"

"We're back on land now, boy."

"Naw! Stop! I want to get out!"

He did not stop the buggy; he did not even turn his head to look at me; he did not understand. I wrenched my leg free with a lunge and leaped headlong out of the buggy, landing in the dust of the road, unhurt. He stopped the buggy.

"Are you really that scared?" he asked softly.

I did not answer; I could not speak. My fear was gone now and he loomed before me like a stranger, like a man I had never seen before, a man with whom I could never share a moment of intimate living.

"Come on, Richard, and get back into the buggy," he said. "I'll take you home now."

I shook my head and began to cry.

"Listen, son, don't you trust me?" he asked. "I was born on that old river. I know that river. There's stone and brick way down under that water. You could wade out for half a mile and it would not come over your head."

His words meant nothing and I would not re-enter the buggy.

"I'd better take you home," he said soberly.

I started down the dusty road. He got out of the buggy and walked beside me. He did not do his shopping that day and when he tried to explain to me what he had been trying to do in frightening me I would not listen or speak to him. I never trusted him after that. Whenever I saw his face the memory of my terror upon the river would come back, vivid and strong, and it stood as a barrier between us.

Each day Uncle Hoskins went to his saloon in the evenings and did not return home until the early hours of the morning. Like my father, he slept in the daytime, but noise never seemed to bother Uncle Hoskins. My brother and I shouted and banged as much as we liked. Often I would creep into his room while he slept and stare at the big shining revolver that lay near his head, within quick reach of his hand. I asked Aunt Maggie why he kept the gun so close to him and she told me that men had threatened to kill him, white men . . .

One morning I awakened to learn that Uncle Hoskins had not come home from the saloon. Aunt Maggie fretted and worried. She wanted to visit the saloon and find out what had happened, but Uncle Hoskins had forbidden her to come to the place. The day wore on and dinnertime came.

"I'm going to find out if anything's happened," Aunt Maggie said.

"Maybe you oughtn't," my mother said. "Maybe it's dangerous."

The food was kept hot on the stove and Aunt Maggie stood on the front porch staring into the deepening dusk. Again she declared that she was going to the saloon, but my mother dissuaded her once more. It grew dark and still he had not come. Aunt Maggie was silent and restless.

"I hope to God the white people didn't bother him," she said.

Later she went into the bedroom and when she came out she whimpered:

"He didn't take his gun. I wonder what could have happened?"

We ate in silence. An hour later there was the sound of heavy footsteps on the front porch and a loud knock came. Aunt Maggie ran to the door and flung it open. A tall black boy stood sweating, panting, and shaking his head. He pulled off his cap.

"Mr. Hoskins . . . he done been shot. Done been shot by a white man," the boy gasped. "Mrs. Hoskins, he dead."

Aunt Maggie screamed and rushed off the porch and down the dusty road into the night.

"Maggie!" my mother screamed.

"Don't you-all go to that saloon," the boy called.

"Maggie!" my mother called, running after Aunt Maggie.

"They'll kill you if you go there!" the boy yelled. "White folks say they'll kill all his kinfolks!"

My mother pulled Aunt Maggie back to the house. Fear drowned out grief and that night we packed clothes and dishes and loaded them into a farmer's wagon. Before dawn we were rolling away, fleeing for our lives. I learned afterwards that Uncle Hoskins had been killed by whites who had long coveted his flourishing liquor business. He had been threatened with death and warned many times to leave, but he had wanted to hold on a while longer to amass more money. We got rooms in West Helena, and Aunt Maggie and my mother kept huddled in the house all day and night, afraid to be seen on the streets. Finally Aunt Maggie defied her fear and made frequent trips back to Elaine, but she went in secret and at night and would tell no one save my mother when she was going.

There was no funeral. There was no music. There was

no period of mourning. There were no flowers. There were only silence, quiet weeping, whispers, and fear. I did not know when or where Uncle Hoskins was buried. Aunt Maggie was not even allowed to see his body nor was she able to claim any of his assets. Uncle Hoskins had simply been plucked from our midst and we, figuratively, had fallen on our faces to avoid looking into that white-hot face of terror that we knew loomed somewhere above us. This was as close as white terror had ever come to me and my mind reeled. Why had we not fought back, I asked my mother, and the fear that was in her made her slap me into silence.

Shocked, frightened, alone without their husbands or friends, my mother and Aunt Maggie lost faith in themselves and, after much debate and hesitation, they decided to return home to Granny and rest, think, map out new plans for living. I had grown used to moving suddenly and the prospects of another trip did not excite me. I had learned to leave old places without regret and to accept new ones for what they looked like. Though I was nearly nine years of age, I had not had a single, unbroken year of school, and I was not conscious of it. I could read and count and that was about as much as most of the people I met could do, grownups or children. Again our household was torn apart; belongings were sold, given away, or simply left behind, and we were off for another long train ride.

A few days later—after we had arrived at Granny's—I was playing alone in a wild field, digging in the ground with an old knife. Suddenly a strange rhythmic sound made me turn my head. Flowing threateningly toward me over the crest of a hill was a wave of black men draped in weird mustard-colored clothing. Unconsciously I jumped to my feet, my heart pounding. What was this? Were these men coming after me? Line by line, row by row, the fantastic men in their wild colors were descending straight at me, trotting, their feet pounding the earth like someone beating a vast drum. I wanted to fly home but, as in a dream, I could not move. I cast about wildly for a clue to tell me what this was, but I could find nothing. The wall of men was drawing closer. My heart was beating so strongly that it shook my body. Again I tried to run, but I could not budge. My mother's name was on the tip of my tongue and I opened my mouth to scream, but no words came, for now the surging men, each looking exactly like the other, parted and poured around me, jarring the earth, their feet stomping in unison. As they flooded past I saw that their black faces were looking at me and that some of them were smiling. Then I noticed that each man was holding a long, dark, heavy, sticklike object upon his shoulder. One of the men yelled something at me which I did not understand. They were past me now, disappearing in a great cloud of brown dust that looked like a part of their clothing, that made them seem akin to the elemental earth itself. As soon as they were far enough away for me to conquer my fear, I dashed home and babbled to my mother what I had seen, asking her who the strange men were.

"Those were soldiers," she said.

"What are soldiers?" I asked.

"Men who fight in wars."

"Why do they fight?"

"Because their country tells them to."

"And what are those long black sticks they have on their shoulders?"

"Rifles."

"What's a rifle?"

"It's a gun that shoots a bullet."

"Like a pistol?"

"Yes."

"Would the bullet kill you?"

"Yes, if it hits you in the right place."

"Who are they going to shoot?"

"Germans."

"Who are Germans?"

"They are the enemy."

"What's an enemy?"

"The people who want to kill you and take your country away from you."

"Where do they live?"

" 'Way across the sea," my mother explained. "Don't you remember that I told you that war has been declared?"

I remembered; but when she had told me, it had not seemed at all important. I asked my mother what the war was about and she spoke of England, France, Russia, Germany, of men dying, but the reality of it was too vast and alien for me to be moved or further interested.

Upon another day I was playing out of doors in front of the house and I accidentally looked down the road and saw what seemed to me to be a herd of elephants coming slowly toward me. There was in me this time none of that naked terror I had felt when I had seen the soldiers, for these strange creatures were moving slowly, silently, with no suggestion of threat. Yet I edged cautiously toward the steps of the house, holding myself ready to run if they should prove to be more violent than they appeared. The strange elephants were a few feet from me now and I saw that their faces were like the faces of men! I stared, my mind trying to adjust memory to reality. What kind of men were these? I saw that there were two lines of creatures that looked like men on either side of the road; that there were a few white faces and a great many black faces. I saw that the white faces were the faces of white men and they were dressed in ordinary clothing; but the black faces were men wearing what seemed to me to be elephant's clothing. As the strange animals came abreast of me I saw that the legs of the black animals were held together by irons and that their arms were linked with heavy chains that clanked softly and musically as they moved. The black creatures were digging a shallow ditch on each side of the road, working silently, grunting as they lifted spades of earth and flung them into the middle of the roadway. One of the strange, striped animals turned a black face upon me.

"What are you doing?" I asked in a whisper, not knowing if one actually spoke to elephants.

He shook his head and cast his eyes guardedly back at a white man, then dug on again. Suddenly I noticed that the white men were holding the long, heavy black sticks—rifles!—on their shoulders. After they had passed I ran breathlessly into the house.

"Mama!" I yelled.

"What?" she answered from the kitchen.

"There are elephants in the street!"

She came to the kitchen door and stared at me.

"Elephants?" she asked.

"Yes. Come and see them. They're digging in the street."

My mother dried her hands on her apron and rushed to the front door. I followed, wanting her to interpret the baffling spectacle I had seen. She looked out of the door and shook her head.

"Those are not elephants," she said.

"What are they?"

"That's a chain gang."

"What's a chain gang?"

"It's just what you see," she said. "A gang of men chained together and made to work."

"Why?"

"Because they've done something wrong and they're being punished."

"What did they do?"

"I don't know."

"But why do they look like that?"

"That's to keep them from running away," she said. "You see, everybody'll know that they're convicts because of their stripes."

"Why don't the white men wear stripes?"

"They're the guards."

"Do white men ever wear stripes?"

"Sometimes."

"Did you ever see any?"

"No."

"Why are there so many black men wearing stripes?"

"It's because . . . Well, they're harder on black people."

"The white people?"

"Yes."

"Then why don't all the black men fight all the white men out there? There are more black men than white men ..."

"But the white men have guns and the black men don't," my mother said. She looked at me and asked: "What made you call them elephants?"

I could not answer her at the moment. But later, brooding over the black-and-white striped clothing of the black men, I remembered that in Elaine I had had a book that carried the gaudy pictures and names of jungle beasts. What had struck me most vividly were the striped zebras that looked as if someone had painted them. The other animals that had gripped my imagination were the elephants, and by association the zebras and the elephants had become linked and identified in my mind to such an extent that when I had seen the convicts dressed in the white and black stripes of zebras, I had thought they were elephants, beasts of the jungle.

Again, after an undetermined stretch of time, my mother announced that we were going to move, that we were going back to West Helena. She had grown tired of the strict religious routine of Granny's home; of the half dozen or more daily family prayers that Granny insisted upon; her fiat that the day began at sunrise and that night commenced at sundown; the long, rambling Bible readings; the individual invocations muttered at each meal; and her declaration that Saturday was the Lord's Sabbath and that no one who lived in her house could work upon that day. In West Helena we could have a home of our own, a condition that now loomed desirable after a few months of Granny's anxiety about the state of our souls. Naturally a trip was agreeable to me. Again we packed. Again we said good-bye. Again we rode the train. Again we were in West Helena.

We rented one half of a double corner house in front of which ran a stagnant ditch carrying sewage. The neighborhood swarmed with rats, cats, dogs, fortunetellers, cripples, blind men, whores, salesmen, rent collectors, and children. In front of our flat was a huge roundhouse where locomotives were cleaned and repaired. There was an eternal hissing of steam, the deep grunting of steel engines, and the tolling of bells. Smoke obscured the vision and cinders drifted into the house, into our beds, into our kitchen, into our food; and a tarlike smell was always in the air.

Bareheaded and barefooted, my brother and I, along with nameless and countless other black children, used to stand and watch the men crawl in, out, over, and under the huge black metal engines. When the men were not looking, we would climb into the engineer's cab and pull our small bodies to the window and look out, imagining that we were grown and had got a job as an engineer running a train and that it was night and there was a storm and we had a long string of passenger cars behind us, trying to get them safely home.

"Whooooooooeeeeeeeee!" we would say.

"Dong! Dong! Dong!"

"Huff-huff! Huff-huff-huff! Huff-huff-huff-huff!" we would say.

But our greatest fun came from wading in the sewage ditch where we found old bottles, tin cans that held tiny crawfish, rusty spoons, bits of metal, old toothbrushes, dead cats and dogs, and occasional pennies. We made wooden boats out of cigar boxes, devised wooden paddles to which we twisted pieces of rubber and sent the cigar-box boats sailing down the ditch under their own power. Many evenings the fathers of the children would come out, take off their shoes, and make and sail the boats themselves.

My mother and Aunt Maggie cooked in the kitchens of white folks and my brother and I were free to wander where we pleased during their working hours. Each day we were left a dime apiece to spend for lunch and all morning we would dream and discuss what we would buy. At ten or eleven o'clock we would go to the corner grocery—owned by a Jew—and buy a nickel's worth of ginger snaps and a bottle of Coca-Cola; that was lunch as we understood it.

I had never seen a Jew before and the proprietor of the corner grocery was a strange thing in my life. Until that time I had never heard a foreign language spoken and I used to linger at the door of the corner grocery to hear the odd sounds that Jews made when they talked. All of us black people who lived in the neighborhood hated Jews, not because they exploited us, but because we had been taught at home and in Sunday school that Jews were "Christ killers." With the Jews thus singled out for us, we made them fair game for ridicule.

We black children—seven, eight, and nine years of age—used to run to the Jew's store and shout:

> *Jew, Jew, Jew*
> *What do you chew?*

Or we would form a long line and weave back and forth in front of the door, singing:

> *Jew, Jew,*
> *Two for five*
> *That's what keeps*
> *Jew alive.*

Or we would chant:

> *Bloody Christ killers*
> *Never trust a Jew*
> *Bloody Christ killers*
> *What won't a Jew do?*

To one of the redheaded Jewish boys we sang:

> *Red head*
> *Jewish bread*
> *Five cents*
> *A Jewish head.*

To the fat Jewish woman we sneered:

> *Red, white, and blue*
> *Your pa was a Jew*
> *Your ma a dirty Dago*
> *What the hell is you?*

And when the baldheaded proprietor would pass by, we black children, poor, half-starved, ignorant, victims of racial prejudice, would sing with a proud lilt:

> *A rotten egg*
> *Never fries*
> *A cheating dog*
> *Never thrives.*

There were many more folk ditties, some mean, others filthy, all of them cruel. No one ever thought of questioning our right to do this; our mothers and parents generally approved, either actively or passively. To hold an attitude of antagonism or distrust toward Jews was bred in us from childhood; it was not merely racial prejudice, it was a part of our cultural heritage.

One afternoon a group of black boys and girls were standing about outside playing, laughing, talking. A black man dressed in overalls went up the steps and into the flat adjoining the one in which I lived.

"This is Saturday," a black girl said to me.

"Yeah. But why you say it?" I asked.

"They gonna make a lotta money in there today," she said, pointing to the door through which the man had disappeared.

"How?"

Another black man went up the steps and into the flat.

"Don't you know?" the girl asked, incredulous.

"Know what?"

"What they selling . . . ?"

"Where?"

"In there where them men went," she said.

"Nobody sells things in there," I said.

"You kidding?" the girl said in honest disbelief.

"I ain't. What they selling? Tell me."

"You know what they selling," she said, looking at me with a teasing smile.

"They don't sell nothing in there," I said.

"Aw, you just a baby," she said, slapping her dingy palm through the air at me in a contemptuous gesture.

I was puzzled. Was there something happening next door to where I lived that I did not know? I thought I had poked my nose into every bit of conceivable business in the neighborhood; if something was being sold next door, then I certainly wanted to know about it. The building in which I lived was a double frame house of one story; the building originally had been a one-dwelling unit and had been converted into two flats, for there were doors in our flat that led into the flat adjoining. These doors had been locked, bolted, and nailed securely. The family next door seemed quiet; men came and went, but that did not seem odd to me. But now the girl's hints made me want to know what was happening over there. I entered our house and locked the door, then put my ear to the thin wall that divided the two flats and listened. I heard faint sounds, but could make nothing of them. I listened at a bolted door and the sounds came a little louder, but I still could understand nothing.

Quietly I pulled up a chair, placed a box upon it, and climbed up and peered through a crack at the top of the door. I saw, in the dim shadows of the room beyond, a naked man and a naked woman upon a bed, the man on top of the woman. I lost my balance and toppled backwards to the floor. I lay still, wondering if the man and woman next door had heard me. But all seemed quiet and my curiosity returned. Just as I had climbed up again to look, a sharp rapping came on the windowpane behind me; I turned my head and saw the landlady from next door looking at me. My heart thumped and I scrambled down. The landlady's black face was pressed hard against the windowpane; her mouth was moving violently and her eyes were glaring. I was afraid to stay in the house or go out. Why had I not thought of lowering the shade? Evidently I had done something terrible, if the wild anger written on the woman's face was any indication. Her face went from the window and a moment later a loud pounding came at the front door.

"Open this door, you boy!"

I trembled and did not answer.

"Open this door or I'll have to break it!"

"My mama ain't here," I said vaguely.

"This is my house and you open this door!" she shouted.

Her voice overpowered me and I opened the door. She rushed in, then stopped and stared at the clumsy scaffolding I had rigged up to look into her flat. Why hadn't I taken it down before I opened the door?

"Boy, what do you mean?" she asked.

I could not answer.

"You scared my customers," she said.

"Customers?" I repeated vaguely.

"You little snot!" she blazed. "I got a good mind to beat you!"

"Naw, you won't!" I said.

"I'm gonna make your folks move outta here," she railed. "I got to make a living and you go and spoil my Saturday for me!"

"I . . . I was just looking . . ."

"Looking . . . ?" She smiled suddenly, relenting a little. "Why don't you come on over like the rest and spend a quarter?"

"I don't want to go to your old house," I told her with my nine-year-old indignation.

"You're a plague," she said, deciding that I would not be a customer. "I'm gonna get you outta here!"

When my mother and Aunt Maggie came home that night, there was a scalding argument. The women shouted at each other over the wooden railings on the front porch and their voices could be heard for half a mile. Neighbors listened. Children gathered and gaped. The argument boiled down to one issue: the landlady demanded that my mother beat me and, for once, my mother refused.

"You oughtn't have *that* in your house," my mother told her.

"It's my house and I'll have in it what I damn please," the landlady said.

"I wouldn't've moved in here if I had thought you were running *that* kind of business," my mother said.

"Don't talk to me like that, you high-toned bitch!" the landlady shouted.

"What do you expect children to do when you do *that*?" my mother asked.

"Them bastard brats of yours ain't no angels!" the landlady said.

"You're just a common prostitute!" Aunt Maggie pitched in.

"And what kind of whore is you?" the landlady shouted.

"Don't you talk to my sister like that!" my mother warned.

"Pack up your rags, you black bastards, and get!" the landlady ordered.

It ended with our packing and moving that night into another frame house on the same street, a few doors away. I still had only a hazy notion of what the landlady was selling. The boys later told me the name of it, but I had no exact conception of it in my mind. Though I knew that others felt it was something terribly bad, I was still curious. In time I would find out what it was.

Something secret was happening in our house and it had reached a serious stage before I knew it. Each night, just as I was dozing off to sleep, I would hear a light tapping on Aunt Maggie's windowpane, a door creaking open, whispers, then long silences. Once I got out of bed and crept to the door of the front room and stole a look. There was a well-dressed black man sitting on the sofa talking in a soft voice to Aunt Maggie. Why was it that I could not meet the man? I crept back to bed, but was awakened later by low voices saying good-bye. The next morning I asked my mother who had been in the house, and she told me that no one had been there.

"But I heard a man talking," I said.

"You didn't," she said. "You were sleeping."

"But I saw a man. He was in the front room."

"You were dreaming," my mother said.

I learned a part of the secret of the night visits one Sunday morning when Aunt Maggie called me and my brother to her room and introduced us to the man who was going to be our new "uncle," a Professor Matthews. He wore a high, snow-white collar and rimless eyeglasses. His lips were thin and his eyelids seemed never to blink. I felt something cold and remote in him and when he called me I would not go to him. He sensed my distrust and softened me up with the gift of a dime, then knelt and prayed for us two "poor fatherless young men," as he called us. After prayer Aunt Maggie told us that she and Professor Matthews were leaving soon for the North. I was saddened, for I had grown to feel that Aunt Maggie was another mother to me.

I did not meet the new "uncle" again, though each morning I saw evidences of his having been in the house. My brother and I were puzzled and we speculated as to what our new "uncle" could be doing. Why did he always come at night? Why did he always speak in so subdued a voice, hardly above a whisper? And how did he get the money to buy such white collars and such nice blue suits? To add to our bewilderment, our mother called us to her one day and cautioned us against telling anyone that "uncle" ever visited us, that people were looking for "uncle."

"What people?" I asked.

"White people," my mother said.

Anxiety entered my body. Somewhere in the unknown the white threat was hovering near again.

"What do they want with him?" I asked.

"You never mind," my mother said.

"What did he do?"

"You keep your mouth shut or the white folks'll get you too," she warned me.

Knowing that we were frightened and baffled about our new "uncle," my mother—I guess—urged Aunt Maggie to tell "uncle" to bribe us into silence and trust. Every morning now was like Christmas; we would climb out of bed and race to the kitchen and look on the table to see what "uncle" had left for us. One morning I found that he had brought me a little female poodle, upon which I bestowed the name of Betsy and she became my pet and companion.

Strangely, "uncle" began visiting us in the daytime now, but when he came all the shades in the house were drawn and we were forbidden to go out of doors until he left. I asked my mother a thousand whispered questions about the silent, black, educated "uncle" and she always replied:

"It's something you can't know. Now keep quiet and go play."

One night the sound of sobbing awakened me. I got up and went softly to the front room and peeped around the jamb of the door; there was "uncle" sitting on the floor by the window, peering into the night from under the lifted curtain. My mother was bent over a small trunk, packing hurriedly. Fear gripped me. Was my mother leaving? Why was Aunt Maggie crying? Were the white people coming after us?

"Hurry up," "uncle" said. "We must get out of here."

"Oh, Maggie," my mother said. "I don't know if you ought to go."

"You keep out of this," "uncle" said, still peering into the dark street.

"But what did you do?" Aunt Maggie asked.

"I'll tell you later," "uncle" said. "We got to get out of here before they come!"

"But you've done something terrible," Aunt Maggie said. "Or you wouldn't be running like this."

"The house is on fire," "uncle" said. "And when they see it, they'll know who did it."

"Did you set the house afire?" my mother asked.

"There was nothing else to do," "uncle" said impatiently. "I took the money. I had hit her. She was unconscious. If they found her, she'd tell. I'd be lost. So I set the fire."

"But she'll burn up," Aunt Maggie said, crying into her hands.

"What could I do?" "uncle" asked. "I had to do it. I couldn't just leave her there and let somebody find her. They'd know somebody hit her. But if she burns, nobody'll ever know."

Fear filled me. What was happening? Were white people coming after all of us? Was my mother going to leave me?

"Mama!" I wailed, running into the room.

"Uncle" leaped to his feet; a gun was in his hand and he was pointing it at me. I stared at the gun, feeling that I was going to die at any moment.

"Richard!" my mother whispered fiercely.

"You're going away!" I yelled.

My mother rushed to me and clapped her hand over my mouth.

"Do you want us all to be killed?" she asked, shaking me.

I quieted.

"Now you go back to sleep," she said.

"You're leaving," I said.

"I'm not."

"You are leaving. I see the trunk!" I wailed.

"You stop that noise," my mother said; and she caught my arms in so tight a grip of fury that my crying ceased because of the pain. "Now you get back in bed."

She led me back to bed and I lay awake, listening to whispers, footsteps, doors creaking in the dark, and the sobs of Aunt Maggie. Finally I heard the sound of a horse and buggy rolling up to the house; I heard the scraping of a trunk being dragged across the floor. Aunt Maggie came into my room, crying softly; she kissed me and whispered good-bye. She kissed my brother, who did not even waken. Then she was gone.

The next morning my mother called me into the kitchen and talked to me for a long time, cautioning me that I must never mention what I had seen and heard, that white people would kill me if they even thought I knew.

"Know what?" I could not help but ask.

"Never you mind, now," she said. "Forget what you saw last night."

"But what did 'uncle' do?"

"I can't tell you."

"He killed somebody," I ventured timidly.

"If anybody heard you say that, you'll die," my mother said.

That settled it for me; I would never mention it. A few days later a tall white man with a gleaming star on his chest and a gun on his hip came to the house. He talked with my mother a long time and all I could hear was my mother's voice:

"I don't know what you're talking about. Search the house if you like."

The tall white man looked at me and my brother, but he said nothing to us. For weeks I wondered what it was that "uncle" had done, but I was destined never to know, not even in all the years that followed.

With Aunt Maggie gone, my mother could not earn enough to feed us and my stomach kept so consistently empty that my head ached most of the day. One afternoon hunger haunted me so acutely that I decided to try to sell my dog Betsy and buy some food. Betsy was a tiny, white, fluffy poodle and when I had washed, dried, and combed her, she looked like a toy. I tucked her under my arm and went for the first time alone into a white neighborhood where there were wide clean streets and big white houses. I went from door to door, ringing the bells. Some white people slammed the door in my face. Others told me to come to the rear of the house, but pride would never let me do that. Finally a young white woman came to the door and smiled.

"What do you want?" she asked.

"Do you want to buy a pretty dog?" I asked.

"Let me see it."

She took the dog into her arms and fondled and kissed it.

"What's its name?"

"Betsy."

"She is cute," she said. "What do you want for her?"

"A dollar," I said.

"Wait a moment," she said. "Let me see if I have a dollar."

She took Betsy into the house with her and I waited on the porch, marveling at the cleanliness, the quietness of the white world. How orderly everything was! Yet I felt out of place. I had no desire to live here. Then I remembered that these houses were the homes in which lived those white people who made Negroes leave their homes and flee into the night. I grew tense. Would someone say that I was a bad nigger and try to kill me here? What was keeping the woman so long? Would she tell other people that a nigger boy had said something wrong to her? Perhaps she was getting a mob? Maybe I ought to leave now and forget about Betsy? My mounting anxieties drowned out my hunger. I wanted to rush back to the safety of the black faces I knew.

The door opened and the woman came out, smiling, still hugging Betsy in her arms. But I could not see her smile now; my eyes were full of the fears I had conjured up.

"I just love this dog," she said, "and I'm going to buy her. I haven't got a dollar. All I have is ninety-seven cents."

Though she did not know it, she was now giving me my opportunity to ask for my dog without saying that I did not want to sell her to white people.

"No, ma'am," I said softly. "I want a dollar."

"But I haven't got a dollar in the house," she said.

"Then I can't sell the dog," I said.

"I'll give you the other three cents when my mother comes home tonight," she said.

"No, ma'am," I said, looking stonily at the floor.

"But, listen, you said you wanted a dollar . . ."

"Yes, ma'am. A dollar."

"Then here is ninety-seven cents," she said, extending a handful of change to me, still holding on to Betsy.

"No, ma'am," I said, shaking my head. "I want a dollar."

"But I'll give you the other three cents!"

"My mama told me to sell her for a dollar," I said, feeling that I was being too aggressive and trying to switch the moral blame for my aggressiveness to my absent mother.

"You'll get a dollar. You'll get the three cents tonight."

"No, ma'am."

"Then leave the dog and come back tonight."

"No, ma'am."

"But what could you want with a dollar *now*?" she asked.

"I want to buy something to eat," I said.

"Then ninety-seven cents will buy you a lot of food," she said.

"No, ma'am. I want my dog."

She stared at me for a moment and her face grew red.

"Here's your dog," she snapped, thrusting Betsy into my arms. "Now, get away from here! You're just about the craziest nigger boy I ever did see!"

I took Betsy and ran all the way home, glad that I had not sold her. But my hunger returned. Maybe I ought to have taken the ninety-seven cents? But it was too late now. I hugged Betsy in my arms and waited. When my mother came home that night, I told her what had happened.

"And you didn't take the money?" she asked.

"No, ma'am."

"Why?"

"I don't know," I said uneasily.

"Don't you know that ninety-seven cents is *almost* a dollar?" she asked.

"Yes, ma'am," I said, counting on my fingers. "Ninety-eight, ninety-nine, one hundred. But I didn't want to sell Betsy to white people."

"Why?"

"Because they're white," I said.

"You're foolish," my mother said.

A week later Betsy was crushed to death beneath the wheels of a coal wagon. I cried and buried her in the back yard and drove a barrel staving into the ground at the head of her grave. My mother's sole comment was:

"You could have had a dollar. But you can't eat a dead dog, can you?"

I did not answer.

Up or down the wet or dusty streets, indoors or out, the days and nights began to spell out magic possibilities.

If I pulled a hair from a horse's tail and sealed it in a jar of my own urine, the hair would turn overnight into a snake.

If I passed a Catholic sister or mother dressed in black and smiled and allowed her to see my teeth, I would surely die.

If I walked under a leaning ladder, I would certainly have bad luck.

If I kissed my elbow, I would turn into a girl.

If my right ear itched, then something good was being said about me by somebody.

If I touched a hunchback's hump, then I would never be sick.

If I placed a safety pin on a steel railroad track and let a train run over it, the safety pin would turn into a pair of bright brandnew scissors.

If I heard a voice and no human being was near, then either God or the Devil was trying to talk to me.

Whenever I made urine, I should spit into it for good luck.

If my nose itched, somebody was going to visit me.

If I mocked a crippled man, then God would make me crippled.

If I used the name of God in vain, then God would strike me dead.

If it rained while the sun was shining, then the Devil was beating his wife.

If the stars twinkled more than usual on any given night, it meant that the angels in heaven were happy and were flitting across the floors of heaven; and since stars were merely holes ventilating heaven, the twinkling came from the angels flitting past the holes that admitted air into the holy home of God.

If I broke a mirror, I would have seven years of bad luck.

If I was good to my mother, I would grow old and rich.

If I had a cold and tied a worn, dirty sock about my throat before I went to bed, the cold would be gone the next morning.

If I wore a bit of asafetida in a little bag tied about my neck, I would never catch a disease.

If I looked at the sun through a piece of smoked glass on Easter Sunday morning, I would see the sun shouting in praise of a Risen Lord.

If a man confessed anything on his deathbed, it was the truth; for no man could stare death in the face and lie.

If you spat on each grain of corn that was planted, the corn would grow tall and bear well.

If I spilt salt, I should toss a pinch over my left shoulder to ward off misfortune.

If I covered a mirror when a storm was raging, the lightning would not strike me.

If I stepped over a broom that was lying on the floor, I would have bad luck.

If I walked in my sleep, then God was trying to lead me somewhere to do a good deed for Him.

Anything seemed possible, likely, feasible, because I wanted everything to be possible . . . Because I had no power to make things happen outside of me in the objective world, I made things happen within. Because my environment was bare and bleak, I endowed it with unlimited potentialities, redeemed it for the sake of my own hungry and cloudy yearning.

A dread of white people now came to live permanently in my feelings and imagination. As the war drew to a close, racial conflict flared over the entire South, and though I did not witness any of it, I could not have been more thoroughly affected by it if I had participated directly in every clash. The war itself had been unreal to me, but I had grown able to respond emotionally to every hint, whisper, word, inflection, news, gossip, and rumor regarding conflicts between the races. Nothing challenged the totality of my personality so much as this pressure of hate and threat that stemmed from the invisible whites. I would stand for hours on the doorsteps of neighbors' houses listening to their talk, learning how a white woman had slapped a black woman, how a white man had killed a black man. It filled me with awe, wonder, and fear, and I asked ceaseless questions.

One evening I heard a tale that rendered me sleepless for nights. It was of a Negro woman whose husband had been seized and killed by a mob. It was claimed that the woman vowed she would avenge her husband's death and she took a shotgun, wrapped it in a sheet, and went humbly to the whites, pleading that she be allowed to take her husband's body for burial. It seemed that she was granted permission to come to the side of her dead husband while the whites, silent and armed, looked on. The woman, so went the story, knelt and prayed, then proceeded to unwrap the sheet; and, before the white men realized what was happening, she had taken the gun from the sheet and had slain four of them, shooting at them from her knees.

I did not know if the story was factually true or not, but it was emotionally true because I had already grown to feel that there existed men against whom I was powerless, men who could violate my life at will.

I resolved that I would emulate the black woman if I were ever faced with a white mob; I would conceal a weapon, pretend that I had been crushed by the wrong done to one of my loved ones; then, just when they thought I had accepted their cruelty as the law of my life, I would let go with my gun and kill as many of them as possible before they killed me. The story of the woman's deception gave form and meaning to confused defensive feelings that had long been sleeping in me.

My imaginings, of course, had no objective value whatever. My spontaneous fantasies lived in my mind because I felt completely helpless in the face of this threat that might come upon me at any time, and because there did not exist to my knowledge any possible course of action which could have saved me if I had ever been confronted with a white mob. My fantasies were a moral bulwark that enabled me to feel I was keeping my emotional integrity whole, a support that enabled my personality to limp through days lived under the threat of violence.

These fantasies were no longer a reflection of my reaction to the white people, they were a part of my living, of my emotional life; they were a culture, a creed, a religion. The hostility of the whites had become so deeply implanted in my mind and feelings that it had lost direct connection with the daily environment in which I lived; and my reactions to this hostility fed upon itself, grew or diminished according to the news that reached me about the whites, according to what I aspired or hoped for. Tension would set in at the mere mention of whites and a vast complex of emotions, involving the whole of my personality, would be aroused. It was as though I was continuously reacting to the threat of some natural force whose hostile behavior could not be predicted. I had never in my life been abused by whites, but I had already become as conditioned to their existence as though I had been the victim of a thousand lynchings.

I lived in West Helena an undeterminedly long time before I returned to school and took up regular study. My mother luckily secured a job in a white doctor's office at the unheard-of wages of five dollars per week and at once she announced that her "sons were going to school again." I was happy. But I was still shy and half paralyzed when in the presence of a crowd, and my first day at the new school made me the laughingstock of the classroom. I was sent to the blackboard to write my name and address; I knew my name and address, knew how to write it, knew how to spell it; but standing at the blackboard with the eyes of the many girls and boys looking at my back made me freeze inside and I was unable to write a single letter.

"Write you name," the teacher called to me.

I lifted the white chalk to the blackboard and, as I was about to write, my mind went blank, empty; I could not remember my name, not even the first letter. Somebody giggled and I stiffened.

"Just forget us and write your name and address," the teacher coaxed.

An impulse to write would flash through me, but my hand would refuse to move. The children began to twitter and I flushed hotly.

"Don't you know your name?" the teacher asked.

I looked at her and could not answer. The teacher rose and walked to my side, smiling at me to give me confidence. She placed her hand tenderly upon my shoulder.

"What's your name?" she asked.

"Richard," I whispered.

"Richard what?"

"Richard Wright."

"Spell it."

I spelled my name in a wild rush of letters, trying desperately to redeem my paralyzing shyness.

"Spell it slowly so I can hear it," she directed me. I did.

"Now, can you write?"

"Yes, ma'am."

"Then write it."

Again I turned to the blackboard and lifted my hand to write, then I was blank and void within. I tried frantically to collect my senses, but I could remember nothing. A sense of the girls and boys behind me filled me to the exclusion of everything. I realized how utterly I was failing and I grew weak and leaned my hot forehead against the cold blackboard. The room burst into a loud and prolonged laugh and my muscles froze.

"You may go to your seat," the teacher said.

I sat and cursed myself. Why did I always appear so dumb when I was called upon to perform something in a crowd? I knew how to write as well as any pupil in the classroom, and no doubt I could read better than any of them, and I could talk fluently and expressively when I was sure of myself. Then why did strange faces make me freeze? I sat with my ears and neck burning, hearing the pupils whisper about me, hating myself, hating them; I sat still as stone and a storm of emotion surged through me.

While sitting in class one day I was startled to hear whistles blowing and bells ringing. Soon the bedlam was deafening. The teacher lost control of her class and the girls and boys ran to the windows. The teacher left the room and when she returned she announced:

"Everybody, pack your things and go home!"

"Why?"

"What's happened?"

"The war is over," the teacher said.

I followed the rest of the children into the streets and saw that white and black people were laughing and singing and shouting. I felt afraid as I pushed through crowds of white people, but my fright left when I entered my neighborhood and saw smiling black faces. I wandered among them, trying to realize what war was, what it meant, and I could not. I noticed that many girls and boys were pointing at something in the sky; I looked up too and saw what seemed to be a tiny bird wheeling and sailing.

"Look!"

"A plane!"

I had never seen a plane.

"It's a bird," I said.

The crowd laughed.

"That's a plane, boy," a man said.

"It's a bird," I said. "I see it."

A man lifted me upon his shoulder.

"Boy, remember this," he said. "You're seeing man fly."

I still did not believe it. It still looked like a bird to me. That night at home my mother convinced me that men could fly.

Christmas came and I had but one orange. I was hurt and would not go out to play with the neighborhood children who were blowing horns and shooting firecrackers. I nursed my orange all of Christmas Day; at night, just before going to bed, I ate it, first taking a bite out of the top and sucking the juice from it as I squeezed it; finally I tore the peeling into bits and munched them slowly.

Chapter Three

HAVING grown taller and older, I now associated with older boys and I had to pay for my admittance into their company by subscribing to certain racial sentiments. The touchstone of fraternity was my feeling toward white people, how much hostility I held toward them, what degrees of value and honor I assigned to race. None of this was premeditated, but sprang spontaneously out of the talk of black boys who met at the crossroads.

It was degrading to play with girls and in our talk we relegated them to a remote island of life. We had somehow caught the spirit of the role of our sex and we flocked together for common moral schooling. We spoke boastfully in bass voices; we used the word "nigger" to prove the tough fiber of our feelings; we spouted excessive profanity as a sign of our coming manhood; we pretended callousness toward the injunctions of our parents; and we strove to convince one another that our decisions stemmed from ourselves and ourselves alone. Yet we frantically concealed how dependent we were upon one another.

Of an afternoon when school had let out I would saunter down the street, idly kicking an empty tin can, or knocking a stick against the palings of a wooden fence, or whistling, until I would stumble upon one or more of the gang loitering at a corner, standing in a field, or sitting upon the steps of somebody's house.

"Hey." Timidly.

"You eat yet?" Uneasily trying to make conversation.

"Yeah, man. I done really fed my face." Casually.

"I had cabbage and potatoes." Confidently.

"I had buttermilk and black-eyed peas." Meekly informational.

"Hell, I ain't gonna stand near you, nigger!" Pronouncement.

"How come?" Feigned innocence.

" 'Cause you gonna smell up this air in a minute!" A shouted accusation.

Laughter runs through the crowd.

"Nigger, your mind's in a ditch." Amusingly moralistic.

"Ditch, nothing! Nigger, you going to break wind any minute now!" Triumphant pronouncement creating suspense.

"Yeah, when them black-eyed peas tell that buttermilk to move over, that buttermilk ain't gonna wanna move and there's gonna be war in your guts and your stomach's gonna swell up and bust!" Climax.

The crowd laughs loud and long.

"Man, them white folks oughta catch you and send you to the zoo and keep you for the next war!" Throwing the subject into a wider field.

"Then when that fighting starts, they oughta feed you on buttermilk and black-eyed peas and let you break wind!" The subject is accepted and extended.

"You'd win the war with a new kind of poison gas!" A shouted climax.

There is high laughter that simmers down slowly.

"Maybe poison gas is something good to have." The subject of white folks is associationally swept into the orbit of talk.

"Yeah, if they hava race riot round here, I'm gonna kill all the white folks with my poison." Bitter pride.

Gleeful laughter. Then silence, each waiting for the other to contribute something.

"Them white folks sure scared of us, though." Sober statement of an old problem.

"Yeah, they send you to war, make you lick them Germans, teach you how to fight and when you come back they scared of you, want to kill you." Half boastful and half complaining.

"My mama says that old white woman where she works talked 'bout slapping her and Ma said: 'Miz Green, if you slaps me, I'll kill you and go to hell and pay for it!' " Extension, development, sacrificial boasting.

"Hell, I woulda just killed her if she hada said that to me." An angry grunt of supreme racial assertion.

Silence.

"Man, them white folks sure is mean." Complaining.

"That's how come so many colored folks leaving the South." Informational.

"And, man, they sure hate for you to leave." Pride of personal and racial worth implied.

"Yeah. They wanna keep you here and work you to death."

"The first white sonofabitch that bothers me is gonna get a hole knocked in his head!" Naïve rebellion.

"That ain't gonna do you no good. Hell, they'll catch you." Rejection of naïve rebellion.

"Ha-ha-ha . . . Yeah, goddammit, they really catch you, now." Appreciation of the thoroughness of white militancy.

"Yeah, white folks set on their white asses day and night, but leta nigger do something, and they get every bloodhound that was ever born and put 'em on his trail." Bitter pride in realizing what it costs to defeat them.

"Man, you reckon these white folks is ever gonna change?" Timid, questioning hope.

"Hell, no! They just born that way." Rejecting hope for fear that it could never come true.

"Shucks, man. I'm going north when I get grown." Rebelling against futile hope and embracing flight.

"A colored man's all right up north." Justifying flight.

"They say a white man hit a colored man up north

and that colored man hit that white man, knocked him cold, and nobody did a damn thing!" Urgent wish to believe in flight.

"Man for man up there." Begging to believe in justice.

Silence.

"Listen, you reckon them buildings up north is as tall as they say they is?" Leaping by association to something concrete and trying to make belief real.

"They say they gotta building in New York forty stories high!" A thing too incredible for belief.

"Man, I'd be scareda them buildings!" Ready to abandon the now suppressed idea of flight.

"You know, they say that them buildings sway and rock in the wind." Stating a miracle.

"Naw, nigger!" Utter astonishment and rejection.

"Yeah, they say they do." Insisting upon the miracle.

"You reckon that could be?" Questioning hope.

"Hell, naw! If a building swayed and rocked in the wind, hell, it'd fall! Any fool knows that! Don't let people maka fool outta you, telling you them things!" Moving body agitatedly, stomping feet impatiently, and scurrying back to safe reality.

Silence. Somebody would pick up a stone and toss it across a field.

"Man, what makes white folks so mean?" Returning to grapple with the old problem.

"Whenever I see one I spit." Emotional rejection of whites.

"Man, ain't they ugly?" Increased emotional rejection.

"Man, you ever get right close to a white man, close enough to smell 'im?" Anticipation of statement.

"They say we stink. But my ma says white folks smell like dead folks." Wishing the enemy was dead.

"Niggers smell from sweat. But white folks smell *all* the time." The enemy is an animal to be killed on sight.

And the talk would weave, roll, surge, spurt, veer, swell, having no specific aim or direction, touching vast areas of life, expressing the tentative impulses of childhood. Money, God, race, sex, color, war, planes, machines, trains, swimming, boxing, anything . . . The culture of one black household was thus transmitted to another black household, and folk tradition was handed from group to group. Our attitudes were made, defined, set, or corrected; our ideas were discovered, discarded, enlarged, torn apart, and accepted. Night would fall. Bats would zip through the air. Crickets would cry from the grass. Frogs would croak. The stars would come out. Dew would dampen the earth. Yellow squares of light would glow in the distance as kerosene lamps were lit in our homes. Finally, from across the fields or down the road a long slow yell would come:

"Youuuuuuuu, Daaaaaaaavee!"

Easy laughter among the boys, but no reply.

"Calling the hogs."

"Go home, pig."

Laughter again. A boy would slowly detach himself from the gang.

"Youuuuuuuu, Daaaaaaaaavee!"

He would not answer his mother's call, for that would have been a sign of dependence.

"I'll do you-all like the farmer did the potato," the boy would say.

"How's that?"

"Plant you now and dig you later!"

The boy would trot home slowly and there would be more easy laughter. More talk. One by one we would be called home to fetch water from the hydrant in the back yard, to go to the store and buy greens and meal for tomorrow, to split wood for kindling.

On Sundays, if our clothes were presentable, my mother would take me and my brother to Sunday school. We did not object, for church was not where we learned of God or His ways, but where we met our school friends and continued our long, rambling talks. Some of the Bible stories were interesting in themselves, but we always twisted them, secularized them to the level of our street life, rejecting all meanings that did not fit into our environment. And we did the same to the beautiful hymns. When the preacher intoned:

Amazing grace, how sweet it sounds

we would wink at one another and hum under our breath:

A bulldog ran my grandma down

We were now large enough for the white boys to fear us and both of us, the white boys and the black boys, began to play our traditional racial roles as though we had been born to them, as though it was in our blood, as though we were being guided by instinct. All the frightful descriptions we had heard about each other, all the violent expressions of hate and hostility that had seeped into us from our surroundings, came now to the surface to guide our actions. The roundhouse was the racial boundary of the neighborhood, and it had been tacitly agreed between the white boys and the black boys that the whites were to keep to the far side of the roundhouse and we blacks were to keep to our side. Whenever we caught a white boy on our side we stoned him; if we strayed to their side, they stoned us.

Our battles were real and bloody; we threw rocks, cinders, coal, sticks, pieces of iron, and broken bottles, and while we threw them we longed for even deadlier weapons. If we were hurt, we took it quietly; there was no crying or whimpering. If our wounds were not truly serious, we hid them from our parents. We did not want to be beaten for fighting. Once, in a battle with a gang of white boys, I was struck behind the ear with a piece of broken bottle; the cut was deep and bled profusely. I tried to stem the flow of blood by dabbing at the cut with a rag and when my mother came from work I was forced to tell her that I was hurt, for I needed medical attention. She rushed me to a doctor who stitched my scalp; but when she took me home she beat me, telling me that I must never fight white boys again, that I might be killed by them, that she had to work and had no time to worry about my fights. Her words did not sink in, for they conflicted with the code of the streets. I promised my mother that I would not fight, but I knew that if I kept my word I would lose my standing in the gang, and the gang's life was my life.

My mother became too ill to work and I began to do chores in the neighborhood. My first job was carrying lunches to the men who worked in the roundhouse, for which I received twenty-five cents a week. When the men did not finish their lunches, I would salvage what few crumbs remained. Later I obtained a job in a small café carting wood in my arms to keep the big stove going and taking trays of food to passengers when trains stopped for a half hour or so in a near-by station. I received a dollar a week for this work, but I was too young and too small to perform the duties; one morning while trying to take a heavily loaded tray up the steps of a train, I fell and dashed the tray of food to the ground.

Inability to pay rent forced us to move into a house perched atop high logs in a section of the town where flood waters came. My brother and I had great fun running up and down the tall, shaky steps.

Again paying rent became a problem and we moved nearer the center of town, where I found a job in a pressing shop, delivering clothes to hotels, sweeping floors, and listening to Negro men boast of their sex lives.

Yet again we moved, this time to the outskirts of town, near a wide stretch of railroad tracks to which, each morning before school, I would take a sack and gather coal to heat our frame house, dodging in and out between the huge, black, puffing engines.

My mother, her health failing rapidly, spoke constantly now of Granny's home, of how ardently she

wanted to see us grow up before she died. Already there
had crept into her speech a halting, lisping quality
that, though I did not know it, was the shadow of her
future. I was more conscious of my mother now than
I had ever been and I was already able to feel what
being completely without her would mean. A slowly
rising dread stole into me and I would look at my
mother for long moments, but when she would look at
me I would look away. Then real fear came as her illness recurred at shorter intervals. Time stood still.
My brother and I waited, hungry and afraid.

One morning a shouting voice awakened me.

"Richard! Richard!"

I rolled out of bed. My brother came running into
the room.

"Richard, you better come and see Mama. She's
very sick," he said.

I ran into my mother's room and saw her lying upon
her bed, dressed, her eyes open, her mouth gaped.
She was very still.

"Mama!" I called.

She did not answer or turn her head. I reached forward to shake her, but drew back, afraid that she was
dead.

"Mama!" I called again, my mind unable to grasp
that she could not answer.

Finally I went to her and shook her. She moved
slightly and groaned. My brother and I called her repeatedly, but she did not speak. Was she dying? It
seemed unthinkable. My brother and I looked at each
other; we did not know what to do.

"We better get somebody," I said.

I ran into the hallway and called a neighbor. A tall,
black woman bustled out of a door.

"Please, won't you come and see my mama? She
won't talk. We can't wake her up. She's terribly sick,"
I told her.

She followed me into our flat.

"Mrs. Wright!" she called to my mother.

My mother lay still, unseeing, silent. The woman felt my mother's hands.

"She ain't dead," she said. "But she's sick, all right. I better get some more of the neighbors."

Five or six of the women came and my brother and I waited in the hallway while they undressed my mother and put her to bed. When we were allowed back in the room, a woman said:

"Looks like a stroke to me."

"Just like paralysis," said another.

"And she's so young," someone else said.

My brother and I stood against a wall while the bustling women worked frantically over my mother. A stroke? Paralysis? What were those things? Would she die? One of the women asked me if there was any money in the house; I did not know. They searched through the dresser and found a dollar or two and sent for a doctor. The doctor arrived. Yes, he told us, my mother had suffered a stroke of paralysis. She was in a serious condition. She needed someone with her day and night; she needed medicine. Where was her husband? I told him the story and he shook his head.

"She'll need all the help that she can get," the doctor said. "Her entire left side is paralyzed. She cannot talk and she will have to be fed."

Later that day I rummaged through drawers and found Granny's address; I wrote to her, pleading with her to come and help us. The neighbors nursed my mother day and night, fed us and washed our clothes. I went through the days with a stunned consciousness, unable to believe what had happened. Suppose Granny did not come? I tried not to think of it. She *had* to come. The utter loneliness was now terrifying. I had been suddenly thrown emotionally upon my own. Within an hour the half-friendly world that I had known had turned cold and hostile. I was too frightened to weep. I was glad that my mother was not dead, but there was the fact that she would be sick for a long, long time, perhaps for the balance of her life. I became morose. Though I was a child, I could no longer feel as a child, could no longer react as a child. The desire for play was gone and I brooded, wondering if Granny would come and help us. I tried not to think of a tomorrow that was neither real nor wanted, for all tomorrows held questions that I could not answer.

When the neighbors offered me food, I refused, already ashamed that so often in my life I had to be fed by strangers. And after I had been prevailed upon to eat I would eat as little as possible, feeling that some of the shame of charity would be taken away. It pained me to think that other children were wondering if I were hungry, and whenever they asked me if I wanted food, I would say no, even though I was starving. I was tense during the days I waited for Granny, and when she came I gave up, letting her handle things, answering questions automatically, obeying, knowing that somehow I had to face things alone. I withdrew into myself.

I wrote letters that Granny dictated to her eight children—there were nine of them, including my mother —in all parts of the country, asking for money with which "to take Ella and her two little children to our home." Money came and again there were days of packing household effects. My mother was taken to the train in an ambulance and put on board upon a stretcher. We rode to Jackson in silence and my mother was put abed upstairs. Aunt Maggie came from Detroit to help nurse and clean. The big house was quiet. We spoke in lowered voices. We walked with soft tread. The odor of medicine hung in the air. Doctors came and went. Night and day I could hear my mother groaning. We thought that she would die at any moment.

Aunt Cleo came from Chicago. Uncle Clark came from Greenwood, Mississippi. Uncle Edward came from Carters, Mississippi. Uncle Charles from Mobile, Alabama. Aunt Addie from a religious school in Huntsville, Alabama. Uncle Thomas from Hazelhurst, Mississippi. The house had an expectant air and I caught whispered talk of "what is to become of her children?" I felt dread, knowing that others—strangers even though they were relatives—were debating my destiny. I had never seen my mother's brothers and sisters before and their presence made live again in me my old shyness. One day Uncle Edward called me to him and he felt my skinny arms and legs.

"He needs more flesh on him," he commented impersonally, addressing himself to his brothers and sisters.

I was horribly embarrassed, feeling that my life had somehow been full of nameless wrong, an unatonable guilt.

"Food will make him pick up in weight," Granny said.

Out of the family conferences it was decided that my brother and I would be separated, that it was too much of a burden for any one aunt or uncle to assume the support of both of us. Where was I to go? Who would take me? I became more anxious than ever. When an aunt or an uncle would come into my presence, I could not look at them. I was always reminding myself that I must not do anything that would make any of them feel they would not want me in their homes.

At night my sleep was filled with wild dreams. Sometimes I would wake up screaming in terror. The grownups would come running and I would stare at them, as though they were figures out of my nightmare, then go back to sleep. One night I found myself standing in the back yard. The moon was shining bright as day. Silence surrounded me. Suddenly I felt that someone was holding my hand. I looked and saw an uncle. He was speaking to me in a low, gentle voice.

"What's the matter, son?"

I stared at him, trying to understand what he was saying. I seemed to be wrapped in a kind of mist.

"Richard, what are you doing?"

I could not answer. It seemed that I could not wake up. He shook me. I came to myself and stared about at the moon-drenched yard.

"Where are we going?" I asked him.

"You were walking in your sleep," he said.

Granny gave me fuller meals and made me take naps in the afternoon and gradually my sleepwalking passed. The uneasy days and nights made me resolve to leave Granny's home as soon as I was old enough to support myself. It was not that they were unkind, but I knew that they did not have money enough to feed me and my brother. I avoided going into my mother's room now; merely to look at her was painful. She had grown very thin; she was still speechless, staring, quiet as stone.

One evening my brother and I were called into the front room where a conference of aunts and uncles was being held.

"Richard," said an uncle, "you know how sick your mother is?"

"Yes, sir."

"Well, Granny's not strong enough to take care of you two boys," he continued.

"Yes, sir," I said, waiting for his decision.

"Well, Aunt Maggie's going to take your brother to Detroit and send him to school."

I waited. Who was going to take me? I had wanted to be with Aunt Maggie, but I did not dare contest the decision.

"Now, where would you like to go?" I was asked.

The question caught me by surprise; I had been waiting for a fiat, and now a choice lay before me. But I did not have the courage to presume that anyone wanted me.

"Anywhere," I said.

"Any of us are willing to take you," he said.

Quickly I calculated which of them lived nearest to Jackson. Uncle Clark lived in Greenwood, which was but a few miles distant.

"I'd like to live with Uncle Clark, since he's close to the home here," I said.

"Is that what you really want?"

"Yes, sir."

.Uncle Clark came to me and placed his hand upon my head.

"All right. I'll take you back with me and send you to school. Tomorrow we'll go and buy clothes."

My tension eased somewhat, but stayed with me. My brother was happy. He was going north. I wanted to go, but I said nothing.

A train ride and I was in yet another little southern town. Home in Greenwood was a four-room bungalow, comprising half of a double house that sat on a quiet shady road. Aunt Jody, a medium-sized, neat, silent, mulatto girl, had a hot supper waiting on the table. She baffled me with her serious, reserved manner; she seemed to be acting in conformity with a code unknown to me, and I assumed that she regarded me as a "wrong one," a boy who for some reason did not have a home; I felt that in her mind she would push me to the outskirts of life and I was awkward and self-conscious in her presence. Both Uncle Clark and Aunt Jody talked to me as though I were a grownup and I wondered if I could do what was expected of me. I had always felt a certain warmth with my mother, even when we had lived in squalor; but I felt none here. Perhaps I was too apprehensive to feel any.

During supper it was decided that I was to be placed in school the next day. Uncle Clark and Aunt Jody both had jobs and I was told that at noon I would find lunch on the stove.

"Now, Richard, this is your new home," Uncle Clark said.

"Yes, sir."

"After school, bring in wood and coal for the fireplaces."

"Yes, sir."

"Split kindling and lay a fire in the kitchen stove."

"Yes, sir."

"Bring in a bucket of water from the yard so that Jody can cook in the mornings."

"Yes, sir."

"After your chores are done, you may spend the afternoon studying."

"Yes, sir."

I had never been assigned definite tasks before and I went to bed a little frightened. I lay sleepless, wondering if I should have come, feeling the dark night holding strange people, strange houses, strange streets. What would happen to me here? How would I get along? What kind of woman was Aunt Jody? How ought I act around here? Would Uncle Clark let me make friends with other boys? I awakened the next morning to see the sun shining into my room; I felt more at ease.

"Richard!" my uncle was calling me.

I washed, dressed, and went into the kitchen and sat wordlessly at the table.

"Good morning, Richard," Aunt Jody said.

"Oh, good morning," I mumbled, wishing that I had thought to say it first.

"Don't people say good morning where you come from?" she asked.

"Yes, ma'am."

"I thought they did," she said pointedly.

Aunt Jody and Uncle Clark began to question me about my life and I grew so self-conscious that my hunger left me. After breakfast, Uncle Clark took me to school, introduced me to the principal. The first half of the school day passed without incident. I sat looking at the strange reading book, following the lessons. The subjects seemed simple and I felt that I could keep up. My anxiety was still in me; I was wondering how I would get on with the boys. Each new school meant a new area of life to be conquered. Were the boys tough? How hard did they fight? I took it for granted that they fought.

At noon recess I went into the school grounds and a group of boys sauntered up to me, looked at me from my head to my feet, whispering among themselves. I leaned against a wall, trying to conceal my uneasiness.

"Where you from?" a boy asked abruptly.

"Jackson," I answered.

"How come they make you people so ugly in Jackson?" he demanded.

There was loud laughter.

"You're not any too good-looking yourself," I countered instantly.

"Oh!"

"Aw!"

"You hear what he told 'im?"

"You think you're smart, don't you?" the boy asked, sneering.

"Listen, I ain't picking a fight," I said. "But if you want to fight, I'll fight."

"Hunh, hard guy, ain't you?"

"As hard as you."

"Do you know who you can tell that to?" he asked me.

"And you know who you can tell it back to?" I asked.

"Are you talking about my mama?" he asked, edging forward.

"If you want it that way," I said.

This was my test. If I failed now, I would have failed at school, for the first trial came not in books, but in how one's fellows took one, what value they placed upon one's willingness to fight.

"Take back what you said," the boy challenged me.

"Make me," I said.

The crowd howled, sensing a fight. The boy hesitated, weighing his chances of beating me.

"You ain't gonna take what that new boy said, is you?" someone taunted the boy.

The boy came close. I stood my ground. Our faces were four inches apart.

"You think I'm scared of you, don't you?" he asked.

"I told you what I think," I said.

Somebody, eager and afraid that we would not fight, pushed the boy and he bumped into me. I shoved him away violently.

"Don't push me!" the boy said.

"Then keep off me!" I said.

He was pushed again and I struck out with my right and caught him in the mouth. The crowd yelled, milled, surging so close that I could barely lift my arm to land a blow. When either of us tried to strike the other, we would be thrown off balance by the screaming boys. Every blow landed elicited shouts of delight. Knowing that if I did not win or make a good showing I would have to fight a new boy each day, I fought tigerishly, trying to leave a scar, seeking to draw blood as proof that I was not a coward, that I could take care of myself. The bell rang and the crowd pulled us apart. The fight seemed a draw.

"I ain't through with you!" the boy shouted.

"Go to hell!" I answered.

In the classroom the boys asked me questions about myself; I was someone worth knowing. When the bell rang for school to be dismissed, I was set to fight again; but the boy was not in sight.

On my way home I found a cheap ring in the streets and at once I knew what I was going to do with it. The ring had a red stone held by tiny prongs which I loosened, took the stone out, leaving the sharp tiny prongs jutting up. I slid the ring on to my finger and shadow boxed. Now, by God, let a goddamn bully come and I would show him how to fight; I would leave a crimson streak on his face with every blow.

But I never had to use the ring. After I had exhibited my new weapon at school, a description of it spread among the boys. I challenged my enemy to another fight, but he would not respond. Fighting was not now necessary. I had been accepted.

No sooner had I won my right to the school grounds than a new dread arose. One evening, before bedtime, I was sitting in the front room, reading, studying. Uncle Clark, who was a contracting carpenter, was at his drawing table, drafting models of houses. Aunt Jody was darning. Suddenly the doorbell rang and Aunt Jody admitted the next-door neighbor, the owner of the house in which we lived and its former occupant. His name was Burden; he was a tall, brown, stooped man and when I was introduced to him I rose and shook his hand.

"Well, son," Mr. Burden told me, "it's certainly a comfort to see another boy in this house."

"Is there another boy here?" I asked eagerly.

"My son was here," Mr. Burden said, shaking his head. "But he's gone now."

"How old is he?" I asked.

"He was about your age," Mr. Burden mumbled sadly.

"Where did he go?" I asked stupidly.

"He's dead," Mr. Burden said.

"Oh," I said.

I had not understood him. There was a long silence. Mr. Burden looked at me wistfully.

"Do you sleep in there?" he asked, pointing to my room.

"Yes, sir."

"That's where my boy slept," he said.

"In *there*?" I asked, just to make sure.

"Yes, right in there."

"On *that* bed?" I asked.

"Yes, that was his bed. When I heard that you were coming, I gave your uncle that bed for you," he explained.

I saw Uncle Clark shaking his head vigorously at Mr. Burden, but he was too late. At once my imagination began to weave ghosts. I did not actually believe in ghosts, but I had been taught that there was a God and I had given a kind of uneasy assent to His existence, and if there was a God, then surely there must be ghosts. In a moment I built up an intense loathing for sleeping in the room where the boy had died. Rationally I knew that the dead boy could not bother me, but he had become alive for me in a way that I could not dismiss. After Mr. Burden had gone, I went timidly to Uncle Clark.

"I'm scared to sleep in there," I told him.

"Why? Because a boy died in there?"

"Yes, sir."

"But, son, that's nothing to be afraid of."

"I know. But I am scared."

"We all must die someday. So why be afraid?"

I had no answer for that.

"When you die, do you want people to be afraid of *you*?"

I could not answer that either.

"This is nonsense," Uncle Clark went on.

"But I'm scared," I told him.

"You'll get over it."

"Can't I sleep somewhere else?"

"There's nowhere else for you to sleep."

"Can I sleep here on the sofa?" I asked.

"*May* I sleep here on the sofa?" Aunt Jody corrected me in a mocking tone.

"May I sleep here on the sofa?" I repeated after her.

"No," Aunt Jody said.

I groped into the dark room and fumbled for the bed; I had the illusion that if I touched it I would encounter the dead boy. I trembled. Finally I jumped roughly into the bed and jerked the covers over my face. I did not sleep that night and my eyes were red and puffy the next morning.

"Didn't you sleep well?" Uncle Clark asked me.

"I can't sleep in that room," I said.

"You slept in it before you heard of that boy who died in there, didn't you?" Aunt Jody asked me.

"Yes, ma'am."

"Then why can't you sleep in it now?"

"I'm just scared."

"You stop being a baby," she told me.

The next night was the same; fear kept me from sleeping. After Uncle Clark and Aunt Jody had gone to bed, I rose and crept into the front room and slept in a tight ball on the sofa, without any cover. I awakened the next morning to find Uncle Clark shaking me.

"Why are you doing this?" he asked.

"I'm scared to sleep in there," I said.

"You go back into that room and sleep tonight," he told me. "You've got to get over this thing."

I spent another sleepless, shivering night in the dead boy's room—it was not my room any longer—and I was so frightened that I sweated. Each creak of the house made my heart stand still. In school the next day I was dull. I came home and spent another long night of wakefulness and the following day I went to sleep in the classroom. When questioned by the teacher, I could give no answer. Unable to free myself from my terror, I began to long for home. A week of sleeplessness brought me near the edge of nervous collapse.

Sunday came and I refused to go to church and Uncle Clark and Aunt Jody were astonished. They did not understand that my refusal to go to church was my way of silently begging them to let me sleep somewhere else. They left me alone in the house and I spent the entire day sitting on the front steps; I did not have enough courage to go into the kitchen to eat. When I became thirsty, I went around the house and drank water from the hydrant in the back yard rather than venture into the house. Desperation made me raise the issue of the room again at bedtime.

"Please, let me sleep on the sofa in the front room," I pleaded.

"You've got to get out of that fear," my uncle said.

I made up my mind to ask to be sent home. I went to Uncle Clark, knowing that he had incurred expense in bringing me here, that he had thought he was helping me, that he had bought my clothes and books.

"Uncle Clark, send me back to Jackson," I said.

He was bent over a little table and he straightened and stared at me.

"You're not happy here?" he asked.

"No, sir," I answered truthfully, fearing that the ceiling would crash down upon my head.

"And you really want to go back?"

"Yes, sir."

"Things will not be as easy for you at home as here," he said. "There's not much money for food and things."

"I want to be where my mother is," I said, trying to strengthen my plea.

"It's really about the room?"

"Yes, sir."

"Well, we tried to make you happy here," my uncle said, sighing. "Maybe we didn't know how. But if you want to go back, then you may go."

"When?" I asked eagerly.

"As soon as school term has ended."

"But I want to go now!" I cried.

"But you'll break up your year's schooling," he said.

"I don't mind."

"You will, in the future. You've never had a single year of steady schooling," he said.

"I want to go home," I said.

"Have you felt this way a long time?" he asked.

"Yes, sir."

"I'll write Granny tonight," he said, his eyes lit with surprise.

Daily I asked him if he had heard from Granny only to learn that there had been no word. My sleeplessness made me feel that my days were a hot, wild dream and my studies suffered at school. I had been making high marks and now I made low ones and finally began to fail altogether. I was fretful, living from moment to moment.

One evening, in doing my chores, I took the water pail to the hydrant in the back yard to fill it. I was half asleep, tired, tense, all but swaying on my feet. I balanced the handle of the pail on the jutting tip of the metal faucet and waited for it to fill; the pail slipped and water drenched my pants and shoes and stockings.

"That goddamn lousy bastard sonofabitching bucket!" I spoke in a whisper of hate and despair.

"Richard!" Aunt Jody's amazed voice sounded in the darkness behind me.

I turned. Aunt Jody was standing on the back steps. She came into the yard.

"What did you say, boy?" she asked.

"Nothing," I mumbled, looking contritely at the ground.

"Repeat what you said!" she demanded.

I did not answer. I stooped and picked up the pail. She snatched it from me.

"What did you say?" she asked again.

I still kept my head down, vaguely wondering if she were intimidating me or if she really wanted me to repeat my curses.

"I'm going to tell your uncle on you," she said at last.

I hated her then. I thought that hanging my head and looking mutely at the ground was a kind of confession and a petition for forgiveness, but she had not accepted it as such.

"I don't care," I said.

She gave me the pail, which I filled with water and carried to the house. She followed me.

"Richard, you are a very bad, bad boy," she said.

"I don't care," I repeated.

I avoided her and went to the front porch and sat. I had had no intention of letting her hear me curse, but since she had heard me and since there was no way to appease her, I decided to let things develop as they would. I would go home. But where was home? Yes, I would run away.

Uncle Clark came and called me into the front room.

"Jody says that you've been using bad language," he said.

"Yes, sir."

"You admit it?"

"Yes, sir."

"Why did you do it?"

"I don't know."

"I'm going to whip you. Pull off your shirt."

Wordlessly I bared my back and he lashed me with a strap. I gritted my teeth and did not cry.

"Are you going to use that language again?" he asked me.

"I want to go home," I said.

"Put on your shirt."

I obeyed.

"I want to go home," I said again.

"But this is your home."

"I want to go to Jackson."

"You have no home in Jackson."

"I want to go to my mother."

"All right," he relented. "I'll send you home Saturday." He looked at me with baffled eyes. "Tell me, where did you learn those words Jody heard you say?"

I looked at him and did not answer; there flashed through my mind a quick, running picture of all the squalid hovels in which I had lived and it made me feel more than ever a stranger as I stood before him. How could I have told him that I had learned to curse before I had learned to read? How could I have told him that I had been a drunkard at the age of six?

When he took me to the train that Saturday morning, I felt guilty and did not want to look at him. He gave me my ticket and I climbed hastily aboard the train. I waved a stiff good-bye to him through the window as the train pulled out. When I could see his face no longer, I wilted, relaxing. Tears blurred my vision. I leaned back and closed my eyes and slept all the way.

I was glad to see my mother. She was much better, though still abed. Another operation had been advised by the doctor and there was hope for recovery. But I was anxious. Why another operation? A victim myself of too many hopes that had never led anywhere, I was for letting my mother remain as she was. My feelings were governed by fear and I spoke to no one about them. I had already begun to sense that my feelings varied too far from those of the people around me for me to blab about what I felt.

I did not re-enter school. Instead, I played alone in the back yard, bouncing a rubber ball off the fence, drawing figures in the soft clay with an old knife, or reading what books I found about the house. I ached to be of an age to take care of myself.

Uncle Edward arrived from Carters to take my mother to Clarksdale for the operation; at the last moment I insisted upon being taken with them. I dressed hurriedly and we went to the station. Throughout the journey I sat brooding, afraid to look at my mother, wanting to return home and yet wanting to go on. We reached Clarksdale and hired a taxi to the doctor's office. My mother was jolly, brave, smiling, but I knew that she was as doubtful as I was. When we reached the doctor's waiting room the conviction settled in me that my mother would never be well again. Finally the doctor came out in his white coat and shook hands with me, then took my mother inside. Uncle Edward left to make arrangements for a room and a nurse. I felt crushed. I waited. Hours later the doctor came to the door.

"How's my mother?"

"Fine!" he said.

"Will she be all right?"

"Everything'll clear up in a few days."

"Can I see her now?"

"No, not now."

Later Uncle Edward returned with an ambulance and two men who carried a stretcher. They entered the doctor's office and brought out my mother; she lay with closed eyes, her body swathed in white. I wanted to run to the stretcher and touch her, but I could not move.

"Why are they taking mama that way?" I asked Uncle Edward.

"There are no hospital facilities for colored, and this is the way we have to do it," he said.

I watched the men take the stretcher down the steps; then I stood on the sidewalk and watched them lift my mother into the ambulance and drive away. I knew that my mother had gone out of my life; I could feel it.

Uncle Edward and I stayed at a boardinghouse; each morning he went to the rooming house to inquire about my mother and each time he returned gloomy and silent. Finally he told me that he was taking my mother back home.

"What chance has mama, really?" I asked him.

"She's very sick," he said.

We left Clarksdale; my mother rode on a stretcher in the baggage car with Uncle Edward attending her. Back home, she lay for days, groaning, her eyes vacant. Doctors visited her and left without making any comment. Granny grew frantic. Uncle Edward, who had gone home, returned and still more doctors were called in. They told us that a blod clot had formed on my mother's brain and that another paralytic stroke had set in.

Once, in the night, my mother called me to her bed and told me that she could not endure the pain, that she wanted to die. I held her hand and begged her to be quiet. That night I ceased to react to my mother; my feelings were frozen. I merely waited upon her, knowing that she was suffering. She remained abed ten years, gradually growing better, but never completely recovering, relapsing periodically into her paralytic state. The family had stripped itself of money to fight my mother's illness and there was no more forthcoming. Her illness gradually became an accepted thing in the house, something that could not be stopped or helped.

My mother's suffering grew into a symbol in my mind, gathering to itself all the poverty, the ignorance, the helplessness; the painful, baffling, hunger-ridden days and hours; the restless moving, the futile seeking, the uncertainty, the fear, the dread; the meaningless pain and the endless suffering. Her life set the emotional tone of my life, colored the men and women I was to meet in the future, conditioned my relation to events that had not yet happened, determined my attitude to situations and circumstances I had yet to face. A somberness of spirit that I was never to lose settled over me during the slow years of my mother's unrelieved suffering, a somberness that was to make me stand apart and look upon excessive joy with suspicion, that was to make me self-conscious, that was to make me keep forever on the move, as though to escape a nameless fate seeking to overtake me.

At the age of twelve, before I had had one full year of formal schooling, I had a conception of life that no experience would ever erase, a predilection for what was real that no argument could ever gainsay, a sense of the world that was mine and mine alone, a notion as to what life meant that no education could ever alter, a conviction that the meaning of living came only when one was struggling to wring a meaning out of meaningless suffering.

At the age of twelve I had an attitude toward life that was to endure, that was to make me seek those areas of living that would keep it alive, that was to make me skeptical of everything while seeking everything, tolerant of all and yet critical. The spirit I had caught gave me insight into the sufferings of others, made me gravitate toward those whose feelings were like my own, made me sit for hours while others told me of their lives, made me strangely tender and cruel, violent and peaceful.

It made me want to drive coldly to the heart of every question and lay it open to the core of suffering I knew I would find there. It made me love burrowing into psychology, into realistic and naturalistic fiction and art, into those whirlpools of politics that had the power to claim the whole of men's souls. It directed my loyalties to the side of men in rebellion; it made me love talk that sought answers to questions that could help nobody, that could only keep alive in me that enthralling sense of wonder and awe in the face of the drama of human feeling which is hidden by the external drama of life.

Chapter Four

GRANNY was an ardent member of the Seventh-Day Adventist Church and I was compelled to make a pretense of worshiping her God, which was her exaction for my keep. The elders of her church expounded a gospel clogged with images of vast lakes of eternal fire, of seas vanishing, of valleys of dry bones, of the sun burning to ashes, of the moon turning to blood, of stars falling to the earth, of a wooden staff being transformed into a serpent, of voices speaking out of clouds, of men walking upon water, of God riding whirlwinds, of water changing into wine, of the dead rising and living, of the blind seeing, of the lame walking; a salvation that teemed with fantastic beasts having multiple heads and horns and eyes and feet; sermons of statues possessing heads of gold, shoulders of silver, legs of brass, and feet of clay; a cosmic tale that began before time and ended with the clouds of the sky rolling away at the Second Coming of Christ; chronicles that concluded with the Armageddon; dramas thronged with all the billions of human beings who had ever lived or died as God judged the quick and the dead . . .

While listening to the vivid language of the sermons I was pulled toward emotional belief, but as soon as I went out of the church and saw the bright sunshine and felt the throbbing life of the people in the streets I knew that none of it was true and that nothing would happen.

Once again I knew hunger, biting hunger, hunger

that made my body aimlessly restless, hunger that kept me on edge, that made my temper flare, hunger that made hate leap out of my heart like the dart of a serpent's tongue, hunger that created in me odd cravings. No food that I could dream of seemed half so utterly delicious as vanilla wafers. Every time I had a nickel I would run to the corner grocery store and buy a box of vanilla wafers and walk back home, slowly, so that I could eat them all up without having to share them with anyone. Then I would sit on the front steps and dream of eating another box; the craving would finally become so acute that I would force myself to be active in order to forget. I learned a method of drinking water that made me feel full temporarily whether I had a desire for water or not; I would put my mouth under a faucet and turn the water on full force and let the stream cascade into my stomach until it was tight. Sometimes my stomach ached, but I felt full for a moment.

No pork or veal was ever eaten at Granny's, and rarely was there meat of any kind. We seldom ate fish and then only those that had scales and spines. Baking powder was never used; it was alleged to contain a chemical harmful to the body. For breakfast I ate mush and gravy made from flour and lard and for hours afterwards I would belch it up into my mouth. We were constantly taking bicarbonate of soda for indigestion. At four o'clock in the afternoon I ate a plate of greens cooked with lard. Sometimes on Sundays we bought a dime's worth of beef which usually turned out to be uneatable. Granny's favorite dish was a peanut roast which she made to resemble meat, but which tasted like something else.

My position in the household was a delicate one; I was a minor, an uninvited dependent, a blood relative who professed no salvation and whose soul stood in mortal peril. Granny intimated boldly, basing her logic on God's justice, that one sinful person in a household could bring down the wrath of God upon the entire establishment, damning both the innocent and the guilty, and on more than one occasion she interpreted my mother's long illness as the result of my faithlessness. I became skilled in ignoring these cosmic threats and developed a callousness toward all metaphysical preachments.

But Granny won an ally in her efforts to persuade me to confess her God; Aunt Addie, her youngest child, had just finished the Seventh-Day Adventist religious school in Huntsville, Alabama, and came home to argue that if the family was compassionate enough to feed me, then the least I could do in return was to follow its guidance. She proposed that, when the fall school term started, I should be enrolled in the religious school rather than a secular one. If I refused, I was placing myself not only in the position of a horrible infidel but of a hardhearted ingrate. I raised arguments and objections, but my mother sided with Granny and Aunt Addie and I had to accept.

The religious school opened and I put in a sullen attendance. Twenty pupils, ranging in age from five to nineteen and in grades from primary to high school, were crowded into one room. Aunt Addie was the only teacher and from the first day an acute, bitter antagonism sprang up between us. This was the first time she had ever taught school and she was nervous, self-conscious because a blood relative of hers—a relative who would not confess her faith and who was not a member of her church—was in her classroom. She was determined that every student should know that I was a sinner of whom she did not approve, and that I was not to be granted consideration of any kind.

The pupils were a docile lot, lacking in that keen sense of rivalry which made the boys and girls who went to public school a crowd—in which a boy was tested and weighed, in which he caught a glimpse of what the world was. These boys and girls were willless, their speech flat, their gestures vague, their personalities devoid of anger, hope, laughter, enthusiasm, passion, or despair. I was able to see them with an objectivity that was inconceivable to them. They were claimed wholly by their environment and could imagine no other, whereas I had come from another plane of living, from the swinging doors of saloons, the railroad yard, the roundhouses, the street gangs, the river levees, an orphan home; had shifted from town to town and home to home; had mingled with grownups more than perhaps was good for me. I had to curb my habit of cursing, but not before I had shocked more than half of them and had embarrassed Aunt Addie to helplessness.

As the first week of school drew to a close, the conflict that smoldered between Aunt Addie and me flared openly. One afternoon she rose from her desk and walked down the aisle and stopped beside me.

"You know better than that," she said, tapping a ruler across my knuckles.

"Better than what?" I asked, amazed, nursing my hand.

"Just look at that floor," she said.

I looked and saw that there were many tiny bits of walnut meat scattered about; some of them had been smeared into grease spots on the clean, white pine boards. At once I knew that the boy in front of me had been eating them; my walnuts were in my pocket, uncracked.

"I don't know anything about that," I said.

"You know better than to eat in the classroom," she said.

"I haven't been eating," I said.

"Don't lie! This is not only a school, but God's holy ground," she said with angry indignation.

"Aunt Addie, my walnuts are here in my pocket . . ."

"I'm Miss Wilson!" she shouted.

I stared at her, speechless, at last comprehending what was really bothering her. She had warned me to call her Miss Wilson in the classroom, and for the most part I had done so. She was afraid that if I called her Aunt Addie I would undermine the morale of the students. Each pupil knew that she was my aunt and many of them had known her longer than I had.

"I'm sorry," I said, and turned from her and opened a book.

"Richard, get up!"

I did not move. The room was tense. My fingers gripped the book and I knew that every pupil in the room was watching. I had not eaten the nuts; I was sorry that I had called her Aunt Addie; but I did not want to be singled out for gratuitous punishment. And, too, I was expecting the boy who sat in front of me to devise some lie to save me, since it was really he who was guilty.

"I asked you to get up!" she shouted.

I still sat, not taking my eyes off my book. Suddenly she caught me by the back of my collar and yanked me from the seat. I stumbled across the room.

"I spoke to you!" she shouted hysterically.

I straightened and looked at her; there was hate in my eyes.

"Don't you look at me that way, boy!"

"I didn't put those walnuts on the floor!"

"Then who did?"

My street gang code was making it hard for me. I had never informed upon a boy in the public school, and I was waiting for the boy in front of me to come to my aid, lying, making up excuses, anything. In the past I had taken punishment that was not mine to protect the solidarity of the gang, and I had seen other boys do the same. But the religious boy, God helping him, did not speak.

"I don't know who did it," I said finally.

"Go to the front of the room," Aunt Addie said.

I walked slowly to her desk, expecting to be lectured; but my heart quickened when I saw her go to the corner and select a long, green, limber switch and come toward me. I lost control of my temper.

"I haven't done anything!" I yelled.

She struck me and I dodged.

"Stand still, boy!" she blazed, her face livid with fury, her body trembling.

I stood still, feeling more defeated by the righteous boy behind me than by Aunt Addie.

"Hold out your hand!"

I held out my hand, vowing that never again would this happen to me, no matter what the price. She stung my palm until it was red, then lashed me across my bare legs until welts rose. I clamped my teeth to keep from uttering a single whimper. When she finished I continued to hold out my hand, indicating to her that her blows could never really reach me, my eyes fixed and unblinking upon her face.

"Put down your hand and go to your seat," she said.

I dropped my hand and turned on my heels, my palm and legs on fire, my body taut. I walked in a fog of anger toward my desk.

"And I'm not through with you!" she called after me.

She had said one word too much; before I knew it, I had whirled and was staring at her with an open mouth and blazing eyes.

"Through with me?" I repeated. "But what have I done to you?"

"Sit down and shut up!" Aunt Addie bellowed.

I sat. I was sure of one thing: I would not be beaten by her again. I had often been painfully beaten, but almost always I had felt that the beatings were somehow right and sensible, that I was in the wrong. Now, for the first time, I felt the equal of an adult; I knew that I had been beaten for a reason that was not right. I sensed some emotional problem in Aunt Addie other than her concern about my eating in school. Did my presence make her feel so insecure that she felt she had to punish me in front of the pupils to impress them? All afternoon I brooded, wondering how I could quit the school.

The moment Aunt Addie came into the house—I reached home before she did—she called me into the kitchen. When I entered, I saw that she was holding another switch. My muscles tightened.

"You're not going to beat me again!" I told her.

"I'm going to teach you some manners!" she said.

I stood fighting, fighting as I had never fought in my life, fighting with myself. Perhaps my uneasy childhood, perhaps my shifting from town to town, perhaps the violence I had already seen and felt took hold of me, and I was trying to stifle the impulse to go to the drawer of the kitchen table and get a knife and defend myself. But this woman who stood before me was my aunt, my mother's sister, Granny's daughter; in her veins my own blood flowed; in many of her actions I could see some elusive part of my own self; and in her speech I could catch echoes of my own speech. I did not want to be violent with her, and yet I did not want to be beaten for a wrong I had not committed.

"You're just mad at me for something!" I said.

"Don't tell me I'm mad!"

"You're too mad to believe anything I say."

"Don't speak to me like that!"

"Then how can I talk to you? You beat me for throwing walnuts on the floor! But I didn't do it!"

"Then who did?"

Since I was alone now with her, and desperate, I cast my loyalties aside and told her the name of the guilty boy, feeling that he merited no consideration.

"Why didn't you tell me before?" she asked.

"I don't want to tell tales on other people."

"So you lied, hunh?"

I could not talk; I could not explain how much I valued my code of solidarity.

"Hold out your hand!"

"You're not going to beat me! I didn't do it!"

"I'm going to beat you for lying!"

"Don't, don't hit me! If you hit me I'll fight you!"

For a moment she hesitated, then she struck at me with the switch and I dodged and stumbled into a corner. She was upon me, lashing me across the face. I leaped, screaming, and ran past her and jerked open the kitchen drawer; it spilled to the floor with a thunderous sound. I grabbed up a knife and held it ready for her.

"Now, I told you to stop!" I screamed.

"You put down that knife!"

"Leave me alone or I'll cut you!"

She stood debating. Then she made up her mind and came at me. I lunged at her with the knife and she grasped my hand and tried to twist the knife loose. I threw my right leg about her legs and gave her a shove, tripping her; we crashed to the floor. She was stronger than I and I felt my strength ebbing; she was still fighting for my knife and I saw a look on her face that made me feel she was going to use it on me if she got possession of it. I bit her hand and we rolled, kicking, scratching, hitting, fighting as though we were strangers, deadly enemies, fighting for our lives.

"Leave me alone!" I screamed at the top of my voice.

"Give me that knife, you boy!"

"I'll kill you! I'll kill you if you don't leave me alone!"

Granny came running; she stood thunderstruck.

"Addie, what are you doing?"

"He's got a knife!" she gasped. "Make 'im put it down!"

"Richard, put down that knife!" Granny shouted.

My mother came limping to the door.

"Richard, stop it!" she shouted.

"I won't! I'm not going to let her beat me!"

"Addie, leave the boy alone," my mother said.

Aunt Addie rose slowly, her eyes on the knife, then she turned and walked out of the kitchen, kicking the door wide open before her as she went.

"Richard, give me that knife," my mother said.

"But, mama, she'll beat me, beat me for nothing," I said. "I'm not going to let her beat me; I don't care what happens!"

"Richard, you are bad, bad," Granny said, weeping.

I tried to explain what had happened, but neither of them would listen. Granny came toward me to take the knife, but I dodged her and ran into the back yard. I sat alone on the back steps, trembling, emotionally spent, crying to myself. Grandpa came down; Aunt Addie had told him what had happened.

"Gimme that knife, mister," he said.

"I've already put it back," I lied, hugging my arm to my side to conceal the knife.

"What's come over you?" he asked.

"I don't want her to beat me," I said.

"You're a child, a boy!" he thundered.

"But I don't want to be beaten!"

"What did you do?"

"Nothing."

"You can lie as fast as a dog can trot," Grandpa said. "And if it wasn't for my rheumatism, I'd take down your pants and tan your backside good and proper. The very idea of a little snot like you threatening somebody with a knife!"

"I'm not going to let her beat me," I said again.

"You're bad," he said. "You better watch your step, young man, or you'll end up on the gallows."

I had long ceased to fear Grandpa; he was a sick old man and he knew nothing of what was happening in the house. Now and then the womenfolk called on him to throw fear into someone, but I knew that he was feeble and was not frightened of him. Wrapped in the misty memories of his young manhood, he sat his days out in his room where his Civil War rifle stood loaded in a corner, where his blue uniform of the Union Army lay neatly folded.

Aunt Addie took her defeat hard, holding me in a cold and silent disdain. I was conscious that she had descended to my own emotional level in her effort to rule me, and my respect for her sank. Until she married, years later, we rarely spoke to each other, though we ate at the same table and slept under the same roof, though I was but a skinny, half-frightened boy and she was the secretary of the church and the church's day-school teacher. God blessed our home with the love that binds . . .

I continued at the church school, despite Aunt Addie's never calling upon me to recite or go to the blackboard. Consequently I stopped studying. I spent my time playing with the boys and found that the only games they knew were brutal ones. Baseball, marbles, boxing, running were tabooed recreations, the Devil's work; instead they played a wildcat game called popping-the-whip, a seemingly innocent diversion whose excitement came only in spurts, but spurts that could hurl one to the edge of death itself. Whenever we were discovered standing idle on the school grounds, Aunt Addie would suggest that we pop-the-whip. It would have been safer for our bodies and saner for our souls had she urged us to shoot craps.

One day at noon Aunt Addie ordered us to pop-the-whip. I had never played the game before and I fell in with good faith. We formed a long line, each boy taking hold of another boy's hand until we were stretched out like a long string of human beads. Although I did not know it, I was on the tip end of the human whip. The leading boy, the handle of the whip, started off at a trot, weaving to the left and to the right, increasing speed until the whip of flesh was curving at breakneck gallop. I clutched the hand of the boy next to me with all the strength I had, sensing that if I did not hold on I would be tossed off. The whip grew taut as human flesh and bone could bear and I felt that my arm was being torn from its socket. Suddenly my breath left me. I was swung in a small, sharp arc. The whip was now being popped and I could hold on no more; the momentum of the whip flung me off my feet into the air, like a bit of leather being flicked off a horsewhip, and I hurtled headlong through space and landed in a ditch. I rolled over, stunned, head bruised and bleeding. Aunt Addie was laughing, the first and only time I ever saw her laugh on God's holy ground.

In the home Granny maintained a hard religious regime. There were prayers at sunup and sundown, at the breakfast table and dinner table, followed by a Bible verse from each member of the family. And it was presumed that I prayed before I got into bed at night. I shirked as many of the weekday church services as possible, giving as my excuse that I had to study; of course, nobody believed me, but my lies were accepted because nobody wanted to risk a row. The daily prayers were a torment and my knees became sore from kneeling so long and often. Finally I devised a method of kneeling that was not really kneeling; I learned, through arduous repetition, how to balance myself on the toes of my shoes and rest my head against a wall in some convenient corner. Nobody, except God, was any the wiser, and I did not think that He cared.

Granny made it imperative, however, that I attend certain all-night ritualistic prayer meetings. She was the oldest member of her church and it would have been unseemly if the only grandchild in her home could not be brought to these important services; she felt that if I were completely remiss in religious conformity it would cast doubt upon the stanchness of her faith, her capacity to convince and persuade, or merely upon her ability to apply the rod to my backside.

Granny would prepare a lunch for the all-night praying session, and the three of us—Granny, Aunt Addie, and I—would be off, leaving my mother and Grandpa at home. During the passionate prayers and the chanted hymns I would sit squirming on a bench, longing to grow up so I could run away, listening indifferently to the theme of cosmic annihilation, loving the hymns for their sensual caress, but at last casting furtive glances at Granny and wondering when it would be safe for me to stretch out on the bench and go to sleep. At ten or eleven I would munch a sandwich and Granny would nod her permission for me to take a nap. I would awaken at intervals to hear snatches of hymns or prayers that would lull me to sleep again. Finally Granny would shake me and I would open my eyes and see the sun streaming through stained-glass windows.

Many of the religious symbols appealed to my sensibilities and I responded to the dramatic vision of life held by the church, feeling that to live day by day with death as one's sole thought was to be so compassionately sensitive toward all life as to view all men as slowly dying, and the trembling sense of fate that welled up, sweet and melancholy, from the hymns blended with the sense of fate that I had already caught from life. But full emotional and intellectual belief never came. Perhaps if I had caught my first sense of life from the church I would have been moved to complete acceptance, but the hymns and sermons of God came into my heart only long after my personality had been shaped and formed by unchartered conditions of life. I felt that I had in me a sense of living as deep as that which the church was trying to give me, and in the end I remained basically unaffected.

My body grew, even on mush and lard gravy, a miracle which the church certainly should have claimed credit for. I survived my twelfth year on a diet that would have stunted an average-sized dog, and my glands began to diffuse through my blood, like sap rising upward in trees in spring, those strange chemicals that made me look curiously at girls and women. The elder's wife sang in the choir and I fell in love with her as only a twelve-year-old can worship a distant and unattainable woman. During the services I would stare at her, wondering what it was like to be married to her, pondering over how passionate she was. I felt no qualms about my first lust for the flesh being born on holy ground; the contrast between budding carnal desires and the aching loneliness of the hymns never evoked any sense of guilt in me.

It was possible that the sweetly sonorous hymns stimulated me sexually, and it might have been that my fleshy fantasies, in turn, having as their foundation my already inflated sensibility, made me love the masochistic prayers. It was highly likely that the serpent of sin that nosed about the chambers of my heart was lashed to hunger by hymns as well as dreams, each reciprocally feeding the other. The church's spiritual life must have been polluted by my base yearnings, by the leaping hunger of my blood for the flesh, because I would gaze at the elder's wife for hours, attempting to draw her eyes to mine, trying to hypnotize her, seeking to communicate with her with my thoughts. If my desires had been converted into a concrete religious symbol, the symbol would have looked something like this: a black imp with two horns; a long, curving, forked tail; cloven hoofs, a scaly, naked body; wet, sticky fingers; moist, sensual lips; and lascivious eyes feasting upon the face of the elder's wife . . .

A religious revival was announced and Granny felt that it was her last chance to bring me to God before I entered the precincts of sin at the public school, for I had already given loud and final notice that I would no longer attend the church school. There was a discernible lessening in Aunt Addie's hostility; perhaps she had come to the conclusion that my lost soul was more valuable than petty pride. Even my mother's attitude was: "Richard, you ought to know God through *some* church."

The entire family became kind and forgiving, but I knew the motives that prompted their change and it drove me an even greater emotional distance from them. Some of my classmates—who had, on the advice of their parents, avoided me—now came to visit and I could tell in a split second that they had been instructed in what to say. One boy, who lived across the street, called on me one afternoon and his self-consciousness betrayed him; he spoke so naïvely and clumsily that I could see the bare bones of his holy plot and hear the creaking of the machinery of Granny's maneuvering.

"Richard, do you know we are all worried about you?" he asked.

"Worried about me? Who's worried about me?" I asked in feigned surprise.

"All of us," he said, his eyes avoiding mine.

"Why?" I asked.

"You're not saved," he said sadly.

"I'm all right," I said, laughing.

"Don't laugh, Richard. It's serious," he said.

"But I tell you that I'm all right."

"Say, Richard, I'd like to be a good friend of yours."

"I thought we were friends already," I said.

"I mean true brothers in Christ," he said.

"We know each other," I said in a soft voice tinged with irony.

"But not in Christ," he said.

"Friendship is friendship with me."

"But don't you want to save your soul?"

"I simply can't feel religion," I told him in lieu of telling him that I did not think I had the kind of soul he thought I had.

"Have you really tried to feel God?" he asked.

"No. But I know I can't feel anything like that."

"You simply can't let the question rest there, Richard."

"Why should I let it rest?"

"Don't mock God," he said.

"I'll never feel God, I tell you. It's no use."

"Would you let the fate of your soul hang upon pride and vanity?"

"I don't think I have any pride in matters like this."

"Richard, think of Christ's dying for you, shedding His blood, His precious blood on the cross."

"Other people have shed blood," I ventured.

"But it's not the same. You don't understand."

"I don't think I ever will."

"Oh, Richard, brother, you are lost in the darkness of the world. You must let the church help you."

"I tell you, I'm all right."

"Come into the house and let me pray for you."

"I don't want to hurt your feelings . . ."

"You can't. I'm talking for God."

"I don't want to hurt God's feelings either," I said, the words slipping irreverently from my lips before I was aware of their full meaning.

He was shocked. He wiped tears from his eyes. I was sorry.

"Don't say that. God may never forgive you," he whispered.

It would have been impossible for me to have told him how I felt about religion. I had not settled in my mind whether I believed in God or not; His existence or nonexistence never worried me. I reasoned that if there did exist an all-wise, all-powerful God who knew the beginning and the end, who meted out justice to all, who controlled the destiny of man, this God would surely know that I doubted His existence and He would laugh at my foolish denial of Him. And if there was no God at all, then why all the commotion? I could not imagine God pausing in His guidance of unimaginably vast worlds to bother with me.

Embedded in me was a notion of the suffering in life, but none of it seemed like the consequences of original sin to me; I simply could not feel weak and lost in a cosmic manner. Before I had been made to go to church, I had given God's existence a sort of tacit assent, but after having seen His creatures serve Him at first hand, I had had my doubts. My faith, such as it was, was welded to the common realities of life, anchored in the sensations of my body and in what my mind could grasp, and nothing could ever shake this faith, and surely not my fear of an invisible power.

"I'm not afraid of things like that," I told the boy.

"Aren't you afraid of God?" he asked.

"No. Why should I be? I've done nothing to Him."

"He's a jealous God," he warned me.

"I hope that He's a kind God," I told him.

"If *you* are kind to Him, He is a kind God," the boy said. "But God will not look at you if you don't look at Him."

During our talk I made a hypothetical statement that summed up my attitude toward God and the suffering in the world, a statement that stemmed from my knowledge of life as I had lived, seen, felt, and suffered it in terms of dread, fear, hunger, terror, and loneliness.

"If laying down my life could stop the suffering in

the world, I'd do it. But I don't believe anything can stop it," I told him.

He heard me but he did not speak. I wanted to say more to him, but I knew that it would have been useless. Though older than I, he had neither known nor felt anything of life for himself; he had been carefully reared by his mother and father and he had always been told what to feel.

"Don't be angry," I told him.

Frightened and baffled, he left me. I felt sorry for him.

Immediately following the boy's visit, Granny began her phase of the campaign. The boy had no doubt conveyed to her my words of blasphemy, for she talked with me for hours, warning me that I would burn forever in the lake of fire. As the day of the revival grew near, the pressure upon me intensified. I would go into the dining room upon some petty errand and find Granny kneeling, her head resting on a chair, uttering my name in a tensely whispered prayer. God was suddenly everywhere in the home, even in Aunt Addie's scowling and brooding face. It began to weigh upon me. I longed for the time when I could leave. They begged me so continuously to come to God that it was impossible for me to ignore them without wounding them. Desperately I tried to think of some way to say no without making them hate me. I was determined to leave home before I would surrender.

Then I blundered and wounded Granny's soul. It was not my intention to hurt or humiliate her; the irony of it was that the plan I conceived had as its purpose the salving of Granny's frustrated feelings toward me. Instead, it brought her the greatest shame and humiliation of her entire religious life.

One evening during a sermon I heard the elder—I took my eyes off his wife long enough to listen, even though she slumbered in my senses all the while—describe how Jacob had seen an angel. Immediately I felt that I had found a way to tell Granny that I needed proof before I could believe, that I could not commit myself to something I could not feel or see. I would tell her that if I were to see an angel I would accept that as infallible evidence that there was a God and would serve Him unhesitatingly; she would surely understand an attitude of that sort. What gave me courage to voice this argument was the conviction that I would never see an angel; if I had ever seen one, I had enough common sense to have gone to a doctor at once. With my bright idea bubbling in my mind, wishing to allay Granny's fears for my soul, wanting to make her know that my heart was not all black and wrong, that I was actually giving serious thought to her passionate pleadings, I leaned to her and whispered:

"You see, Granny, if I ever saw an angel like Jacob did, then I'd believe."

Granny stiffened and stared at me in amazement; then a glad smile lit up her old wrinkled white face and she nodded and gently patted my hand. That ought to hold her for a while, I thought. During the sermon Granny looked at me several times and smiled. Yes, she knows now that I'm not dismissing her pleas from my mind . . . Feeling that my plan was working, I resumed my worship of the elder's wife with a cleansed conscience, wondering what it would be like to kiss her, longing to feel some of the sensuous emotions of which my reading had made me conscious. The service ended and Granny rushed to the front of the church and began talking excitedly to the elder; I saw the elder looking at me in surprise. Oh, goddamn, she's telling him! I thought with anger. But I had not guessed one-thousandth of it.

The elder hurried toward me. Automatically I rose. He extended his hand and I shook it.

"Your grandmother told me," he said in awed tones.

I was speechless with anger.

"I didn't want her to tell you that," I said.

"She says that you have seen an angel." The words literally poured out of his mouth.

I was so overwhelmed that I gritted my teeth. Finally I could speak and i grabbed his arm.

"No . . . N-nooo, sir! No, sir!" I stammered. "I didn't say that. She misunderstood me."

The last thing on earth I wanted was a mess like this. The elder blinked his eyes in bewilderment.

"What did you tell her?" he asked.

"I told her that if I ever saw an angel, then I would believe," I said, feeling foolish, ashamed, hating and pitying my believing granny. The elder's face became bleak and stricken. He was stunned with disappointment.

"You . . . you didn't see an angel?" he asked.

"No, *sir*!" I said emphatically, shaking my head vigorously so that there could be no possible further misunderstanding.

"I see," he breathed in a sigh.

His eyes looked longingly into a corner of the church.

"With God, you know, anything is possible," he hinted hopefully.

"But I didn't see *anything*," I said. "I'm sorry about this."

"If you pray, then God will come to you," he said.

The church grew suddenly hot. I wanted to bolt out of it and never see it again. But the elder took hold of my arm and would not let me move.

"Elder, this is all a mistake. I didn't want anything like this to happen," I said.

"Listen, I'm older than you are, Richard," he said. "I think that you have in your heart the gift of God." I must have looked dubious, for he said: "Really, I do."

"Elder, please don't say anything to anybody about this," I begged.

Again his face lit with vague hope.

"Perhaps you don't want to tell me because you are bashful?" he suggested. "Look, this is serious. If you saw an angel, then tell me."

I could not deny it verbally any more; I could only shake my head at him. In the face of his hope, words seemed useless.

"Promise me you'll pray. If you pray, then God will answer," he said.

I turned my head away, ashamed for him, feeling that I had unwittingly committed an obscene act in rousing his hopes so wildly high, feeling sorry for his having such hopes. I wanted to get out of his presence. He finally let me go, whispering:

"I want to talk to you sometime."

The church members were staring at me. My fists doubled. Granny's wide and innocent smile was shining on me and I was filled with dismay. That she could make such a mistake meant that she lived in a daily atmosphere that urged her to expect something like this to happen. She had told the other members and everybody knew it, including the elder's wife! There they stood, the church members, with joyous astonishment written on their faces, whispering among themselves. Perhaps at that moment I could have mounted the pulpit and led them all; perhaps that was to be my greatest moment of triumph!

Granny rushed to me and hugged me violently, weeping tears of joy. Then I babbled, speaking with emotional reproof, censuring her for having misunderstood me; I must have spoken more loudly and harshly than was called for—the others had now gathered about me and Granny—for Granny drew away from me abruptly and went to a far corner of the church and stared at me with a cold, set face. I was crushed. I went to her and tried to tell her how it had happened.

"You shouldn't've spoken to me," she said in a breaking voice that revealed the depths of her disillusionment.

On our way home she would not utter a single word. I walked anxiously beside her, looking at her tired old white face, the wrinkles that lined her neck, the deep, waiting black eyes, and the frail body, and I knew more than she thought I knew about the meaning of religion, the hunger of the human heart for that which is not and can never be, the thirst of the human spirit to conquer and transcend the implacable limitations of human life.

Later, I convinced her that I had not wanted to hurt her and she immediately seized upon my concern for her feelings as an opportunity to have one more try at bringing me to God. She wept and pleaded with me to pray, really to pray, to pray hard, to pray until tears came . . .

"Granny, don't make me promise," I begged.

"But you must, for the sake of your soul," she said.

I promised; after all, I felt that I owed her something for inadvertently making her ridiculous before the members of her church.

Daily I went into my room upstairs, locked the door, knelt, and tried to pray, but everything I could think of saying seemed silly. Once it all seemed so absurd that I laughed out loud while on my knees. It was no use. I could not pray. I could never pray. But I kept my failure a secret. I was convinced that if I ever succeeded in praying, my words would bound noiselessly against the ceiling and rain back down upon me like feathers.

My attempts at praying became a nuisance, spoiling my days; and I regretted the promise I had given Granny. But I stumbled on a way to pass the time in my room, a way that made the hours fly with the speed of the wind. I took the Bible, pencil, paper, and a rhyming dictionary and tried to write verses for hymns. I justified this by telling myself that, if I wrote a really good hymn, Granny might forgive me. But I failed even in that; the Holy Ghost was simply nowhere near me . . .

One day while killing my hour of prayer, I remembered a series of volumes of Indian history I had read the year before. Yes, I knew what I would do; I would write a story about the Indians . . . But what about them? Well, an Indian girl . . . I wrote of an Indian maiden, beautiful and reserved, who sat alone upon the bank of a still stream, surrounded by eternal twilight and ancient trees, waiting . . . The girl was keeping some·vow which I could not describe and, not knowing how to develop the story, I resolved that the girl had to die. She rose slowly and walked toward the dark stream, her face stately and cold; she entered the water and walked on until the water reached her shoulders, her chin; then it covered her. Not a murmur or a gasp came from her, even in dying.

"And at last the darkness of the night descended and softly kissed the surface of the watery grave and the only sound was the lonely rustle of the ancient trees," I wrote as I penned the final line.

I was excited; I read it over and saw that there was a yawning void in it. There was no plot, no action, nothing save atmosphere and longing and death. But I had never in my life done anything like it; I had made something, no matter how bad it was; and it was mine . . . Now, to whom could I show it? Not my relatives; they would think I had gone crazy. I decided to read it to a young woman who lived next door. I interrupted her as she was washing dishes and, swearing her to secrecy, I read the composition aloud. When I finished she smiled at me oddly, her eyes baffled and astonished.

"What's that for?" she asked.

"Nothing," I said.

"But why did you write it?"

"I just wanted to."

"Where did you get the idea?"

I wagged my head, pulled down the corners of my mouth, stuffed my manuscript into my pocket and looked at her in a cocky manner that said: Oh, it's nothing at all. I write stuff like this all the time. It's easy, if you know how. But I merely said in an humble, quiet voice:

"Oh, I don't know. I just thought it up."

"What're you going to do with it?"

"Nothing."

God only knows what she thought. My environment contained nothing more alien than writing or the desire to express one's self in writing. But I never forgot the look of astonishment and bewilderment on the young woman's face when I had finished reading and glanced at her. Her inability to grasp what I had done or was trying to do somehow gratified me. Afterwards whenever I thought of her reaction I smiled happily for some unaccountable reason.

Chapter Five

NO longer set apart for being sinful, I felt that I could breathe again, live again, that I had been released from a prison. The cosmic images of dread were now gone and the external world became a reality, quivering daily before me. Instead of brooding and trying foolishly to pray, I could run and roam, mingle with boys and girls, feel at home with people, share a little of life in common with others, satisfy my hunger to be and live.

Granny and Aunt Addie changed toward me, giving me up for lost; they told me that they were dead to the world, and those of their blood who lived in that world were therefore dead to them. From urgent solicitude they dropped to coldness and hostility. Only my mother, who had in the meantime recovered somewhat, maintained her interest in me, urging me to study hard and make up for squandered time.

Freedom brought problems; I needed textbooks and had to wait for months to obtain them. Granny said that she would not buy worldly books for me. My clothes were a despair. So hostile did Granny and Aunt Addie become that they ordered me to wash and iron my own clothes. Eating was still skimpy, but I had now adjusted myself to the starch, lard, and greens diet. I went to school, feeling that my life depended not so much upon my learning as upon getting into another world of people.

Until I entered Jim Hill public school, I had had but

one year of unbroken study; with the exception of
one year at the church school, each time I had begun a
school term something happened to disrupt it. Already
my personality was lopsided; my knowledge of feeling
was far greater than my knowledge of fact. Though I
was not aware of it, the next four years were to be
the only opportunity for formal study in my life.

The first school day presented the usual problem and
I was emotionally prepared to meet it. Upon what
terms would I be allowed to remain upon the school
grounds? With pencil and tablet, I walked nonchalantly
into the schoolyard, wearing a cheap, brand-new straw
hat. I mingled with the boys, hoping to pass unnoticed,
but knowing that sooner or later I would be spotted for
a newcomer. And trouble came quickly. A black boy
bounded past me, thumping my straw hat to the ground,
and yelling:

"Straw katy!"

I picked up my hat and another boy ran past,
slapping my hat even harder.

"Straw katy!"

Again I picked up my hat and waited. The cry
spread. Boys gathered around, pointing, chanting:

"Straw katy! Straw katy!"

I did not feel that I had been really challenged so
far; no particular boy had stood his ground and
taunted me. I was hoping that the teasing would cease,
and tomorrow I would leave my straw hat at home.
But the boy who had begun the game came close.

"Mama bought me a straw hat," he sneered.

"Watch what you're saying," I warned him.

"Oh, look! He talks!" the boy said.

The crowd howled with laughter, waiting, hoping.

"Where you from?" the boy asked me.

"None of your business," I said.

"Now, look, don't you go and get sassy, or I'll cut
you down," he said.

"I'll say what I please," I said.

The boy picked up a tiny rock and put it on his
shoulder and walked close again.

"Knock it off," he invited me.

I hesitated for a moment, then acted; I brushed the rock from his shoulder and ducked and grabbed him about the legs and dumped him to the ground. A volcano of screams erupted from the crowd. I jumped upon the fallen boy and started pounding him. Then I was jerked up. Another boy had begun to fight me. My straw hat had been crushed and forgotten.

"Don't you hit my brother!" the new boy yelled.

"Two fighting one ain't fair!" I yelled.

Both of them now closed in on me. A blow landed on the back of my head. I turned and saw a brick rolling away and I felt blood oozing down my back. I looked around and saw several brickbats scattered about. I scooped up a handful. The two boys backed away. I took aim as they circled me; I made a motion as if to throw and one of the boys turned and ran. I let go with the brick and caught him in the middle of his back. He screamed. I chased the other halfway around the schoolyard. The boys howled their delight; they crowded around me, telling me that I had fought with two bullies. Then suddenly the crowd quieted and parted. I saw a woman teacher bearing down upon me. I dabbed at the blood on my neck.

"Was it you who threw that brick?" she asked.

"Two boys were fighting me," I told her.

"Come," she said, taking my hand.

I entered school escorted by the teacher, under arrest. I was taken to a room and confronted with the two brothers.

"Are these the boys?" she asked.

"Both of 'em fought me," I said. "I had to fight back."

"He hit me first!" one brother yelled.

"You're lying!" I yelled back.

"Don't you use that language in here," the teacher said.

"But they're not telling the truth," I said. "I'm new here and they tore up my hat."

"He hit me first," the boy said again.

I reached around the teacher, who stood between us, and smacked the boy. He screamed and started at me. The teacher grabbed us.

"The very idea of you!" the teacher shouted at me. "You are trying to fight right in school! What's the matter with you?"

"He's not telling the truth," I maintained.

She ordered me to sit down; I did, but kept my eyes on the two brothers. The teacher dragged them out of the room and I sat until she returned.

"I'm in a good mind not to let you off this time," she said.

"It wasn't my fault," I said.

"I know. But you hit one of those boys right in here," she said.

"I'm sorry."

She asked me my name and sent me to a room. For a reason I could not understand, I was assigned to the fifth grade. Would they detect that I did not belong there? I sat and waited. When I was asked my age I called it out and was accepted.

I studied night and day and within two weeks I was promoted to the sixth grade. Overjoyed, I ran home and babbled the news. The family had not thought it possible. How could a bad, bad boy do that? I told the family emphatically that I was going to study medicine, engage in research, make discoveries. Flushed with success, I had not given a second's thought to how I would pay my way through a medical school. But since I had leaped a grade in two weeks, anything seemed possible, simple, easy.

I was now with boys and girls who were studying, fighting, talking; it revitalized my being, whipped my senses to a high, keen pitch of receptivity. I knew that my life was revolving about a world that I had to encounter and fight when I grew up. Suddenly the future loomed tangibly for me, as tangible as a future can loom for a black boy in Mississippi.

Most of my schoolmates worked mornings, evenings, and Saturdays; they earned enough to buy their clothes

and books, and they had money in their pockets at
school. To see a boy go into a grocery store at noon
recess and let his eyes roam over filled shelves and
pick out what he wanted—even a dime's worth—was
a hairbreadth short of a miracle to me. But when I
broached the idea of my working to Granny, she would
have none of it; she laid down the injunction that I
could not work on Saturdays while I slept under her
roof. I argued that Saturdays were the only days on
which I could earn any worth-while sum, and Granny
looked me straight in the eyes and quoted Scripture:

*But the seventh day is the sabbath of the Lord thy
God: in it thou shalt not do any work, thou, nor
thy son, nor thy daughter, nor thy manservant, nor
thy maidservant, nor thine ox, nor thine ass, nor any
of thy cattle, nor thy stranger that is within thy
gates; that thy manservant and thy maidservant may
rest as well as thou . . .*

And that was the final word. Though we lived just
on the borders of actual starvation, I could not bribe
Granny with a promise of half or two-thirds of my salary; her answer was no and never. Her refusal
wrought me up to a high pitch of nervousness and I
cursed myself for being made to live a different and
crazy life. I told Granny that she was not responsible for my soul, and she replied that I was a minor,
that my soul's fate rested in her hands, that I had
no word to say in the matter.

To protect myself against pointed questions about
my home and my life, to avoid being invited out when
I knew that I could not accept, I was reserved with
the boys and girls at school, seeking their company but
never letting them guess how much I was being kept
out of the world in which they lived, valuing their
casual friendships but hiding it, acutely self-conscious
but covering it with a quick smile and a ready phrase.
Each day at noon I would follow the boys and girls
into the corner store and stand against a wall and
watch them buy sandwiches, and when they would ask
me: "Why don't you eat a lunch?" I would answer with

a shrug of my shoulders: "Aw, I'm not hungry at noon, ever." And I would swallow my saliva as I saw them split open loaves of bread and line them with juicy sardines. Again and again I vowed that someday I would end this hunger of mine, this apartness, this eternal difference; and I did not suspect that I would never get intimately into their lives, that I was doomed to live with them but not of them, that I had my own strange and separate road, a road which in later years would make them wonder how I had come to tread it.

I now saw a world leap to life before my eyes because I could explore it, and that meant not going home when school was out, but wandering, watching, asking, talking. Had I gone home to eat my plate of greens, Granny would not have allowed me out again, so the penalty I paid for roaming was to forfeit my food for twelve hours. I would eat mush at eight in the morning and greens at seven or later at night. To starve in order to learn about my environment was irrational, but so were my hungers. With my books slung over my shoulder, I would tramp with a gang into the woods, to rivers, to creeks, into the business district, to the doors of poolrooms, into the movies when we could slip in without paying, to neighborhood ball games, to brick kilns, to lumberyards, to cotton-seed mills to watch men work. There were hours when hunger would make me weak, would make me sway while walking, would make my heart give a sudden wild spurt of beating that would shake my body and make me breathless; but the happiness of being free would lift me beyond hunger, would enable me to discipline the sensations of my body to the extent that I could temporarily forget.

In my class was a tall, black, rebellious boy who was bright in his studies and yet utterly fearless in his assertion of himself; he could break the morale of the class at any moment with his clowning and the teacher never found an adequate way of handling him. It was he who detected my plaguing hunger and suggested to me a way to earn some money.

"You can't sit in school all day and not eat," he said.

"What am I going to eat?" I asked.

"Why don't you do like me?"

"What do you do?"

"I sell papers."

"I tried to get a paper route, but they're all full," I said. "I'd like to sell papers because I could read them. I can't find things to read."

"You too?" he asked, laughing.

"What do you mean?" I asked.

"That's why I sell papers. I like to read 'em and that's the only way I can get hold of 'em," he explained.

"Do your parents object to your reading?" I asked.

"Yeah. My old man's a damn crackpot," he said.

"What papers are you selling?"

"It's a paper published in Chicago. It comes out each week and it has a magazine supplement," he informed me.

"What kind of a paper is it?"

"Well, I never read the newspaper. It isn't much. But, boy, the magazine supplement! What stories . . . I'm reading the serial of Zane Grey's *Riders of the Purple Sage.*"

I stared at him in complete disbelief.

"Riders of the Purple Sage!" I exclaimed.

"Yes."

"Do you think I can sell those papers?"

"Sure. I make over fifty cents a week and have stuff to read," he explained.

I followed him home and he gave me a copy of the newspaper and the magazine supplement. The newspaper was thin, ill-edited, and designed to circulate among rural, white Protestant readers.

"Hurry up and start selling 'em," he urged me. "I'd like to talk to you about the stories."

I promised him that I would order a batch of them that night. I walked home through the deepening twilight, reading, lifting my eyes now and then from the print in order not to collide with strangers. I was absorbed in the tale of a renowned scientist who had rigged up a mystery room made of metal in the basement of his palatial home. Prompted by some obscure motive, he would lure his victims into this room and then throw an electric switch. Slowly, with heart-racking agony, the air would be sucked from the metal room and his victims would die, turning red, blue, then black. This was what I wanted, tales like this. I had not read enough to have developed any taste in reading. Anything that interested me satisfied me.

Now, at last, I could have my reading in the home, could have it there with the approval of Granny. She had already given me permission to sell papers. Oh, boy, how lucky it was for me that Granny could not read! She had always burned the books I had brought into the house, branding them as worldly; but she would have to tolerate these papers if she was to keep her promise to me. Aunt Addie's opinion did not count, and she never paid any attention to me anyway. In her eyes, I was dead. I told Granny that I planned to make some money by selling papers and she agreed, thinking that at last I was becoming a serious, right-thinking boy. That night I ordered the papers and waited anxiously.

The papers arrived and I scoured the Negro area, slowly building up a string of customers who bought the papers more because they knew me than from any desire to read. When I returned home at night, I would go to my room and lock the door and revel in outlandish exploits of outlandish men in faraway, outlandish cities. For the first time in my life I became aware of the life of the modern world, of vast cities, and I was claimed by it; I loved it. Though they were merely stories, I accepted them as true because I wanted to believe them, because I hungered for a different life, for something new. The cheap pulp tales enlarged my knowledge of the world more than anything I had encountered so far. To me, with my roundhouse, saloon-door, and river-levee background, they were revolutionary, my gateway to the world.

I was happy and would have continued to sell the newspaper and its magazine supplement indefinitely had it not been for the racial pride of a friend of the family. He was a tall, quiet, sober, soft-spoken black man, a carpenter by trade. One evening I called at his home with the paper. He gave me a dime, then looked at me oddly.

"You know, son," he said, "I sure like to see you make a little money each week."

"Thank you, sir," I said.

"But tell me, who told you to sell these papers?" he asked.

"Nobody."

"Where do you get them from?"

"Chicago."

"Do you ever read 'em?"

"Sure. I read the stories in the magazine supplement," I explained. "But I never read the newspaper."

He was silent a moment.

"Did a white man ask you to sell these papers?" he asked.

"No, sir," I answered, puzzled now. "Why do you ask?"

"Do your folks know you are selling these papers?"

"Yes, sir. But what's wrong?"

"How did you know where to write for these papers?" he asked, ignoring my questions.

"A friend of mine sells them. He gave me the address."

"Is this friend of yours a white man?"

"No, sir. He's colored. But why are you asking me all this?"

He did not answer. He was sitting on the steps of his front porch. He rose slowly.

"Wait right here a minute, son," he said. "I want to show you something."

Now what was wrong? The papers were all right; at least they seemed so to me. I waited, annoyed, eager to be gone on my rounds so that I could have time to get home and lie in bed and read the next installment of a thrilling horror story. The man returned with a carefully folded copy of the newspaper. He handed it to me.

"Did you see this?" he asked, pointing to a lurid cartoon.

"No, sir," I said. "I don't read the newspaper; I only read the magazine."

"Well, just look at that. Take your time and tell me what you think," he said.

It was the previous week's issue and I looked at the picture of a huge black man with a greasy, sweaty face, thick lips, flat nose, golden teeth, sitting at a polished, wide-topped desk in a swivel chair. The man had on a pair of gleaming yellow shoes and his feet were propped upon the desk. His thick lips nursed a big, black cigar that held white ashes an inch long. In the man's red-dotted tie was a dazzling horseshoe stickpin, glaring conspicuously. The man wore red suspenders and his shirt was striped silk and there were huge diamond rings on his fat black fingers. A chain of gold girded his belly and from the fob of his watch a rabbit's foot dangled. On the floor at the side of the desk was a spittoon overflowing with mucus. Across the wall of the room in which the man sat was a bold sign, reading:

THE WHITE HOUSE

Under the sign was a portrait of Abraham Lincoln, the features distorted to make the face look like that of a gangster. My eyes went to the top of the cartoon and I read:

> The only dream of a nigger is to be president and to sleep with white women! Americans, do we want this in our fair land? Organize and save white womanhood!

I stared, trying to grasp the point of the picture

and the captions, wondering why it all seemed so strange and yet familiar.

"Do you know what this means?" the man asked me.

"Gee, I don't know," I confessed.

"Did you ever hear of the Ku Klux Klan?" he asked me softly.

"Sure. Why?"

"Do you know what the Ku Kluxers do to colored people?"

"They kill us. They keep us from voting and getting good jobs," I said.

"Well, the paper you're selling preaches the Ku Klux Klan doctrines," he said.

"Oh, no!" I exclaimed.

"Son, you're holding it in your hands," he said.

"I read the magazine, but I never read the paper," I said vaguely, thoroughly rattled.

"Listen, son," he said. "Listen. You're a black boy and you're trying to make a few pennies. All right. I don't want to stop you from selling these papers, if you want to sell 'em. But I've read these papers now for two months and I know what they're trying to do. If you sell 'em, you're just helping white people to kill you."

"But these papers come from Chicago," I protested naïvely, feeling unsure of the entire world now, feeling that racial propaganda surely could not be published in Chicago, the city to which Negroes were fleeing by the thousands.

"I don't care where the paper comes from," he said. "Just you listen to this."

He read aloud a long article in which lynching was passionately advocated as a solution for the problem of the Negro. Even though I heard him reading it, I could not believe it.

"Let me see that," I said.

I took the paper from him and sat on the edge of the steps; in the paling light I turned the pages and read articles so brutally anti-Negro that goose pimples broke out over my skin.

"Do you like that?" he asked me.

"No, sir," I breathed.

"Do you see what you are doing?"

"I didn't know," I mumbled.

"Are you going to sell those papers now?"

"No, sir. Never again."

"They tell me that you are smart in school, and when I read those papers you were selling I didn't know what to make of it. Then I said to myself that that boy doesn't know what he's selling. Now, a lot of folks wanted to speak to you about these papers, but they were scared. They thought you were mixed up with some white Ku Kluxers and if they told you to stop you would put the Kluxers on 'em. But I said, shucks, that boy just don't know what he's doing."

I handed him his dime, but he would not take it.

"Keep the dime, son," he said. "But for God's sake, find something else to sell."

I did not try to sell any more of the papers that night; I walked home with them under my arm, feeling that some Negro would leap from a bush or fence and waylay me. How on earth could I have made so grave a mistake? The way I had erred was simple but utterly unbelievable. I had been so enthralled by reading the serial stories in the magazine supplement that I had not read a single issue of the newspaper. I decided to keep my misadventure secret, that I would tell no one that I had been unwittingly an agent for pro-Ku Klux Klan literature. I tossed the papers into a ditch and when I reached home I told Granny, in a quiet, offhand way, that the company did not want to send me any more papers because they already had too many agents in Jackson, a lie which I thought was an understatement of the actual truth. Granny did not care one way or the other, since I had been making so little money in selling them that I had not been able to help much with household expenses.

The father of the boy who had urged me to sell the

papers also found out their propagandistic nature and
forbade his son to sell them. But the boy and I never
discussed the subject; we were too ashamed of ourselves. One day he asked me guardedly:

"Say, are you still selling those papers?"

"Oh, no. I don't have time," I said, my eyes avoiding his.

"I'm not either," he said, pulling down the corners
of his mouth. "I'm too busy."

I burned at my studies. At the beginning of the
school term I read my civics and English and geog-
raphy volumes through and only referred to them
when in class. I solved all my mathematical problems
far in advance; then, during school hours, when I
was not called on to recite, I read tattered, secondhand copies of *Flynn's Detective Weekly* or the *Argosy
All-Story Magazine,* or dreamed, weaving fantasies
about cities I had never seen and about people I had
never met.

School ended. I could not get a job that would let
me rest on Granny's holy Sabbath. The long hot idle
summer days palled on me. I sat at home brooding,
nursing bodily and spiritual hunger. In the afternoons, after the sun had spent its force, I played ball
with the neighborhood boys. At night I sat on the
front steps and stared blankly at the passing people,
wagons, cars . . .

On one such lazy, hot summer night Granny, my
mother, and Aunt Addie were sitting on the front
porch, arguing some obscure point of religious doctrine. I sat huddled on the steps, my cheeks resting
sullenly in my palms, half listening to what the grownups were saying and half lost in a daydream. Suddenly
the dispute evoked an idea in me and, forgetting that
I had no right to speak without permission, I piped
up and had my say. I must have sounded reekingly
blasphemous, for Granny said, "Shut up, you!" and
leaned forward promptly to chastise me with one of
her casual, back-handed slaps on my mouth. But I had

by now become adept at dodging blows and I nimbly ducked my head. She missed me; the force of her blow was so strong that she fell down the steps, headlong, her aged body wedged in a narrow space between the fence and the bottom step. I leaped up. Aunt Addie and my mother screamed and rushed down the steps and tried to pull Granny's body out. But they could not move her. Grandpa was called and he had to tear the fence down to rescue Granny. She was barely conscious. They put her to bed and summoned a doctor.

I was frightened. I ran to my room and locked the door, fearing that Grandpa would rend me to pieces. Had I done right or had I done wrong? If I had held still and let Granny slap me, she would not have fallen. But was it not natural to dodge a blow? I waited, trembling. But no one came to my room. The house was quiet. Was Granny dead? Hours later I unlocked the door and crept downstairs. Well, I told myself, if Granny died, I would leave home. There was nothing else to do. Aunt Addie confronted me in the hallway with burning, black eyes.

"You see what you've done to Granny," she said.

"I didn't touch her," I said. I had wanted to ask how Granny was, but my fear made me forget that.

"You were trying to kill her," Aunt Addie said.

"I didn't touch Granny, and you know it!"

"You are evil. You bring nothing but trouble!"

"I was trying to dodge her. She was trying to hit me. I had done nothing wrong . . ."

Her lips moved silently as she sought to formulate words to place me in a position of guilt.

"Why do you butt in when grown people are talking?" she demanded, finding her weapon at last.

"I just wanted to talk," I mumbled sullenly. "I sit in this house for hours and I can't even talk."

"Hereafter, you keep your mouth shut until you're spoken to," she advised me.

"But Granny oughtn't always be hitting at me like that," I said as delicately as possible.

"Boy, don't you stand there and say what Granny

ought to do," she blazed, finding her ground of accusation. "If you don't keep your mouth shut, then *I'll* hit you!" she continued.

"I'm only trying to explain why Granny fell," I said.

"Shut up, now! Or I'll wring your neck, you fool!"

"You're another fool!" I came back at her, angry now.

She trembled with fury.

"I'll fix you this night!" she said, rushing at me.

I dodged her and ran into the kitchen and grabbed the long bread knife. She followed me and I confronted her. I was so hysterical that I was crying.

"If you touch me, I'll cut you, so help me," I said in gasps. "I'm going to leave here as soon as I can work and make a living. But as long's I'm here, you better not touch me."

We stood looking into each other's eyes, our bodies trembling with hate.

"I'm going to get you for this," she vowed in a low, serious voice. "I'll get you when you haven't got a knife."

"I'll always keep a knife for you," I told her.

"You've got to sleep at night," she whimpered with rage. "I'll get you then."

"If you touch me when I'm sleeping, I'll kill you," I told her.

She walked out of the kitchen, kicking the door open before her as she went. Aunt Addie had a habit of kicking doors; she always paused before a partly opened door and kicked it open; if the door swung in, she flung it back with her foot; or, if the door was shut, she opened it with her hand for an inch or two, then opened it the rest of the way with her foot; she acted as though she wanted to get a glimpse into the room beyond before she entered it, perhaps to see if it contained anything dreadful or unholy.

For a month after that I took a kitchen knife to bed with me each night, hiding it under my pillow so that when Aunt Addie came I could protect myself. But she never came. Perhaps she prayed.

Granny was abed for six weeks; she had wrenched her back when her slap missed me.

There were more violent quarrels in our deeply religious home than in the home of a gangster, a burglar, or a prostitute, a fact which I used to hint gently to Granny and which did my cause no good. Granny bore the standard for God, but she was always fighting. The peace that passes understanding never dwelt with us. I, too, fought; but I fought because I felt I had to keep from being crushed, to fend off continuous attack. But Granny and Aunt Addie quarreled and fought not only with me, but with each other over minor points of religious doctrine, or over some imagined infraction of what they chose to call their moral code. Wherever I found religion in my life I found strife, the attempt of one individual or group to rule another in the name of God. The naked will to power seemed always to walk in the wake of a hymn.

As summer waned I obtained a strange job. Our next-door neighbor, a janitor, decided to change his profession and become an insurance agent. He was handicapped by illiteracy and he offered me the job of accompanying him on trips into the delta plantation area to write and figure for him, at wages of five dollars a week. I made several trips with Brother Mance, as he was called, to plantation shacks, sleeping on shuck mattresses, eating salt pork and black-eyed peas for breakfast, dinner, and supper; and drinking, for once, all the milk I wanted.

I had all but forgotten that I had been born on a plantation and I was astonished at the ignorance of the children I met. I had been pitying myself for not having books to read, and now I saw children who had never read a book. Their chronic shyness made me seem bold and city-wise; a black mother would try to lure her brood into the room to shake hands with me and they would linger at the jamb of the door, peering at me with one eye, giggling hysterically.

At night, seated at a crude table, with a kerosene lamp spluttering at my elbow, I would fill out insurance applications, and a share-cropper family, fresh from laboring in the fields, would stand and gape. Brother Mance would pace the floor, extolling my abilities with pen and paper. Many of the naïve black families bought their insurance from us because they felt that they were connecting themselves with something that would make their children "write 'n speak lak dat pretty boy from Jackson."

The trips were hard. Riding trains, autos, or buggies, moving from morning till night, we went from shack to shack, plantation to plantation. Exhausted, I filled out applications. I saw a bare, bleak pool of black life and I hated it; the people were alike, their homes were alike, and their farms were alike. On Sundays Brother Mance would go to the nearest country church and give his sales talk, preaching it in the form of a sermon, clapping his hands as he did so, spitting on the floor to mark off his paragraphs, and stomping his feet in the spit to punctuate his sentences, all of which captivated the black sharecroppers. After the performance the wall-eyed yokels would flock to Brother Mance, and I would fill out applications until my fingers ached.

I returned home with a pocketful of money that melted into the bottomless hunger of the household. My mother was proud; even Aunt Addie's hostility melted temporarily. To Granny, I had accomplished a miracle and some of my sinful qualities evaporated, for she felt that success spelled the reward of righteousness and that failure was the wages of sin. But God called Brother Mance to heaven that winter and, since the insurance company would not accept a minor as an agent, my status reverted to a worldly one; the holy household was still burdened with a wayward boy to whom, in spite of all, sin somehow insisted upon clinging.

School opened and I began the seventh grade. My old hunger was still with me and I lived on what I did not eat. Perhaps the sunshine, the fresh air, and the pot liquor from greens kept me going. Of an evening I would sit in my room reading, and suddenly I would become aware of smelling meat frying in a neighbor's kitchen and would wonder what it was like to eat as much meat as one wanted. My mind would drift into a fantasy and I would imagine myself a son in a family that had meat on the table at each meal; then I would become disgusted with my futile daydreams and would rise and shut the window to bar the torturing scent of meat.

When I came downstairs one morning and went into the dining room for my bowl of mush and lard gravy I felt at once that something serious was happening in the family. Grandpa, as usual, was not at the table; he always had his meals in his room. Granny nodded me to my seat; I sat and bowed my head. From under my brows I saw my mother's tight face. Aunt Addie's eyes were closed, her forehead furrowed, her lips trembling. Granny buried her face in her hands. I wanted to ask what had happened, but I knew that I would not get an answer.

Granny prayed and invoked the blessings of God for each of us, asking Him to guide us if it was His will, and then she told God that "my poor old husband lies sick this beautiful morning" and asked God, if it was His will, to heal him. That was how I learned of Grandpa's final illness. On many occasions I learned of some event, a death, a birth, or an impending visit, some happening in the neighborhood, at her church, or at some relative's home, first through Granny's informative prayers at the breakfast or dinner table.

Grandpa was a tall, black, lean man with a long face, snow-white teeth, and a head of woolly white hair. In anger he bared his teeth—a habit, Granny said, that he had formed while fighting in the trenches of the Civil War—and hissed, while his fists would clench until the veins swelled. In his rare laughs he bared his teeth in the same way, only now his teeth did not flash long and his body was relaxed. He owned a sharp pocketknife—which I had been forbidden to touch—and sat for long hours in the sun, whittling, whistling quietly, or maybe, if he was feeling well, humming some strange tune.

I had often tried to ask him about the Civil War, how he had fought, how he had felt, had he seen Lincoln, but he would never respond.

"You, git 'way frum me, you young'un," was all that he would ever say.

From Granny I learned—over a course of years—that he had been wounded in the Civil War and had never received his disability pension, a fact which he hugged close to his heart with bitterness. I never heard him speak of white people; I think he hated them too much to talk of them. In the process of being discharged from the Union Army, he had gone to a white officer to seek help in filling out his papers. In filling out the papers, the white officer misspelled Grandpa's name, making him Richard Vinson instead of Richard Wilson. It was possible that Grandpa's southern accent and his illiteracy made him mispronounce his own name. It was rumored that the white officer had been a Swede and had had a poor knowledge of English. Another rumor had it that the white officer had been a Southerner and had deliberately falsified Grandpa's papers. Anyway, Grandpa did not discover that he had been discharged in the name of Richard Vinson until years later; and when he applied to the War Department for a pension, no trace could be found of his ever having served in the Union Army under the name of Richard Wilson.

I asked endless questions about Grandpa's pension, but information was always denied me on the grounds that I was too young to know what was involved. For decades a long correspondence took place between Grandpa and the War Department; in letter after letter Grandpa would recount events and conversations (always dictating these long accounts to others); he would name persons long dead, citing their ages and descriptions, reconstructing battles in which he had fought, naming towns, rivers, creeks, roads, cities, villages, citing the names and numbers of regiments and companies with which he had fought, giving the exact day and the exact hour of the day of certain occurrences, and send it all to the War Department in Washington.

I used to get the mail early in the morning and whenever there was a long, businesslike envelope in the stack, I would know that Grandpa had got an answer from the War Department and I would run upstairs with it. Grandpa would lift his head from the pillow, take the letter from me and open it himself. He would stare at the black print for a long time, then reluctantly, distrustfully hand the letter to me.

"Well?" he would say.

And I would read him the letter—reading slowly and pronouncing each word with extreme care—telling him that his claims for a pension had not been substantiated and that his application had been rejected. Grandpa would not blink an eye, then he would curse softly under his breath.

"It's them goddamn rebels," he would hiss.

As though doubting what I had read, he would dress up and take the letter to at least a dozen of his friends in the neighborhood and ask them to read it to him; finally he would know it from memory. At last he would put the letter away carefully and begin his brooding again, trying to recall out of his past some telling fact that might help him in getting his pension. Like "K" of Kafka's novel, *The Castle,* he tried desperately to persuade the authorities of his true identity right up to the day of his death, and failed.

Often, when there was no food in the house, I would dream of the Government's sending a letter that would read something like this:

Dear Sir:
Your claim for a pension has been verified. The matter

of your name has been satisfactorily cleared up. In accordance with official regulations, we are hereby instructing the Secretary of the Treasury to compile and compute and send to you, as soon as it is convenient, the total amount of all moneys past due, together with interest, for the past ————years, the amount being $————.

We regret profoundly that you have been so long delayed in this matter. You may be assured that your sacrifice has been a boon and a solace to your country.

But no letter like that ever came, and Grandpa was so sullen most of the time that I stopped dreaming of him and his hopes. Whenever he walked into my presence I became silent, waiting for him to speak, wondering if he were going to upbraid me for something. I would relax when he left. My will to talk to him gradually died.

It was from Granny's conversations, year after year, that the meager details of Grandpa's life came to me. When the Civil War broke out, he ran off from his master and groped his way through the Confederate lines to the North. He darkly boasted of having killed "mo'n mah fair share of them damn rebels" while en route to enlist in the Union Army. Militantly resentful of slavery, he joined the Union Army to kill southern whites; he waded in icy streams; slept in mud; suffered, fought . . . Mustered out, he returned to the South and, during elections, guarded ballot boxes with his army rifle so that Negroes could vote. But when the Negro had been driven from political power, his spirit had been crushed. He was convinced that the war had not really ended, that it would start again.

And now as we ate breakfast—we ate in silence; there was never any talk at our table; Granny said that talking while eating was sinful, that God might make the food choke you—we thought of Grandpa's pension. During the days that followed letters were written, affidavits were drawn up and sworn to, conferences were held, but nothing came of it all. (It was my conviction, supported by no evidence save my own emotional fear of whites, that Grandpa had been cheated out of his pension because of his opposition to white supremacy.)

I came in from school one afternoon and Aunt Addie met me in the hallway. Her face was trembling and her eyes were red.

"Go upstairs and say good-bye to your grandpa," she said.

"What's happened?"

She did not answer. I ran upstairs and was met by Uncle Clark, who had come from Greenwood. Granny caught my hand.

"Come and say good-bye to your grandpa," she said.

She led me to Grandpa's room; he was lying fully dressed upon the bed, looking as well as he ever looked. His eyes were open, but he was so still that I did not know if he was dead or alive.

"Papa, here's Richard," Granny whispered.

Grandpa looked at me, flashed his white teeth for a fraction of a second.

"Good-bye, grandpa," I whispered.

"Good-bye, son," he spoke hoarsely. "Rejoice, for God has picked out my s-s-e . . . in-in h-heaven . . ."

His voice died. I had not understood what he had said and I wondered if I should ask him to repeat it. But Granny took my hand and led me from the room. The house was quiet; there was no crying. My mother sat silent in her rocking chair, staring out the window; now and then she would lower her face to her hands. Granny and Aunt Addie moved silently about the house. I sat mute, waiting for Grandpa to die. I was still puzzled about what he had tried to say to me; it seemed important that I should know his final words. I followed Granny into the kitchen.

"Granny, what did Grandpa say? I didn't quite hear him," I whispered.

She whirled and gave me one of her back-handed slaps across my mouth.

"Shut up! The angel of death's in the house!"

"I just wanted to know," I said, nursing my bruised lips.

She looked at me and relented.

"He said that God had picked out his seat in heaven," she said. "Now you know. So sit down and quit asking fool questions."

When I awakened the next morning my mother told me that Grandpa had "gone home."

"Get on your hat and coat," Granny said.

"What do you want me to do?" I asked.

"Quit asking questions and do what you are told," she said.

I dressed for the outdoors.

"Go to Tom and tell him that Papa's gone home. Ask him to come here and take charge of things," Granny said.

Tom, her eldest son, had recently moved from Hazelhurst to Jackson and lived near the outskirts of town. Feeling that I was bearing an important message, I ran every inch of the two miles; I thought that news of a death should be told at once. I came in sight of my uncle's house with a heaving chest; I bounded up the steps and rapped on the door. My little cousin, Maggie, opened the door.

"Where's Uncle Tom?" I asked.

"He's sleeping," she said.

I ran into his room, went to his bed, and shook him.

"Uncle Tom, Granny says to come at once. Grandpa's dead," I panted.

He stared at me a long time.

"You certainly are a prize fool," he said quietly. "Don't you know that that's no way to tell a person that his father's dead?"

I stared at him, baffled, panting.

"I ran all the way out here," I gasped. "I'm out of breath. I'm sorry."

He rose slowly and began to dress, ignoring me; he did not utter a word for five minutes.

"What're you waiting for?" he asked me.

"Nothing," I said.

I walked home slowly, asking myself what on earth was the matter with me, why it was I never seemed to do things as people expected them to be done. Every word and gesture I made seemed to provoke hostility. I had never been able to talk to others, and I had to guess at their meanings and motives. I had not intentionally tried to shock Uncle Tom, and yet his anger at me seemed to outweigh his sorrow for his father. Finding no answer, I told myself that I was a fool to worry about it, that no matter what I did I would be wrong somehow as far as my family was concerned.

I was not allowed to go to Grandpa's funeral; I was ordered to stay home "and mind the house." I sat reading detective stories until the family returned from the graveyard. They told me nothing and I asked no questions. The routine of the house flowed on as usual; for me there was sleep, mush, greens, school, study, loneliness, yearning, and then sleep again.

My clothing became so shabby that I was ashamed to go to school. Many of the boys in my class were wearing their first long-pants suits. I grew so bitter that I decided to have it out with Granny; I would tell her that if she did not let me work on Saturdays I would leave home. But when I opened the subject, she would not listen. I followed her about the house, demanding the right to work on Saturday. Her answer was no and no and no.

"Then I'll quit school," I declared.

"Quit then. See how much I care," she said.

"I'll go away from here and you'll never hear from me!"

"No, you won't," she said tauntingly.

"How can I ever learn enough to get a job?" I asked her, switching my tactics. I showed her my ragged stockings, my patched pants. "Look, I won't go to school like this! I'm not asking you for money or to do anything. I only want to work!"

"I have nothing to do with whether you go to school or not," she said. "You left the church and you are on your own. You are with the world. You're dead to me, dead to Christ."

"That old church of yours is messing up my life," I said.

"Don't you say that in this house!"

"It's true and you know it!"

"God's punishing you," she said. "And you're too proud to ask Him for help."

"I'm going to get a job anyway."

"Then you can't live here," she said.

"Then I'll leave," I said, trembling violently.

"You won't leave," she repeated.

"You think I'm joking, don't you?" I asked, determined to make her know how I felt. "I'll leave this minute!"

I ran to my room, got a battered suitcase, and began packing my ragged clothes. I did not have a penny, but I was going to leave. She came to the door.

"You little fool! Put that suitcase down!"

"I'm going where I can work!"

She snatched the suitcase out of my hands; she was trembling.

"All right," she said. "If you want to go to hell, then go. But God'll know that it was not my fault. He'll forgive me, but He won't forgive you."

Weeping, she rushed from the door. Her humanity had triumphed over her fear. I emptied the suitcase, feeling spent. I hated these emotional outbursts, these tempests of passion, for they always left me tense and weak. Now I was truly dead to Granny and Aunt Addie, but my mother smiled when I told her that I had defied them. She rose and hobbled to me on her paralytic legs and kissed me.

Chapter Six

THE next day at school I inquired among the students about jobs and was given the name of a white family who wanted a boy to do chores. That afternoon, as soon as school had let out, I went to the address. A tall, dour white woman talked to me. Yes, she needed a boy, an honest boy. Two dollars a week. Mornings, evenings, and all day Saturdays. Washing dishes. Chopping wood. Scrubbing floors. Cleaning the yard. I would get my breakfast and dinner. As I asked timid questions, my eyes darted about. What kind of food would I get? Was the place as shabby as the kitchen indicated?

"Do you want this job?" the woman asked.

"Yes, ma'am," I said, afraid to trust my own judgment.

"Now, boy, I want to ask you one question and I want you to tell me the truth," she said.

"Yes, ma'am," I said, all attention.

"Do you steal?" she asked me seriously.

I burst into a laugh, then checked myself.

"What's so damn funny about that?" she asked.

"Lady, if I was a thief, I'd never tell anybody."

"What do you mean?" she blazed with a red face.

I had made a mistake during my first five minutes in the white world. I hung my head.

"No, ma'am," I mumbled. "I don't steal."

She stared at me, trying to make up her mind.

"Now, look, we don't want a sassy nigger around here," she said.

"No, ma'am," I assured her. "I'm not sassy."

Promising to report the next morning at six o'clock, I walked home and pondered on what could possibly have been in the woman's mind to have made her ask me point-blank if I stole. Then I recalled hearing that white people looked upon Negroes as a variety of children, and it was only in the light of that that her question made any sense. If I had been planning to murder her, I certainly would not have told her and, rationally, she no doubt realized it. Yet habit had overcome her rationality and had made her ask me: "Boy, do you steal?" Only an idiot would have answered: "Yes, ma'am. I steal."

What would happen now that I would be among white people for hours at a stretch? Would they hit me? Curse me? If they did, I would leave at once. In all my wishing for a job I had not thought of how I would be treated, and now it loomed important, decisive, sweeping down beneath every other consideration. I would be polite, humble, saying yes sir and no sir, yes ma'am and no ma'am, but I would draw a line over which they must not step. Oh, maybe I'm just thinking up trouble, I told myself. They might like me . . .

The next morning I chopped wood for the cook stove, lugged in scuttles of coal for the grates, washed the front porch and swept the back porch, swept the kitchen, helped wait on the table, and washed the dishes. I was sweating. I swept the front walk and ran to the store to shop. When I returned the woman said:

"Your breakfast is in the kitchen."

"Thank you, ma'am."

I saw a plate of thick, black molasses and a hunk of white bread on the table. Would I get no more than this? They had had eggs, bacon, coffee . . . I picked up the bread and tried to break it; it was stale and hard. Well, I would drink the molasses. I lifted the plate and brought it to my lips and saw floating on the surface of the black liquid green and white bits of mold. Goddamn . . . I can't eat this, I told myself. The food was not even clean. The woman came into the kitchen as I was putting on my coat.

"You didn't eat," she said.

"No, ma'am," I said. "I'm not hungry."

"You'll eat at home?" she asked hopefully.

"Well, I just wasn't hungry this morning, ma'am," I lied.

"You don't like molasses and bread," she said dramatically.

"Oh, yes, ma'am, I do," I defended myself quickly, not wanting her to think that I dared criticize what she had given me.

"I don't know what's happening to you niggers nowadays," she sighed, wagging her head. She looked closely at the molasses. "It's a sin to throw out molasses like that. I'll put it up for you this evening."

"Yes, ma'am," I said heartily.

Neatly she covered the plate of molasses with another plate, then felt the bread and dumped it into the garbage. She turned to me, her face lit with an idea.

"What grade are you in school?"

"Seventh, ma'am."

"Then why are you going to school?" she asked in surprise.

"Well, I want to be a writer," I mumbled, unsure of myself; I had not planned to tell her that, but she had made me feel so utterly wrong and of no account that I needed to bolster myself.

"A what?" she demanded.

"A writer," I mumbled.

"For what?"

"To write stories," I mumbled defensively.

"You'll never be a writer," she said. "Who on earth put such ideas into your nigger head?"

"Nobody," I said.

"I didn't think anybody ever would," she declared indignantly.

As I walked around her house to the street, I knew that I would not go back. The woman had assaulted my ego; she had assumed that she knew my place in life, what I felt, what I ought to be, and I resented it with all my heart. Perhaps she was right; perhaps I would never be a writer; but I did not want her to say so.

Had I kept the job I would have learned quickly just how white people acted toward Negroes, but I was too naïve to think that there were many white people like that. I told myself that there were good white people, people with money and sensitive feelings. As a whole, I felt that they were bad, but I would be lucky enough to find the exceptions.

Fearing that my family might think I was finicky, I lied to them, telling them that the white woman had already hired a boy. At school I continued to ask about jobs and was directed to another address. As soon as school was out I made for the house. Yes, the woman said that she wanted a boy who could milk a cow, feed chickens, gather vegetables, help serve breakfast and dinner.

"But I can't milk a cow, ma'am," I said.

"Where are you from?" she asked incredulously.

"Here in Jackson," I said.

"You mean to stand there, nigger, and tell me that you live in Jackson and don't know how to milk a cow?" she demanded in surprise.

I said nothing, but I was quickly learning the reality —a Negro's reality—of the white world. One woman had assumed that I would tell her if I stole, and now this woman was amazed that I could not milk a cow, I, a nigger who dared live in Jackson . . . They were all turning out to be alike, differing only in detail. I faced a wall in the woman's mind, a wall that she did not know was there.

"I just never learned," I said finally.

"I'll show you how to milk," she said, as though glad

to be charitable enough to repair a nigger's knowledge on that score. "It's easy."

The place was large; they had a cow, chickens, a
garden, all of which spelled food and that decided me.
I told her that I would take the job and I reported for
work the next morning. My tasks were simple but
many; I milked the cow under her supervision, gathered eggs, swept, and was through in time to serve
breakfast. The dining-room table was set for five; there
were eggs, bacon, toast, jam, butter, milk, apples . . .
That seemed promising. The woman told me to bring
the food in as they called for it, and I familiarized myself with the kitchen so that I could act quickly when
called upon. Finally the woman came into the dining
room followed by a pale young man who sat down and
stared at the food.

"What the hell!" he snarled. "Every morning it's
these damn eggs for breakfast."

"Listen, you sonofabitch," the woman said, sitting
too, "you don't have to eat 'em."

"You might try serving some dirt," he said, and
forked up the bacon.

I felt that I was dreaming. Were they like that all the
time? If so, I would not stay here. A young girl came
and flopped into her chair.

"That's right, you bitch," the young man said.
"Knock the food right out of my goddamn mouth."

"You know what you can do," the girl said.

I stared at them so intently that I was not aware that
the young man was watching me.

"Say, what in hell are you glaring at me for, you nigger bastard?" he demanded. "Get those goddamn biscuits off that stove and put 'em on the table."

"Yes, sir."

Two middle-aged men came in and sat down. I never
learned who was in the family, who was related to
whom, or if it was a family. They cursed each other in
an amazingly offhand manner and nobody seemed to
mind. As they hurled invectives, they barely looked at
each other. I was tense each moment, trying to anti-

cipate their wishes and avoid a curse, and I did not suspect that the tension I had begun to feel that morning would lift itself into the passion of my life. Perhaps I had waited too long to start working for white people; perhaps I should have begun earlier, when I was younger—as most of the other black boys had done—and perhaps by now the tension would have become an habitual condition, contained and controlled by reflex. But that was not to be my lot; I was always to be conscious of it, brood over it, carry it in my heart, live with it, sleep with it, fight with it.

The morning was physically tiring, but the nervous strain, the fear that my actions would call down upon my head a storm of curses, was even more damaging. When the time came for me to go to school, I was emotionally spent. But I clung to the job because I got enough to eat and no one watched me closely and measured out my food. I had rarely tasted eggs and I would put hunks of yellow butter into a hot skillet and hurriedly scramble three or four eggs at a time and gobble them down in huge mouthfuls so that the woman would not see me. And I would take tumblers of milk behind a convenient door and drain them in a swallow, as though they contained water.

Though the food I ate strengthened my body, I acquired another problem: I had fallen down in my studies at school. Had I been physically stronger, had not my new tensions sapped my already limited energy, I might have been able to work mornings and evenings and still carry my studies successfully. But in the middle of the day I would grow groggy; in the classroom I would feel that the teacher and the pupils were receding from me and I would know that I was drifting off to sleep. I would go to the water fountain in the corridor and let cold water run over my wrists, chilling my blood, hoping in that way to keep awake.

But the job had its boon. At the midday recess I would crowd gladly into the corner store and eat sandwiches with the boys, slamming down my own money on the counter for what I wanted, swapping descriptions of the homes of white folks in which we worked. I used to divert them with vivid word pictures of the cursing family, their brooding silences, their indifference toward one another. I told them of the food I managed to eat when the woman's back was turned, and they were filled with friendly envy.

The boys would now examine some new article of clothing I had bought; none of us allowed a week to pass without buying something new, paying fifty cents down and fifty cents per week. We knew that we were being cheated, but we never had enough cash to buy in any other way.

My mother began a rapid recovery. I was happy when she expressed the hope that someday soon we might have a home of our own. Though Granny was angry and disgusted, my mother began to attend a Methodist church in the neighborhood, and I went to Sunday school, not because my mother begged me to —which she did—but to meet and talk with my classmates.

In the black Protestant church I entered a new world: prim, brown, puritanical girls who taught in the public schools; black college students who tried to conceal their plantation origin; black boys and girls emerging self-consciously from adolescence; wobbly-bosomed black and yellow church matrons; black janitors and porters who sang proudly in the choir; subdued redcaps and carpenters who served as deacons; meek, blank-eyed black and yellow washerwomen who shouted and moaned and danced when hymns were sung; jovial, potbellied black bishops; skinny old maids who were constantly giving rallies to raise money; snobbery, clannishness, gossip, intrigue, petty class rivalry, and conspicuous displays of cheap clothing . . . I liked it and I did not like it; I longed to be among them, yet when with them I looked at them as if I were a million miles away. I had been kept out of their world too long ever to be able to become a real part of it.

Nevertheless, I was so starved for association with people that I allowed myself to be seduced by it all, and for a few months I lived the life of an optimist. A revival began at the church and my classmates at school urged me to attend. More because I liked them than from any interest in religion, I consented. As the services progressed night after night, my mother tried to persuade me to join, to save my soul at last, to become a member of a responsible community church. Despite the fact that I told them I could never feel any religion, the boys of my gang begged me to "come to God."

"You believe in God, don't you?" they asked.

I evaded the question.

"But this is a new day," they said, pulling down the corners of their lips. "We don't holler and moan in church no more. Come to church and be a member of the community."

"Oh, I don't know," I said.

"We don't want to push you," they said delicately, implying that if I wanted to associate with them I would have to join.

On the last night of the revival, the preacher asked all those who were members of the church to stand. A good majority of those present rose. Next the preacher called upon the Christians who were not members of any church to stand. More responded. There remained now but a few young men who, belonging to no church and professing no religion, were scattered sheepishly about the pews. Having thus isolated the sinners, the preacher told the deacons to prevail upon those who lived "in darkness to discuss the state of their souls with him." The deacons sped to their tasks and asked us to go into a room and talk with a man "chosen and anointed of God." They held our arms and smiled as they bent and talked to us. Surrounded by people I knew and liked, with my mother's eyes looking pleadingly into mine, it was hard to refuse. I followed the others into a room where the preacher stood; he smiled and shook our hands.

"Now, you young men," he began in a brisk, clipped tone, "I want all of you to know God. I'm not asking you to join the church, but it's my duty as a man of God to tell you that you are in danger. Your peril is great; you stand in the need of prayer. Now, I'm going to ask each of you a personal favor. I want you to let the members of this church send up a prayer to God for you. Now, is there any soul here so cold, so hard, so lost, that he would say no to that? Can you refuse to let the good people of this community pray for you?"

He paused dramatically and no one answered. All the techniques of his appeal were familiar to me and I sat there feeling foolish, wanting to leap through the window and go home and forget about it. But I sat still, filled more with disgust than sin.

"Would any man in this room dare fling no into God's face?" the preacher asked.

There was silence.

"Now, I'm going to ask all of you to rise and go into the church and take a seat on the front bench," he said, edging on to more definite commitments. "Just stand up," he said, lifting his hands, palms up, as though he had the power to make us rise by magic. "That's it, young man," he encouraged the first boy who rose.

I followed them and we sat like wet ducks on a bench facing the congregation. Some part of me was cursing. A low, soft hymn began.

This may be the last time, I don't know . . .

They sang it, hummed it, crooned it, moaned it, implying in sweet, frightening tones that if we did not join the church then and there we might die in our sleep that very night and go straight to hell. The church members felt the challenge and the volume of song swelled. Could they sing so terrifyingly sweet as to

make us join, burst into tears and drop to our knees?
A few boys rose and gave their hands to the preacher.
A few women shouted and danced with joy. Another
hymn began.

> *It ain't my brother, but it's me, Oh, Lord,*
> *Standing in the need of prayer . . .*

During the singing the preacher tried yet another
ruse; he intoned mournfully, letting his voice melt into
the singing, yet casting his words above it:

"How many mothers of these young men are here
tonight?"

Among others, my mother rose and stood proudly.

"Now, good sweet mothers, come right down in
front here," said the preacher.

Hoping that this was the night of my long-deferred
salvation, my mother came forward, limping, weeping,
smiling. The mothers ringed their sons around, whispering, pleading.

"Now, you good sweet mothers, symbols of Mother
Mary at the tomb, kneel and pray for your sons, your
only sons," the preacher chanted.

The mothers knelt. My mother grabbed my hands
and I felt hot tears scalding my fingers. I tried to stifle
my disgust. We young men had been trapped by the
community, the tribe in which we lived and of which
we were a part. The tribe, for its own safety, was asking us to be at one with it. Our mothers were kneeling
in public and praying for us to give the sign of alle-
giance. The hymn ended and the preacher launched
into a highly emotional and symbolic sermon, recount-
ing how our mothers had given birth to us, how they
had nursed us from infancy, how they had tended us
when we were sick, how they had seen us grow up,
how they had watched over us, how they had always
known what was best for us. He then called for yet
another hymn, which was hummed. He chanted above
it in a melancholy tone:

"Now, I'm asking the first mother who really loves her son to bring him to me for baptism!"

Goddamn, I thought. It had happened quicker than I had expected. My mother was looking steadily at me.

"Come, son, let your old mother take you to God," she begged. "I brought you into the world, now let me help to save you."

She caught my hand and I held back.

"I've been as good a mother as I could," she whispered through her tears.

"God is hearing every word," the preacher underscored her plea.

This business of saving souls had no ethics; every human relationship was shamelessly exploited. In essence, the tribe was asking us whether we shared its feelings; if we refused to join the church, it was equivalent to saying no, to placing ourselves in the position of moral monsters. One mother led her beaten and frightened son to the preacher amid shouts of amen and hallelujah.

"Don't you love your old crippled mother, Richard?" my mother asked. "Don't leave me standing here with my empty hands," she said, afraid that I would humiliate her in public.

It was no longer a question of my believing in God; it was no longer a matter of whether I would steal or lie or murder; it was a simple, urgent matter of public pride, a matter of how much I had in common with other people. If I refused, it meant that I did not love my mother, and no man in that tight little black community had ever been crazy enough to let himself be placed in such a position. My mother pulled my arm and I walked with her to the preacher and shook his hand, a gesture that made me a candidate for baptism. There were more songs and prayers; it lasted until well after midnight. I walked home limp as a rag; I had not felt anything except sullen anger and a crushing sense of shame. Yet I was somehow glad that I had got it over with; no barriers now stood between me and the community.

"Mama, I don't feel a thing," I told her truthfully.

"Don't you worry; you'll grow into feeling it," she assured me.

And when I confessed to the other boys that I felt nothing, they too admitted that they felt nothing.

"But the main thing is to be a member of the church," they said.

The Sunday of the baptism arrived. I dressed in my best and showed up sweating. The candidates were huddled together to listen to a sermon in which the road of salvation was mapped out from the cradle to the grave. We were then called to the front of the church and lined up. The preacher, draped in white robes, dipped a small branch of a tree in a huge bowl of water and hovered above the head of the first candidate.

"I baptize thee in the name of the Father, the Son, and the Holy Ghost," he pronounced sonorously as he shook the wet branch. Drops trickled down the boy's face.

From one boy to another he went, dipping the branch each time. Finally my turn came and I felt foolish, tense; I wanted to yell for him to stop; I wanted to tell him that all this was so much nonsense. But I said nothing. The dripping branch was shaken above my head and drops of water wet my face and scalp, some of it rolling down my neck and wetting my back, like insects crawling. I wanted to squirm, but I held still. Then it was over. I relaxed. The preacher was now shaking the branch over another boy's head. I sighed. I had been baptized.

Even after receiving the "right hand of fellowship," Sunday school bored me. The Bible stories seemed slow and meaningless when compared to the bloody thunder of pulp narrative. And I was not alone in feeling this; other boys went to sleep in Sunday school. Finally the boldest of us confessed that the entire thing was a fraud and we played hooky from church.

As summer neared, my mother suffered yet another stroke of paralysis and again I had to watch her suffer, listen to her groans, powerless to help. I used to lie awake nights and think back to the early days in Arkansas, tracing my mother's life, reliving events, wondering why she had apparently been singled out for so much suffering, meaningless suffering, and I would feel more awe than I had ever felt in church. My mind could find no answer and I would feel rebellious against all life. But I never felt humble.

Another change took place at home. We needed money badly and Granny and Aunt Addie decided that we could no longer share the entire house, and Uncle Tom and his family were invited to live upstairs at a nominal rental. The dining room and the living room were converted into bedrooms and for the first time we were squeezed for living space. We began to get on each other's nerves. Uncle Tom had taught school in country towns for thirty years and as soon as he was under the roof he proceeded to tell me what was wrong with my life. I ignored him and he resented it.

Rattling pots and pans in the kitchen would now awaken me in the mornings and I would know that Uncle Tom and his family were getting breakfast. One morning I was roused by my uncle's voice calling gently but persistently. I opened my eyes and saw the dim blob of his face peering from behind the jamb of the kitchen door.

"What time have you?" I thought he asked me, but I was not sure.

"Hunh?" I mumbled sleepily.

"What time have you got?" he repeated.

I lifted myself on my elbow and looked at my dollar watch, which lay on the chair at the bedside.

"Eighteen past five," I mumbled.

"Eighteen past five?" he asked.

"Yes, sir."

"Now, is that the right time?" he asked again.

I was tired, sleepy; I did not want to look at the

watch again, but I was satisfied that, on the whole, I had given him the correct time.

"It's right," I said, snuggling back down into my pillow. "If it's a little slow or fast, it's not far wrong."

There was a short silence; I thought he had gone.

"What on earth do you mean, boy?" he asked in loud anger.

I sat up, blinking, staring into the shadows of the room, trying to see the expression on his face.

"What do I mean?" I asked, bewildered. "I mean what I said." Had I given him the wrong time? I looked again at my watch. "It's twenty past now."

"Why, you impudent black rascal!" he thundered.

I pushed back the covers of the bed, sensing trouble.

"What are you angry about?" I asked.

"I never heard a sassier black imp than you in all my life," he spluttered.

I swung my feet to the floor so that I could watch him.

"What are you talking about?" I asked. "You asked me the time and I told you."

" 'If it's a little fast or slow, it's not far wrong,' " he said, imitating me in an angry, sarcastic voice. "I've taught school for thirty years, and by God I've never had a boy say anything like that to me."

"But what's wrong with what I said?" I asked, amazed.

"Shut up!" he shouted. "Or I'll take my fist and ram it down your sassy throat! One more word out of you, and I'll get a limb and teach you a lesson."

"What's the matter with you, Uncle Tom?" I asked. "What's wrong with what I said?"

I could hear his breath whistling in his throat; I knew that he was furious.

"This day I'm going to give you the whipping some man ought to have given you long ago," he vowed.

I got to my feet and grabbed my clothes; the whole thing seemed unreal. I had been confronted so suddenly with struggle that I could not pull all the strings of the situation together at once. I did not feel that I had given him cause to say I was sassy. I had spoken to him just as I spoke to everybody. Others did not resent my words, so why should he? I heard him go out of the kitchen door and I knew that he had gone into the back yard. I pulled on my clothes and ran to the window; I saw him tearing a long, young, green switch from the elm tree. My body tightened. I was damned if he was going to beat me with it. Until a few days ago he had never lived near me, had never had any say in my rearing or lack of rearing. I was working, eating my meals out, buying my own clothes, giving what few pennies I could to Granny to help out in the house. And now a strange uncle who felt that I was impolite was going to teach me to act as I had seen the backward black boys act on the plantations, was going to teach me to grin, hang my head, and mumble apologetically when I was spoken to.

My senses reeled in protest. No, that could not be. He would not beat me. He was only bluffing. His anger would pass. He would think it over and realize that it was not worth all the bother. Dressed, I sat on the edge of the bed and waited. I heard his footsteps come onto the back porch. I felt weak all over. How long was this going to last? How long was I going to be beaten for trifles and less than trifles? I was already so conditioned toward my relatives that when I passed them I actually had a nervous tic in my muscles, and now I was going to be beaten by someone who did not like the tone of voice in which I spoke. I ran across the room and pulled out the dresser drawer and got my pack of razor blades; I opened it and took a thin blade of blue steel in each hand. I stood ready for him. The door opened. I was hoping desperately that this was not true, that this dream would end.

"Richard!" he called me in a cold, even tone.

"Yes, sir!" I answered, striving to keep my tension out of my voice.

"Come here."

I walked into the kitchen, my eyes upon him, my hands holding the razors behind my back.

"Now, Uncle Tom, what do you want with me?" I asked him.

"You need a lesson in how to live with people," he said.

"If I do need one, you're not going to give it to me," I said.

"You'll swallow those words before I'm through with you," he vowed.

"Now, listen, Uncle Tom," I said, "you're not going to whip me. You're a stranger to me. You don't support me. I don't live with you."

"You shut that foul mouth of yours and get into the back yard," he snapped.

He had not seen the razors in my hand. I ducked out the kitchen door and jumped lightly off the porch to the ground. He ran down the steps and advanced with the lifted switch.

"I've got a razor in each hand!" I warned in a low, charged voice. "If you touch me, I'll cut you! Maybe I'll get cut too, but I'll cut you, so help me God!"

He paused, staring at my lifted hands in the dawning light of morning. I held a sharp blue edge of steel tightly between thumb and forefinger of each fist.

"My God," he gasped.

"I didn't mean to hurt your feelings this morning," I told him. "You insist I did. Now, I'll be damned if I'm going to be beaten because of your hurt feelings."

"You're the worst criminal I ever saw," he exclaimed softly.

"If you want to fight, I'll fight. That's the way it'll be between us," I told him.

"You'll never amount to anything," he said, shaking his head and blinking his eyes in astonishment.

"I'm not worried about that," I said. "All I want you to do is keep away from me, now and always . . ."

"You'll end on the gallows," he predicted.

"If I do, you'll have nothing to do with it," I said.

He stared at me in silence; evidently he did not believe me, for he took a step forward to test me.

"Put those razors down," he commanded.

"I'll cut you! I'll cut you!" I said, hysteria leaping into my voice, my hands slicing out with points of steel as I backed away.

He stopped; he had never in his life faced a person more grimly determined. Now and then he blinked his eyes and shook his head.

"You fool!" he bellowed suddenly.

"I'll make you bloody if you hit me!" I warned him. His chest heaved and his body seemed to droop.

"Somebody will yet break your spirit," he said.

"It won't be you!"

"You'll get yours someday!"

"You won't be the one to give it to me!"

"And you've just been baptized," he said heavily.

"The hell with that," I said.

We stood in the early morning light and a touch of sun broke on the horizon. Roosters were crowing. A bird chirped near-by somewhere. Perhaps the neighbors were listening. Finally Uncle Tom's face began to twitch. Tears rolled down his cheeks. His lips trembled.

"Boy, I'm sorry for you," he said at last.

"You'd better be sorry for yourself," I said.

"You think you're a man," he said, dropping his arm and letting the switch drag in the dust of the yard. His lips moved as he groped for words. "But you'll learn, and you'll learn the hard way. I wish I could be an example to you . . ."

I knew that I had conquered him, had rid myself of him mentally and emotionally; but I wanted to be sure.

"You are not an example to me; you could never be," I spat at him. "You're a *warning*. Your life isn't so hot that you can tell me what to do." He repaired chairs for a living now, since he had retired from teaching. "Do you think I want to grow up and weave the bottoms of chairs for people to sit in?"

He twitched violently, trying to control himself.

"You'll be sorry you said that," he mumbled.

He turned his tall, lean, bent body and walked

slowly up the steps. I sat on the porch a long time, waiting for my emotions to ebb. Then I crept cautiously into the house, got my hat, coat, books, and went to work, went to face the whims of the white folks.

Chapter Seven

SUMMER. Bright hot days. Hunger still a vital part of my consciousness. Passing relatives in the hallways of the crowded home and not speaking. Eating in silence at a table where prayers are said. My mother recovering slowly, but now definitely crippled for life. Will I be able to enter school in September? Loneliness. Reading. Job hunting. Vague hopes of going north. But what would become of my mother if I left her in this queer house? And how would I fare in a strange city? Doubt. Fear. My friends are buying long-pants suits that cost from seventeen to twenty dollars, a sum as huge to me as the Alps! This was my reality in 1924.

Word came that a near-by brickyard was hiring and I went to investigate. I was frail, not weighing a hundred pounds. At noon I sneaked into the yard and walked among the aisles of damp, clean-smelling clay and came to a barrow full of wet bricks just taken from the machine that shaped them. I caught hold of the handles of the barrow and was barely able to lift it; it weighed perhaps four times as much as I did. If I were only stronger and heavier!

Later I asked questions and found that the water boy was missing; I ran to the office and was hired. I walked in the hot sun lugging a big zinc pail from one laboring gang of black men to another for a dollar a day; a man would lift the tin dipper to his lips, take a swallow, rinse out his mouth, spit, and then drink in long, slow gulps as sweat dripped into the dipper. And off again I would go, chanting:

"Water!"

And somebody would yell:

"Here, boy!"

Deep into wet pits of clay, into sticky ditches, up slippery slopes I would struggle with the pail. I stuck it out, reeling at times from hunger, pausing to get my breath before clambering up a hill. At the end of the week the money sank into the endless expenses at home. Later I got a job in the yard that paid a dollar and a half a day, that of bat boy. I went between the walls of clay and picked up bricks that had cracked open; when my barrow was full, I would wheel it out onto a wooden scaffold and dump it into a pond.

I had but one fear here: a dog. He was owned by the boss of the brickyard and he haunted the clay aisles, snapping, growling. The dog had been wounded many times, for the black workers were always hurling bricks at it. Whenever I saw the animal, I would take a brick from my load and toss it at him; he would slink away, only to appear again, showing his teeth. Several of the Negroes had been bitten and had been ill; the boss had been asked to leash the dog, but he had refused. One afternoon I was wheeling my barrow toward the pond when something sharp sank into my thigh. I whirled; the dog crouched a few feet away, snarling. I had been bitten. I drove the dog away and opened my trousers; teeth marks showed deep and red.

I did not mind the stinging hurt, but I was afraid of an infection. When I went to the office to report that the boss's dog had bitten me, I was met by a tall blonde white girl.

"What do you want?" she asked.

"I want to see the boss, ma'am."

"For what?"

"His dog bit me, ma'am, and I'm afraid I might get an infection."

"Where did he bite you?"

"On my leg," I lied, shying from telling her where the bite was.

"Let's see," she said.

"No, ma'am. Can't I see the boss?"

"He isn't here now," she said, and went back to her typing.

I returned to work, stopping occasionally to examine the teeth marks; they were swelling. Later in the afternoon a tall white man wearing a cool white suit, a Panama hat, and white shoes came toward me.

"Is this the nigger?" he asked a black boy as he pointed at me.

"Yes, sir," the black boy answered.

"Come here, nigger," he called me.

I went to him.

"They tell me my dog bit you," he said.

"Yes, sir."

I pulled down my trousers and he looked.

"Humnnn," he grunted, then laughed. "A dog bite can't hurt a nigger."

"It's swelling and it hurts," I said.

"If it bothers you, let me know," he said. "But I never saw a dog yet that could really hurt a nigger."

He turned and walked away and the black boys gathered to watch his tall form disappear down the aisles of wet bricks.

"Sonofabitch!"

"He'll get his someday!"

"Boy, their hearts are hard!"

"Lawd, a white man'll do anything!"

"Break up that prayer meeting!" the white straw boss yelled.

The wheelbarrows rolled again. A boy came close to me.

"You better see a doctor," he whispered.

"I ain't got no money," I said.

Two days passed and luckily the redness and swelling went away.

Summer wore on and the brickyard closed; again I was out of work. I heard that caddies were wanted and I tramped five miles to the golf links. I was hired by a florid-faced white man at the rate of fifty cents for nine holes. I did not know the game and I lost three balls in as many minutes; it seemed that my eyes could not trace the flight of the balls. The man dismissed me. I watched the other boys do their jobs and within half an hour I had another golf bag and was following a ball. I made a dollar. I returned home, disgusted, tired, hungry, hating the sight of a golf course.

School opened and, though I had not prepared myself, I enrolled. The school was far across town and the walking distance alone consumed my breakfast of mush and lard gravy. I attended classes without books for a month, then got a job working mornings and evenings for three dollars a week.

I grew silent and reserved as the nature of the world in which I lived became plain and undeniable; the bleakness of the future affected my will to study. Granny had already thrown out hints that it was time for me to be on my own. But what had I learned so far that would help me to make a living? Nothing. I could be a porter like my father before me, but what else? And the problem of living as a Negro was cold and hard. What was it that made the hate of whites for blacks so steady, seemingly so woven into the texture of things? What kind of life was possible under that hate? How had this hate come to be? Nothing about the problems of Negroes was ever taught in the classrooms at school; and whenever I would raise these questions with the boys, they would either remain silent or turn the subject into a joke. They were vocal about the petty individual wrongs they suffered, but they possessed no desire for a knowledge of the picture as a whole. Then why was I worried about it?

Was I really as bad as my uncles and aunts and Granny repeatedly said? Why was it considered wrong to ask questions? Was I right when I resisted punishment? It was inconceivable to me that one should surrender to what seemed wrong, and most of the people

I had met seemed wrong. Ought one to surrender to authority even if one believed that that authority was wrong? If the answer was yes, then I knew that I would always be wrong, because I could never do it. Then how could one live in a world in which one's mind and perceptions meant nothing and authority and tradition meant everything? There were no answers.

The eighth grade days flowed in their hungry path and I grew more conscious of myself; I sat in classes, bored, wondering, dreaming. One long dry afternoon I took out my composition book and told myself that I would write a story; it was sheer idleness that led me to it. What would the story be about? It resolved itself into a plot about a villain who wanted a widow's home and I called it *The Voodoo of Hell's Half-Acre*. It was crudely atmospheric, emotional, intuitively psychological, and stemmed from pure feeling. I finished it in three days and then wondered what to do with it.

The local Negro newspaper! That's it . . . I sailed into the office and shoved my ragged composition book under the nose of the man who called himself the editor.

"What is that?" he asked.

"A story," I said.

"A news story?"

"No, fiction."

"All right. I'll read it," he said.

He pushed my composition book back on his desk and looked at me curiously, sucking at his pipe.

"But I want you to read it *now*." I said.

He blinked. I had no idea how newspapers were run. I thought that one took a story to an editor and he sat down then and there and read it and said yes or no.

"I'll read this and let you know about it tomorrow," he said.

I was disappointed; I had taken time to write it and he seemed distant and uninterested.

"Give me the story," I said, reaching for it.

He turned from me, took up the book and read ten pages or more.

"Won't you come in tomorrow?" he asked. "I'll have it finished then."

I honestly relented.

"All right," I said. "I'll stop in tomorrow."

I left with the conviction that he would not read it. Now, where else could I take it after he had turned it down? The next afternoon, en route to my job, I stepped into the newspaper office.

"Where's my story?" I asked.

"It's in galleys," he said.

"What's that?" I asked; I did not know what galleys were.

"It's set up in type," he said. "We're publishing it."

"How much money will I get?" I asked, excited.

"We can't pay for manuscript," he said.

"But you sell your papers for money," I said with logic.

"Yes, but we're young in business," he explained.

"But you're asking me to *give* you my story, but you don't *give* your papers away," I said.

He laughed.

"Look, you're just starting. This story will put your name before our readers. Now, that's something," he said.

"But if the story is good enough to sell to your readers, then you ought to give me some of the money you get from it," I insisted.

He laughed again and I sensed that I was amusing him.

"I'm going to offer you something more valuable than money," he said. "I'll give you a chance to learn to write."

I was pleased, but I still thought he was taking advantage of me.

"When will you publish my story?"

"I'm dividing it into three installments," he said.

"The first installment appears this week. But the main thing is this: Will you get news for me on a space rate basis?"

"I work mornings and evenings for three dollars a week," I said.

"Oh," he said. "Then you better keep that. But what are you doing this summer?"

"Nothing:"

"Then come to see me before you take another job," he said. "And write some more stories."

A few days later my classmates came to me with baffled eyes, holding copies of the *Southern Register* in their hands.

"Did you really write that story?" they asked me.

"Yes."

"Why?"

"Because I wanted to."

"Where did you get it from?"

"I made it up."

"You didn't. You copied it out of a book."

"If I had, no one would publish it."

"But what are they publishing it for?"

"So people can read it."

"Who told you to do that?"

"Nobody."

"Then why did you do it?"

"Because I wanted to," I said again.

They were convinced that I had not told them the truth. We had never had any instruction in literary matters at school; the literature of the nation or the Negro had never been mentioned. My schoolmates could not understand why anyone would want to write a story; and, above all, they could not understand why I had called it *The Voodoo of Hell's Half-Acre.* The mood out of which a story was written was the most alien thing conceivable to them. They looked at me with new eyes, and a distance, a suspiciousness came between us. If I had thought anything in writing the story, I had thought that perhaps it would make me more acceptable to them, and now it was cutting me off from them more completely than ever.

At home the effects were no less disturbing. Granny came into my room early one morning and sat on the edge of my bed.

"Richard, what is this you're putting in the papers?" she asked.

"A story," I said.

"About what?"

"It's just a story, granny."

"But they tell me it's been in three times."

"It's the same story. It's in three parts."

"But what is it about?" she insisted.

I hedged, fearful of getting into a religious argument.

"It's just a story I made up," I said.

"Then it's a lie," she said.

"Oh, Christ," I said.

"You must get out of this house if you take the name of the Lord in vain," she said.

"Granny, please . . . I'm sorry," I pleaded. "But it's hard to tell you about the story. You see, granny, everybody knows that the story isn't true, but . . ."

"Then why write it?" she asked.

"Because people might want to read it."

"That's the Devil's work," she said and left.

My mother also was worried.

"Son, you ought to be more serious," she said. "You're growing up now and you won't be able to get jobs if you let people think that you're weak-minded. Suppose the superintendent of schools would ask you to teach here in Jackson, and he found out that you had been writing stories?"

I could not answer her.

"I'll be all right, mama," I said.

Uncle Tom, though surprised, was highly critical and contemptuous. The story had no point, he said. And whoever heard of a story by the title of *The Voodoo of Hell's Half-Acre*? Aunt Addie said that it was a sin for anyone to use the word "hell" and that what was wrong with me was that I had nobody to guide me. She blamed the whole thing upon my upbringing.

In the end I was so angry that I refused to talk about the story. From no quarter, with the exception of the Negro newspaper editor, had there come a single encouraging word. It was rumored that the principal wanted to know why I had used the word "hell." I felt that I had committed a crime. Had I been conscious of the full extent to which I was pushing against the current of my environment, I would have been frightened altogether out of my attempts at writing. But my reactions were limited to the attitude of the people about me, and I did not speculate or generalize.

I dreamed of going north and writing books, novels. The North symbolized to me all that I had not felt and seen; it had no relation whatever to what actually existed. Yet, by imagining a place where everything was possible, I kept hope alive in me. But where had I got this notion of doing something in the future, of going away from home and accomplishing something that would be recognized by others? I had, of course, read my Horatio Alger stories, my pulp stories, and I knew my Get-Rich-Quick Wallingford series from cover to cover, though I had sense enough not to hope to get rich; even to my naïve imagination that possibility was too remote. I knew that I lived in a country in which the aspirations of black people were limited, marked-off. Yet I felt that I had to go somewhere and do something to redeem my being alive.

I was building up in me a dream which the entire educational system of the South had been rigged to stifle. I was feeling the very thing that the state of Mississippi had spent millions of dollars to make sure that I would never feel; I was becoming aware of the thing that the Jim Crow laws had been drafted and passed to keep out of my consciousness; I was acting on impulses that southern senators in the nation's capital had striven to keep out of Negro life; I was beginning to dream the dreams that the state had said were wrong, that the schools had said were taboo.

Had I been articulate about my ultimate aspirations, no doubt someone would have told me what I was bargaining for; but nobody seemed to know, and least of all did I. My classmates felt that I was doing something that was vaguely wrong, but they did not know how to express it. As the outside world grew more meaningful, I became more concerned, tense; and my classmates and my teachers would say: "Why do you ask so many questions?" Or: "Keep quiet."

I was in my fifteenth year; in terms of schooling I was far behind the average youth of the nation, but I did not know that. In me was shaping a yearning for a kind of consciousness, a mode of being that the way of life about me had said could not be, must not be, and upon which the penalty of death had been placed. Somewhere in the dead of the southern night my life had switched onto the wrong track and, without my knowing it, the locomotive of my heart was rushing down a dangerously steep slope, heading for a collision, heedless of the warning red lights that blinked all about me, the sirens and the bells and the screams that filled the air.

Chapter Eight

SUMMER again. The old problem of hunting for a job. I told the woman for whom I was working, a Mrs. Bibbs, that I needed an all-day job that would pay me enough money to buy clothes and books for the next school term. She took the matter up with her husband, who was a foreman in a sawmill.

"So you want to work in the mill, hunh?" he asked.

"Yes, sir."

He came to me and put his hands under my arms and lifted me from the floor, as though I were a bundle of feathers.

"You're too light for our work," he said.

"But maybe I could do *something* there," I said.

"That's the problem," he said soberly. "The work's heavy and dangerous." He was silent and I knew that he considered the matter closed. That was the way things were between whites and blacks in the South; many of the most important things were never openly said; they were understated and left to seep through to one. I, in turn, said nothing; but I did not leave the room; my standing silent was a way of asking him to reconsider, telling him that I wanted ever so much to try for a job in his mill. "All right," he said finally. "Come to the mill in the morning. I'll see what I can do. But I don't think that you'll like it."

I was at the mill at dawn the next morning and saw men lifting huge logs with tackle blocks. There

were scores of buzzing steel saws biting into green
wood with loud whines.

"Watch out!" somebody yelled.

I looked around and saw a black man pointing
above my head; I glanced up. A log was swinging toward me. I scrambled out of its path. The black man
came to my side.

"What do you want here, boy?"

"Mr. Bibbs, the foreman, told me to look around.
I'm looking for a job," I said.

The man gazed at me intently.

"I wouldn't try for this if I was you," he said. "If
you know this game, all right. But this is dangerous
stuff for a guy that's green." He held up his right
hand from which three fingers were missing. "See?"

I nodded and left.

Empty days. Long days. Bright hot days. The sun
heated the pavements until they felt like the top of an
oven. I spent the morning hunting for jobs and I read
during the afternoons. One morning I was walking
toward the center of town and passed the home of a
classmate, Ned Greenley. He was sitting on his porch,
looking glum.

"Hello, Ned. What's new?" I asked.

"You've heard, haven't you?" he asked.

"About what?"

"My brother, Bob?"

"No, what happened?"

Ned began to weep softly.

"They killed him," he managed to say.

"The white folks?" I asked in a whisper, guessing.

He sobbed his answer. Bob was dead; I had met him
only a few times, but I felt that I had known him
through his brother.

"What happened?"

"Th-they t-took him in a c-car . . . Out on a c-
country road . . . Th-they shot h-him," Ned whimpered.

I had heard that Bob was working at one of the
hotels in town.

"Why?"

"Th-they said he was fooling with a white prostitute there in the hotel," Ned said.

Inside of me my world crashed and my body felt heavy. I stood looking down the quiet, sun-filled street. Bob had been caught by the white death, the threat of which hung over every male black in the South. I had heard whispered tales of black boys having sex relations with white prostitutes in the hotels in town, but I had never paid any close attention to them; now those tales came home to me in the form of the death of a man I knew.

I did not search for a job that day; I returned home and sat on my porch too, and stared. What I had heard altered the look of the world, induced in me a temporary paralysis of will and impulse. The penalty of death awaited me if I made a false move and I wondered if it was worth-while to make any move at all. The things that influenced my conduct as a Negro did not have to happen to me directly; I needed but to hear of them to feel their full effects in the deepest layers of my consciousness. Indeed, the white brutality that I had not seen was a more effective control of my behavior than that which I knew. The actual experience would have let me see the realistic outlines of what was really happening, but as long as it remained something terrible and yet remote, something whose horror and blood might descend upon me at any moment, I was compelled to give my entire imagination over to it, an act which blocked the springs of thought and feeling in me, creating a sense of distance between me and the world in which I lived.

A few days later I sought out the editor of the local Negro newspaper and found that he could not hire me. I had doubts now about my being able to enter school that fall. The empty days of summer rolled on. Whenever I met my classmates they would tell me about the jobs they had found, how some of them had left town to work in summer resorts in the North. Why did they not tell me of these jobs? I demanded of them. They said that they simply had not thought of it, and as I heard the words fall from their lips my sense of isolation became doubly acute. But, after all, what would make them think of me in connection with jobs when for years I had encountered them only casually in the classroom? I had had no association with them; the religious home in which I lived, my mush-and-lard-gravy poverty had cut me off from the normal processes of the lives of black boys my own age.

One afternoon I made a discovery in the home that stunned me. I was talking to my cousin, Maggie, who was a few months younger than I, when Uncle Tom entered the room. He paused, stared at me with silent hostility, then called his daughter. I gave the matter no thought. A few moments later I rose from my chair, where I had been reading, and was on my way down the hall when I heard Uncle Tom scolding his daughter. I caught a few phrases:

"Do you want me to break your neck? Didn't I tell you to stay away from him? That boy's a dangerous fool, I tell you! Then why don't you keep away from him? And make the other children keep away from him! Ask me no questions, but do as I tell you! Keep away from him, or I'll skin you!"

And I could hear my cousin's whimpering replies. My throat grew tight with anger. I wanted to rush into the room and demand an explanation, but I held still. How long had this been going on? I thought back over the time since Uncle Tom and his family had moved into the house, and I was filled with dismay as I recalled that on scarcely any occasion had any of his children ever been alone with me. Be careful now, I told myself; don't see what isn't there . . . But no matter how carefully I weighed my memories, I could recall no innocent intimacy, no games, no playing, none of the association that usually exists between young people living in the same house. Then suddenly I was reliving that early morning when I had held

Uncle Tom at bay with my razors. Though I must have seemed brutal and desperate to him, I had never thought of myself as being so, and now I was appalled at how I was regarded. It was a flash of insight which revealed to me the true nature of my relations with my family, an insight which altered the entire course of my life. I was now definitely decided upon leaving home. But I would remain until the ninth grade term had ended. There were many days when I spoke to no one in the home except my mother. My life was falling to pieces and I was acutely aware of it. I was poised for flight, but I was waiting for some event, some word, some act, some circumstance to furnish the impetus.

I returned to my job at Mrs. Bibbs's and bought my schoolbooks; my clothing remained little better than rags. Luckily the studies in the ninth—my last year at school—were light; and, during a part of the term the teacher turned over the class to my supervision, an honor that helped me emotionally and made me hope faintly. It was even hinted that, if I kept my grades high, it would be possible for me to teach in the city school system.

During that winter my brother came home from Chicago; I was glad to see him, though we were strangers. But it was not long before I felt that the affection shown him by the family was far greater than that which I had ever had from them. Slowly my brother grew openly critical of me, taking his cue from those about him, and it hurt. My loneliness became organic. I felt walled in and I grew irritable. I associated less and less with my classmates, for their talk was now full of the schools they planned to attend when the term was over. The cold days dragged mechanically: up early and to my job, splitting wood, carrying coal, sweeping floors, then off to school and boredom.

The school term ended. I was selected as valedictorian of my class and assigned to write a paper to be delivered at one of the public auditoriums. One morning the principal summoned me to his office.

"Well, Richard Wright, here's your speech," he said with smooth bluntness and shoved a stack of stapled sheets across his desk.

"What speech?" I asked as I picked up the papers.

"The speech you're to say the night of graduation," he said.

"But, professor, I've written my speech already," I said.

He laughed confidently, indulgently.

"Listen, boy, you're going to speak to both *white* and colored people that night. What can you alone think of saying to them? You have no experience . . ."

I burned.

"I know that I'm not educated, professor," I said. "But the people are coming to hear the students, and I won't make a speech that you've written."

He leaned back in his chair and looked at me in surprise.

"You know, we've never had a boy in this school like you before," he said. "You've had your way around here. Just how you managed to do it, I don't know. But, listen, take this speech and say it. I know what's best for you. You can't afford to just say *anything* before those white people that night." He paused and added meaningfully: "The superintendent of schools will be there; you're in a position to make a good impression on him. I've been a principal for more years than you are old, boy. I've seen many a boy and girl graduate from this school, and none of them was too proud to recite a speech I wrote for them."

I had to make up my mind quickly; I was faced with a matter of principle. I wanted to graduate, but I did not want to make a public speech that was not my own.

"Professor, I'm going to say my own speech that night," I said.

He grew angry.

"You're just a young, hotheaded fool," he said. He

toyed with a pencil and looked up at me. "Suppose you don't graduate?"

"But I passed my examinations," I said.

"Look, mister," he shot at me, "I'm the man who says who passes at this school."

I was so astonished that my body jerked. I had gone to this school for two years and I had never suspected what kind of man the principal was; it simply had never occurred to me to wonder about him.

"Then I don't graduate," I said flatly.

I turned to leave.

"Say, you. Come here," he called.

I turned and faced him; he was smiling at me in a remote, superior sort of way.

"You know, I'm glad I talked to you," he said. "I was seriously thinking of placing you in the school system, teaching. But, now, I don't think that you'll fit."

He was tempting me, baiting me; this was the technique that snared black young minds into supporting the southern way of life.

"Look, professor, I may never get a chance to go to school again," I said. "But I like to do things right."

"What do you mean?"

"I've no money. I'm going to work. Now, this ninth-grade diploma isn't going to help me much in life. I'm not bitter about it; it's not your fault. But I'm just not going to do things this way."

"Have you talked to anybody about this?" he asked me.

"No, why?"

"Are you sure?"

"This is the first I've heard of it, professor," I said, amazed again.

"You haven't talked to any white people about this?"

"No, sir!"

"I just wanted to know," he said.

My amazement increased; the man was afraid now for his job!

"Professor, you don't understand me." I smiled.

"You're just a young, hot fool," he said, confident

again. "Wake up, boy. Learn the world you're living in. You're smart and I know what you're after. I've kept closer track of you than you think. I know your relatives. Now, if you play safe," he smiled and winked, "I'll help you to go to school, to college."

"I want to learn, professor," I told him. "But there are some things I don't want to know."

"Good-bye," he said.

I went home, hurt but determined. I had been talking to a "bought" man and he had tried to "buy" me. I felt that I had been dealing with something unclean. That night Griggs, a boy who had gone through many classes with me, came to the house.

"Look, Dick, you're throwing away your future here in Jackson," he said. "Go to the principal, talk to him, take his speech and say it. I'm saying the one he wrote. So why can't you? What the hell? What can you lose?"

"No," I said.

"Why?"

"I know only a hell of a little, but my speech is going to reflect that," I said.

"Then you're going to be blacklisted for teaching jobs," he said.

"Who the hell said I was going to teach?" I asked.

"God, but you've got a will," he said.

"It's not will. I just don't want to do things that way," I said.

He left. Two days later Uncle Tom came to me. I knew that the principal had called him in.

"I hear that the principal wants you to say a speech which you've rejected," he said.

"Yes, sir. That's right," I said.

"May I read the speech you've written?" he asked.

"Certainly," I said, giving him my manuscript.

"And may I see the one that the principal wrote?"

I gave him the principal's speech too. He went to his room and read them. I sat quiet, waiting. He returned.

"The principal's speech is the better speech," he said.

"I don't doubt it," I replied. "But why did they ask me to write a speech if I can't deliver it?"

"Would you let me work on your speech?" he asked.

"No, sir."

"Now, look, Richard, this is your future . . ."

"Uncle Tom, I don't care to discuss this with you," I said.

He stared at me, then left. The principal's speech was simpler and clearer than mine, but it did not say anything; mine was cloudy, but it said what I wanted to say. What could I do? I had half a mind not to show up at the graduation exercises. I was hating my environment more each day. As soon as school was over, I would get a job, save money, and leave.

Griggs, who had accepted a speech written by the principal, came to my house each day and we went off into the woods to practice orating; day in and day out we spoke to the trees, to the creeks, frightening the birds, making the cows in the pastures stare at us in fear. I memorized my speech so thoroughly that I could have recited it in my sleep.

The news of my clash with the principal had spread through the class and the students became openly critical of me.

"Richard, you're a fool. You're throwing away every chance you've got. If they had known the kind of fool boy you are, they would never have made you valedictorian," they said.

I gritted my teeth and kept my mouth shut, but my rage was mounting by the hour. My classmates, motivated by a desire to "save" me, pestered me until I all but reached the breaking point. In the end the principal had to caution them to let me alone, for fear I would throw up the sponge and walk out.

I had one more problem to settle before I could make my speech. I was the only boy in my class wearing short pants and I was grimly determined to leave school in long pants. Was I not going to work? Would I not be on my own? When my desire for long pants became known at home, yet another storm shook the house.

"You're trying to go too fast," my mother said.

"You're nothing but a child," Uncle Tom pronounced.

"He's beside himself," Granny said.

I served notice that I was making my own decisions from then on. I borrowed money from Mrs. Bibbs, my employer, made a down payment on a pearl-gray suit. If I could not pay for it, I would take the damn thing back after graduation.

On the night of graduation I was nervous and tense; I rose and faced the audience and my speech rolled out. When my voice stopped there was some applause. I did not care if they liked it or not; I was through. Immediately, even before I left the platform, I tried to shunt all memory of the event from me. A few of my classmates managed to shake my hand as I pushed toward the door, seeking the street. Somebody invited me to a party and I did not accept. I did not want to see any of them again. I walked home, saying to myself: The hell with it! With almost seventeen years of baffled living behind me, I faced the world in 1925.

Chapter Nine

MY life now depended upon my finding work, and I was so anxious that I accepted the first offer, a job as a porter in a clothing store selling cheap goods to Negroes on credit. The shop was always crowded with black men and women pawing over cheap suits and dresses. And they paid whatever price the white man asked. The boss, his son, and the clerk treated the Negroes with open contempt, pushing, kicking, or slapping them. No matter how often I witnessed it, I could not get used to it. How can they accept it? I asked myself. I kept on edge, trying to stifle my feelings and never quite succeeding, a prey to guilt and fear because I felt that the boss suspected that I resented what I saw.

One morning, while I was polishing brass out front, the boss and his son drove up in their car. A frightened black woman sat between them. They got out and half dragged and half kicked the woman into the store. White people passed and looked on without expression. A white policeman watched from the corner, twirling his night stick; but he made no move. I watched out of the corner of my eyes, but I never slackened the strokes of my chamois upon the brass. After a moment or two I heard shrill screams coming from the rear room of the store; later the woman stumbled out, bleeding, crying, holding her stomach, her clothing torn. When she reached the sidewalk, the policeman met her, grabbed her, accused her of being drunk, called a patrol wagon and carted her away.

When I went to the rear of the store, the boss and his son were washing their hands at the sink. They looked at me and laughed uneasily. The floor was bloody, strewn with wisps of hair and clothing. My face must have reflected my shock, for the boss slapped me reassuringly on the back.

"Boy, that's what we do to niggers when they don't pay their bills," he said.

His son looked at me and grinned.

"Here, hava cigarette," he said.

Not knowing what to do, I took it. He lit his and held the match for me. This was a gesture of kindness, indicating that, even if they had beaten the black woman, they would not beat me if I knew enough to keep my mouth shut.

"Yes, sir," I said.

After they had gone, I sat on the edge of a packing box and stared at the bloody floor until the cigarette went out.

The store owned a bicycle which I used in delivering purchases. One day, while returning from the suburbs, my bicycle tire was punctured. I walked along the hot, dusty road, sweating and leading the bicycle by the handle bars.

A car slowed at my side.

"What's the matter there, boy?" a white man called.

I told him that my bicycle was broken and that I was walking back to town.

"That's too bad," he said. "Hop on the running board."

He stopped the car. I clutched hard at my bicycle with one hand and clung to the side of the car with the other.

"All set?"

"Yes, sir."

The car started. It was full of young white men. They were drinking. I watched the flask pass from mouth to mouth.

"Wanna drink, boy?" one asked.

The memory of my six-year-old drinking came back and filled me with caution. But I laughed, the wind whipping my face.

"Oh, no!" I said.

The words were barely out of my mouth before I felt something hard and cold smash me between the eyes. It was an empty whisky bottle. I saw stars, and fell backwards from the speeding car into the dust of the road, my feet becoming entangled in the steel spokes of the bicycle. The car stopped and the white men piled out and stood over me.

"Nigger, ain't you learned no better sense'n that yet?" asked the man who hit me. "Ain't you learned to say *sir* to a white man yet?"

Dazed, I pulled to my feet. My elbows and legs were bleeding. Fists doubled, the white man advanced, kicking the bicycle out of the way.

"Aw, leave the bastard alone. He's got enough," said one.

They stood looking at me. I rubbed my shins, trying to stop the flow of blood. No doubt they felt a sort of contemptuous pity, for one asked:

"You wanna ride to town now, nigger? You reckon you know enough to ride now?"

"I wanna walk," I said simply.

Maybe I sounded funny. They laughed.

"Well, walk, you black sonofabitch!"

Before they got back into their car, they comforted me with:

"Nigger, you sure ought to be glad it was us you talked to that way. You're a lucky bastard, 'cause if you'd said that to some other white man, you might've been a dead nigger now."

I was learning rapidly how to watch white people, to observe their every move, every fleeting expression, how to interpret what was said and what left unsaid.

Late one Saturday night I made some deliveries in a white neighborhood. I was pedaling my bicycle back to the store as fast as I could when a police car, swerving toward me, jammed me into the curbing.

"Get down, nigger, and put up your hands!" they ordered.

I did. They climbed out of the car, guns drawn, faces set, and advanced slowly.

"Keep still!" they ordered.

I reached my hands higher. They searched my pockets and packages. They seemed dissatisfied when they could find nothing incriminating. Finally, one of them said:

"Boy, tell your boss not to send you out in white neighborhoods at this time of night."

"Yes, sir," I said.

I rode off, feeling that they might shoot at me, feeling that the pavement might disappear. It was like living in a dream, the reality of which might change at any moment.

Each day in the store I watched the brutality with growing hate, yet trying to keep my feelings from registering in my face. When the boss looked at me I would avoid his eyes. Finally the boss's son cornered me one morning.

"Say, nigger, look here," he began.

"Yes, sir."

"What's on your mind?"

"Nothing, sir," I said, trying to look amazed, trying to fool him.

"Why don't you laugh and talk like the other niggers?" he asked.

"Well, sir, there's nothing much to say or smile about," I said, smiling.

His face was hard, baffled; I knew that I had not convinced him. He whirled from me and went to the front of the store; he came back a moment later, his face red. He tossed a few green bills at me.

"I don't like your looks, nigger. Now, get!" he snapped.

I picked up the money and did not count it. I grabbed my hat and left.

I held a series of petty jobs for short periods, quitting some to work elsewhere, being driven off others because of my attitude, my speech, the look in my eyes. I was no nearer than ever to my goal of saving enough money to leave. At times I doubted if I could ever do it.

One jobless morning I went to my old classmate, Griggs, who worked for a Capitol Street jeweler. He was washing the windows of the store when I came upon him.

"Do you know where I can find a job?" I asked.

He looked at me with scorn.

"Yes, I know where you can find a job," he said, laughing.

"Where?"

"But I wonder if you can hold it," he said.

"What do you mean?" I asked. "Where's the job?"

"Take your time," he said. "You know, Dick, I know you. You've been trying to hold a job all summer, and you can't. Why? Because you're impatient. That's your big fault."

I said nothing, because he was repeating what I had already heard him say. He lit a cigarette and blew out smoke leisurely.

"Well," I said, egging him on to speak.

"I wish to hell I could talk to you," he said.

"I think I know what you want to tell me," I said.

He clapped me on the shoulder; his face was full of fear, hate, concern for me.

"Do you want to get killed?" he asked me.

"Hell, no!"

"Then, for God's sake, learn how to live in the South!"

"What do you mean?" I demanded. "Let white people tell me that. Why should you?"

"See?" he said triumphantly, pointing his finger at me. "There it is, *now*! It's in your face. You won't let people tell you things. You rush too much. I'm trying to help you and you won't let me." He paused and looked about; the streets were filled with white people. He spoke to me in a low, full tone. "Dick, look, you're black, black, *black,* see? Can't you understand that?"

"Sure, I understand it," I said.

"You don't act a damn bit like it," he spat.

He then reeled off an account of my actions on every job I had held that summer.

"How did you know that?" I asked.

"White people make it their business to watch niggers," he explained. "And they pass the word around. Now, my boss is a Yankee and he tells me things. You're marked already."

Could I believe him? Was it true? How could I ever learn this strange world of white people?

"Then tell me how must I act?" I asked humbly. "I just want to make enough money to leave."

"Wait and I'll tell you," he said.

At that moment a woman and two men stepped from the jewelry store; I moved to one side to let them pass, my mind intent upon Griggs's words. Suddenly Griggs reached for my arm and jerked me violently, sending me stumbling three or four feet across the pavement. I whirled.

"What's the matter with you?" I asked.

Griggs glared at me, then laughed.

"I'm teaching you how to get out of white people's way," he said.

I looked at the people who had come out of the store; yes, they were *white,* but I had not noticed it.

"Do you see what I mean?" he asked. "White people want you out of their way." He pronounced the words slowly so that they would sink into my mind.

"I know what you mean," I breathed.

"Dick, I'm treating you like a brother," he said. "You act around white people as if you didn't know that they were white. And they *see* it."

"Oh, Christ, I can't be a slave," I said hopelessly.

"But you've got to eat," he said.

"Yes, I got to eat."

"Then start acting like it," he hammered at me, pounding his fist in his palm. "When you're in front of white people, *think* before you act, *think* before you speak. Your way of doing things is all right among *our* people, but not for *white* people. They won't stand for it."

I stared bleakly into the morning sun. I was nearing my seventeenth birthday and I was wondering if I would ever be free of this plague. What Griggs was saying was true, but it was simply utterly impossible for me to calculate, to scheme, to act, to plot all the time. I would remember to dissemble for short periods, then I would forget and act straight and human again, not with the desire to harm anybody, but merely forgetting the artificial status of race and class. It was the same with whites as with blacks; it was my way with everybody. I sighed, looking at the glittering diamonds in the store window, the rings and the neat rows of golden watches.

"I guess you're right," I said at last. "I've got to watch myself, break myself . . ."

"No," he said quickly, feeling guilty now. Someone —a white man—went into the store and we paused in our talk. "You know, Dick, you may think I'm an Uncle Tom, but I'm not. I hate these white people, hate 'em with all my heart. But I can't show it; if I did, they'd kill me." He paused and looked around to see if there were any white people within hearing distance. "Once I heard an old drunk nigger say:

> *All these white folks dressed so fine*
> *Their ass-holes smell just like mine . . ."*

I laughed uneasily, looking at the white faces that passed me. But Griggs, when he laughed, covered his mouth with his hand and bent at the knees, a gesture which was unconsciously meant to conceal his excessive joy in the presence of whites.

"That's how I feel about 'em," he said proudly after he had finished his spasm of glee. He grew sober. "There's an optical company upstairs and the boss is a Yankee from Illinois. Now, he wants a boy to work all day in summer, mornings and evenings in winter. He wants to break a colored boy into the optical trade. You know algebra and you're just cut out for the work. I'll tell Mr. Crane about you and I'll get in touch with you."

"Do you suppose I could see him now?" I asked.

"For God's sake, take your *time!*" he thundered at me.

"Maybe that's what's wrong with Negroes," I said. "They take too much time."

I laughed, but he was disturbed. I thanked him and left. For a week I did not hear from him and I gave up hope. Then one afternoon Griggs came to my house.

"It looks like you've got a job," he said. "You're going to have a chance to learn a trade. But remember to keep your head. Remember you're black. You start tomorrow."

"What will I get?"

"Five dollars a week to start with; they'll raise you if they like you," he explained.

My hopes soared. Things were not quite so bad, after all. I would have a chance to learn a trade. And I need not give up school. I told him that I would take the job, that I would be humble.

"You'll be working for a Yankee and you ought to get along," he said.

The next morning I was outside the office of the optical company long before it opened. I was reminding myself that I must be polite, must think before I spoke, must think before I acted, must say "yes sir, no sir," that I must so conduct myself that white people would not think that I thought I was as good as they. Suddenly a white man came up to me.

"What do you want?" he asked me.

"I'm reporting for a job, sir," I said.

"O.K. Come on."

I followed him up a flight of steps and he unlocked the door of the office. I was a little tense, but the young white man's manner put me at ease and I sat and held my hat in my hand. A white girl came and began punching the typewriter. Soon another white man, thin and gray, entered and went into the rear room. Finally a tall, red-faced white man arrived, shot me a quick glance and sat at his desk. His brisk manner branded him a Yankee.

"You're the new boy, eh?"

"Yes, sir."

"Let me get my mail out of the way and I'll talk with you," he said pleasantly.

"Yes, sir."

I even pitched my voice to a low plane, trying to rob it of any suggestion or overtone of aggressiveness.

Half an hour later Mr. Crane called me to his desk and questioned me closely about my schooling, about how much mathematics I had had. He seemed pleased when I told him that I had had two years of algebra.

"How would you like to learn this trade?" he asked.

"I'd like it fine, sir. I'd like nothing better," I said.

He told me that he wanted to train a Negro boy in the optical trade; he wanted to help him, guide him. I tried to answer in a way that would let him know that I would try to be worthy of what he was doing. He took me to the stenographer and said:

"This is Richard. He's going to be with us."

He then led me into the rear room of the office, which turned out to be a tiny factory filled with many strange machines smeared with red dust.

"Reynolds," he said to a young white man, "this is Richard."

"What you saying there, boy!" Reynolds grinned and boomed at me.

Mr. Crane took me to the older man.

"Pease, this is Richard, who'll work with us."

Pease looked at me and nodded. Mr. Crane then held forth to the two white men about my duties; he told them to break me in gradually to the workings of the shop, to instruct me in the mechanics of grinding and polishing lenses. They nodded their assent.

"Now, boy, let's see how clean you can get this place," Mr. Crane said.

"Yes, sir."

I swept, mopped, dusted, and soon had the office and the shop clean. In the afternoons, when I had caught up with my work, I ran errands. In an idle moment I would stand and watch the two white men grinding lenses on the machines. They said nothing to me and I said nothing to them. The first day passed, the second, the third, a week passed and I received my five dollars. A month passed. But I was not learning anything and nobody had volunteered to help me. One afternoon I walked up to Reynolds and asked him to tell me about the work.

"What are you trying to do, get smart, nigger?" he asked me.

"No, sir," I said.

I was baffled. Perhaps he just did not want to help me. I went to Pease, reminding him that the boss had said that I was to be given a chance to learn the trade.

"Nigger, you think you're white, don't you?"

"No, sir."

"You're acting mighty like it," he said.

"I was only doing what the boss told me to do," I said.

Pease shook his fist in my face.

"This is a *white* man's work around here," he said.

From then on they changed toward me; they said good morning no more. When I was just a bit slow in performing some duty, I was called a lazy black son-ofabitch. I kept silent, striving to offer no excuse for worsening of relations. But one day Reynolds called me to his machine.

"Nigger, you think you'll ever amount to anything?" he asked in a slow, sadistic voice.

"I don't know, sir," I answered, turning my head away.

"What do niggers think about?" he asked.

"I don't know, sir," I said, my head still averted.

"If I was a nigger, I'd kill myself," he said.

I said nothing. I was angry.

"You know why?" he asked.

I still said nothing.

"But I don't reckon niggers mind being niggers," he said suddenly and laughed.

I ignored him. Mr. Pease was watching me closely; then I saw them exchange glances. My job was not leading to what Mr. Crane had said it would. I had been humble, and now I was reaping the wages of humility.

"Come here, boy," Pease said.

I walked to his bench.

"You didn't like what Reynolds just said, did you?" he asked.

"Oh, it's all right," I said smiling.

"You didn't like it. I could see it on your face," he said.

I stared at him and backed away.

"Did you ever get into any trouble?" he asked.

"No, sir."

"What would you do if you got into trouble?"

"I don't know, sir."

"Well, watch yourself and don't get into trouble," he warned.

I wanted to report these clashes to Mr. Crane, but the thought of what Pease or Reynolds would do to me if they learned that I had "snitched" stopped me. I worked through the days and tried to hide my resentment under a nervous, cryptic smile.

The climax came at noon one summer day. Pease called me to his workbench; to get to him I had to go between two narrow benches and stand with my back against a wall.

"Richard, I want to ask you something," Pease began pleasantly, not looking up from his work.

"Yes, sir."

Reynolds came over and stood blocking the narrow passage between the benches; he folded his arms and stared at me solemnly. I looked from one to the other, sensing trouble. Pease looked up and spoke slowly, so there would be no possibility of my not understanding.

"Richard, Reynolds here tells me that you called me Pease," he said.

I stiffened. A void opened up in me. I knew that this was the showdown.

He meant that I had failed to call him Mr. Pease. I looked at Reynolds; he was gripping a steel bar in his hand. I opened my mouth to speak, to protest, to assure Pease that I had never called him simply *Pease,* and that I had never had any intention of doing so, when Reynolds grabbed me by the collar, ramming my head against a wall.

"Now, be careful, nigger," snarled Reynolds, baring his teeth. "I heard you call 'im *Pease.* And if you say you didn't, you're calling me a liar, see?" He waved the steel bar threateningly.

If I had said: No, sir, Mr. Pease, I never called you *Pease,* I would by inference have been calling Reynolds a liar; and if I had said: Yes, sir, Mr. Pease, I called you *Pease,* I would have been pleading guilty to the worst insult that a Negro can offer to a southern white man. I stood trying to think of a neutral course that would resolve this quickly risen nightmare, but my tongue would not move.

"Richard, I asked you a question!" Pease said. Anger was creeping into his voice.

"I don't remembering calling you *Pease,* Mr. Pease," I said cautiously. "And if I did, I sure didn't mean . . ."

"You black sonofabitch! You called me *Pease,* then!" he spat, rising and slapping me till I bent sideways over a bench.

Reynolds was up on top of me demanding:

"Didn't you call him *Pease*? If you say you didn't, I'll rip your gut string loose with this f--k--g bar, you black granny dodger! You can't call a white man a liar and get away with it!"

I wilted. I begged them not to hit me. I knew what they wanted. They wanted me to leave the job.

"I'll leave," I promised. "I'll leave right now!"

They gave me a minute to get out of the factory, and warned me not to show up again or tell the boss. Reynolds loosened his hand on my collar and I ducked out of the room. I did not see Mr. Crane or the stenographer in the office. Pease and Reynolds had so timed it that Mr. Crane and the stenographer would be out when they turned on the terror. I went to the street and waited for the boss to return. I saw Griggs wiping glass shelves in the jewelry store and I beckoned to him. He came out and I told him what had happened.

"Then what are you standing there like a fool for?" he demanded. "Won't you ever learn? Get home! They might come down!"

I walked down Capitol Street feeling that the sidewalk was unreal, that I was unreal, that the people were unreal, yet expecting somebody to demand to know what right I had to be on the streets. My wound went deep; I felt that I had been slapped out of the human race. When I reached home, I did not tell the family what had happened; I merely told them that I had quit, that I was not making enough money, that I was seeking another job.

That night Griggs came to my house; we went for a walk.

"You got a goddamn tough break," he said.

"Can you say it was my fault?" I asked.

He shook his head.

"Well, what about your goddamn philosophy of meekness?" I asked him bitterly.

"These things just happen," he said, shrugging.

"They owe me money," I said.

"That's what I came about," he said. "Mr. Crane wants you to come in at ten in the morning. Ten sharp, now, mind you, because he'll be there and those guys won't gang up on you again."

The next morning at ten I crept up the stairs and peered into the office of the optical shop to make sure that Mr. Crane was in. He was at his desk. Pease and Reynolds were at their machines in the rear.

"Come in, Richard," Mr. Crane said.

I pulled off my hat and walked into the office; I stood before him.

"Sit down," he said.

I sat. He stared at me and shook his head.

"Tell me, what happened?"

An impulse to speak rose in me and died with the realization that I was facing a wall that I would never breech. I tried to speak several times and could make no sounds. I grew tense and tears burnt my cheeks.

"Now, just keep control of yourself," Mr. Crane said.

I clenched my fists and managed to talk.

"I tried to do my best here," I said.

"I believe you," he said. "But I want to know what happened. Which one bothered you?"

"Both of 'em," I said.

Reynolds came running to the door and I rose. Mr. Crane jumped to his feet.

"Get back in there," he told Reynolds.

"That nigger's lying!" Reynolds said. "I'll kill 'im if he lies on me!"

"Get back in there or get out," Mr. Crane said. Reynolds backed away, keeping his eyes on me.

"Go ahead," Mr. Crane said. "Tell me what happened."

Then again I could not speak. What could I accomplish by telling him? I was black; I lived in the South. I would never learn to operate those machines as long as those two white men in there stood by them. Anger and fear welled in me as I felt what I had missed; I leaned forward and clapped my hands to my face.

"No, no, now," Mr. Crane said. "Keep control of yourself. No matter what happens, keep control . . ."

"I know," I said in a voice not my own. "There's no use of my saying anything."

"Do you want to work here?" he asked me.

I looked at the white faces of Pease and Reynolds; I imagined their waylaying me, killing me. I was remembering what had happened to Ned's brother.

"No, sir," I breathed.

"Why?"

"I'm scared," I said. "They would kill me."

Mr. Crane turned and called Pease and Reynolds into the office.

"Now, tell me which one bothered you. Don't be afraid. Nobody's going to hurt you," Mr. Crane said.

I stared ahead of me and did not answer. He waved the men inside. The white stenographer looked at me with wide eyes and I felt drenched in shame, naked to my soul. The whole of my being felt violated, and I knew that my own fear had helped to violate it. I was breathing hard and struggling to master my feelings.

"Can I get my money, sir?" I asked at last.

"Just sit a minute and take hold of yourself," he said.

I waited and my roused senses grew slowly calm.

"I'm awfully sorry about this," he said.

"I had hoped for a lot from this job," I said. "I'd wanted to go to school, to college . . ."

"I know," he said. "But what are you going to do now?"

My eyes traveled over the office, but I was not seeing.

"I'm going away," I said.

"What do you mean?"

"I'm going to get out of the South," I breathed.

"Maybe that's best," he said. "I'm from Illinois. Even for me, it's hard here. I can do just so much."

He handed me my money, more than I had earned for the week. I thanked him and rose to leave. He rose. I went into the hallway and he followed me. He reached out his hand.

"It's tough for you down here," he said.

I barely touched his hand. I walked swiftly down the hall, fighting against crying again. I ran down the steps, then paused and looked back up. He was standing at the head of the stairs, shaking his head. I went into the sunshine and walked home like a blind man.

Chapter Ten

FOR weeks after that I could not believe in my feelings. My personality was numb, reduced to a lumpish, loose, dissolved state. I was a non-man, something that knew vaguely that it was human but felt that it was not. As time separated me from the experience, I could feel no hate for the men who had driven me from the job. They did not seem to be individual men, but part of a huge, implacable, elemental design toward which hate was futile. What I did feel was a longing to attack. But how? And because I knew of no way to grapple with this thing, I felt doubly cast out.

I went to bed tired and got up tired, though I was having no physical exercise. During the day I overacted to each event, my banked emotions spilling around it. I refused to talk to anyone about my affairs, because I knew that I would only hear a justification of the ways of the white folks and I did not want to hear it. I lived carrying a huge wound, tender, festering, and I shrank when I came near anything that I thought would touch it.

But I had to work because I had to eat. My next job was that of a helper in a drugstore, and the night before I reported for work I fought with myself, telling myself that I had to master this thing, that my life depended upon it. Other black people worked, got along somehow, then I must, *must*, MUST get along until I could get my hands on enough money to leave.

I would make myself fit in. Others had done it. I would do it. I had to do it.

I went to the job apprehensive, resolving to watch my every move. I swept the sidewalk, pausing when a white person was twenty feet away. I mopped the store, cautiously waiting for the white people to move out of my way in their own good time. I cleaned acres of glass shelving, changing my tempo now to work faster, holding every nuance of reality within the focus of my consciousness. Noon came and the store was crowded; people jammed to the counters for food. A white man behind the counter ran up to me and shouted:

"A jug of Coca-Cola, quick, boy!"

My body jerked taut and I stared at him. He stared at me.

"What's wrong with you?"

"Nothing," I said.

"Well, move! Don't stand there gaping!"

Even if I had tried, I could not have told him what was wrong. My sustained expectation of violence had exhausted me. My preoccupation with curbing my impulses, my speech, my movements, my manner, my expressions had increased my anxiety. I became forgetful, concentrating too much upon trivial tasks. The men began to yell at me and that made it worse. One day I dropped a jug of orange syrup in the middle of the floor. The boss was furious. He caught my arm and jerked me into the back of the drugstore. His face was livid. I expected him to hit me. I was braced to defend myself.

"I'm going to deduct that from your pay, you black bastard!" he yelled.

Words had come instead of blows and I relaxed.

"Yes, sir," I said placatingly. "It was my fault."

My tone whipped him to a frenzy.

"You goddamn right it was!" he yelled louder.

"I'm new at this," I mumbled, realizing that I had said the wrong thing, though I had been striving to say the right.

"We're only trying you out," he warned me.

"Yes, sir. I understand," I said.

He stared at me, speechless with rage. Why could I not learn to keep my mouth shut at the right time? I had said just one short sentence too many. My words were innocent enough, but they indicated, it seemed, a consciousness on my part that infuriated white people.

Saturday night came and the boss gave me my money and snapped: "Don't come back. You won't do."

I knew what was wrong with me, but I could not correct it. The words and actions of white people were baffling signs to me. I was living in a culture and not a civilization and I could learn how that culture worked only by living with it. Misreading the reactions of whites around me made me say and do the wrong things. In my dealing with whites I was conscious of the entirety of my relations with them, and they were conscious only of what was happening at a given moment. I had to keep remembering what others took for granted; I had to think out what others felt.

I had begun coping with the white world too late. I could not make subservience an automatic part of my behavior. I had to feel and think out each tiny item of racial experience in the light of the whole race problem, and to each item I brought the whole of my life. While standing before a white man I had to figure out how to perform each act and how to say each word. I could not help it. I could not grin. In the past I had always said too much, now I found that it was difficult to say anything at all. I could not react as the world in which I lived expected me to; that world was too baffling, too uncertain.

I was idle for weeks. The summer waned. Hope for school was now definitely gone. Autumn came and many of the boys who held jobs returned to school. Jobs were now numerous. I heard that hallboys were needed at one of the hotels, the hotel in which Ned's brother had lost his life. Should I go there? Would I, too, make a fatal slip? But I had to earn money. I applied and was accepted to mop long white tiled hallways that stretched around the entire perimeter of the office floors of the building. I reported each night at ten, got a huge pail of water, a bushel of soap flakes and, with a gang of moppers, I worked. All the boys were Negroes and I was happy; at least I could talk, joke, laugh, sing, say what I pleased.

I began to marvel at how smoothly the black boys acted out the roles that the white race had mapped out for them. Most of them were not conscious of living a special, separate, stunted way of life. Yet I knew that in some period of their growing up—a period that they had no doubt forgotten—there had been developed in them a delicate, sensitive controlling mechanism that shut off their minds and emotions from all that the white race had said was taboo. Although they lived in an America where in theory there existed equality of opportunity, they knew unerringly what to aspire to and what not to aspire to. Had a black boy announced that he aspired to be a writer, he would have been unhesitatingly called crazy by his pals. Or had a black boy spoken of yearning to get a seat on the New York Stock Exchange, his friends—in the boy's own interest—would have reported his odd ambition to the white boss.

There was a pale-yellow boy who had gonorrhea and was proud of it.

"Say," he asked me one night, "you ever have the clap?"

"God, no," I said. "Why do you ask?"

"I got it," he said matter-of-factly. "I thought you could tell me something to use."

"Haven't you been to a doctor?" I asked.

"Aw, hell. Them doctors ain't no good."

"Don't be foolish," I said.

"What's the matter with you?" he demanded of me. "You talk like you'd be 'shamed of the clap."

"I would," I said.

"Hell, you ain't a man 'less you done had it three times," he said.

"Don't brag about it," I said.

" 'Tain't nothing worse'n a bad cold," he said.

But I noticed that when he urinated he would grab hold of a steam pipe, a doorjamb, or a window sill and strain with tear-filled eyes and a tortured face, as though he were attempting to lift the hotel up from its foundations. I laughed to cover my disgust.

When I was through mopping, I would watch the never-ending crap games that went on in the lockers, but I could never become interested enough to participate. Gambling had never appealed to me. I could not conceive of any game holding more risks than the life I was living. Curses and sex stories sounded round the clock and blue smoke choked the air. I would sit listening for hours, wondering how on earth they could laugh so freely, trying to grasp the miracle that gave their debased lives the semblance of a human existence.

Several Negro girls were employed as maids in the hotel, some of whom I knew. One night when I was about to go home I saw a girl who lived in my direction and I fell in beside her to walk part of the distance together. As we passed the white night watchman, he slapped her playfully on her buttocks. I turned around, amazed. The girl twisted out of his reach, tossed her head saucily, and went down the hallway. I had not moved from my tracks.

"Nigger, you look like you don't like what I did," he said.

I could not move or speak. My immobility must have seemed a challenge to him, for he pulled his gun.

"Don't you like it, nigger?"

"Yes, sir," I whispered with a dry throat.

"Well, talk like it, then, goddammit!"

"Oh, yes, sir!" I said with as much heartiness as I could muster.

I walked down the hall, knowing that the gun was pointed at me, but afraid to look back. When I was out of the door, my throat felt as though it were swelling and bursting with fire. The girl was waiting for me. I walked past her. She caught up with me.

"God, how could you let him do that?" I exploded.

"It don't matter. They do that all the time," she said.

"i wanted to do something," I said.

"You woulda been a fool if you had," she said.

"But how must you feel?"

"They never get any further with us than that, if we don't want 'em to," she said dryly.

"Yes, I would've been a fool," I said, but she did not catch the point.

I was afraid to go to work the following night. What would the watchman think? Would he decide to teach me a lesson? I walked slowly through the door, wondering if he would continue his threat. His eyes looked at and through me. Evidently he considered the matter closed, or else he had had so many experiences of that kind that he had already forgotten it.

Out of my salary I had begun to save a few dollars, for my determination to leave had not lessened. But I found the saving exasperatingly slow. I pondered continuously ways of making money, and the only ways that I could think of involved transgressions of the law. No, I must not do that, I told myself. To go to jail in the South would mean the end. And there was the possibility that if I were ever caught I would never reach jail.

This was the first time in my life that I had ever consciously entertained the idea of violating the laws of the land. I had felt that my intelligence and industry could cope with all situations, and, until that time, I had never stolen a penny from anyone. Even hunger had never driven me to appropriate what was not my own. The mere idea of stealing had been repugnant. I had not been honest from deliberate motives, but being dishonest had simply never occurred to me.

Yet, all about me, Negroes were stealing. More than once I had been called a "dumb nigger" by black boys who discovered that I had not availed myself of a chance to snatch some petty piece of white property that had been carelessly left within my reach.

"How in hell you gonna git ahead?" I had been asked when I had said that one ought not steal.

I knew that the boys in the hotel filched whatever they could. I knew that Griggs, my friend who worked in the Capitol Street jewelry store, was stealing regularly and successfully. I knew that a black neighbor of mine was stealing bags of grain from a wholesale house where he worked, though he was a stanch deacon in his church and prayed and sang on Sundays. I knew that the black girls who worked in white homes stole food daily to supplement their scanty wages. And I knew that the very nature of black and white relations bred this constant thievery.

No Negroes in my environment had ever thought of organizing, no matter in how orderly a fashion, and petitioning their white employers for higher wages. The very thought would have been terrifying to them, and they knew that the whites would have retaliated with swift brutality. So, pretending to conform to the laws of the whites, grinning, bowing, they let their fingers stick to what they could touch. And the whites seemed to like it.

But I, who stole nothing, who wanted to look them straight in the face, who wanted to talk and act like a man, inspired fear in them. The southern whites would rather have had Negroes who stole, work for them than Negroes who knew, however dimly, the worth of their own humanity. Hence, whites placed a premium upon black deceit; they encouraged irresponsibility; and their rewards were bestowed upon us blacks in the degree that we could make them feel safe and superior.

My objections to stealing were not moral. I did not approve of it because I knew that, in the long run, it was futile, that it was not an effective way to alter one's relationship to one's environment. Then, how could I change my relationship to my environment? Almost my entire salary went to feed the eternally hungry stomachs at home. If I saved a dollar a week, it would take me two years to amass a hundred dollars, the amount which for some reason I had decided was necessary to stake me in a strange city. And, God knows, anything could happen to me in two years . . .

I did not know when I would be thrown into a situation where I would say the wrong word to the wrong white man and find myself in trouble. And, above all, I wanted to avoid trouble, for I feared that if I clashed with whites I would lose control of my emotions and spill out words that would be my sentence of death. Time was not on my side and I had to make some move. Often, when perplexed, I longed to be like the smiling, lazy, forgetful black boys in the noisy hotel locker rooms, with no torrential conflicts to resolve. Many times I grew weary of the secret burden I carried and longed to cast it down, either in action or in resignation. But I was not made to be a resigned man and I had only a limited choice of actions, and I was afraid of all of them.

A new anxiety was created in me by my desire to leave quickly. I had now seen at close quarters the haughty white men who made the laws; I had seen how they acted, how they regarded black people, how they regarded me; and I no longer felt bound by the laws which white and black were supposed to obey in common. I was outside those laws; the white people had told me so. Now when I thought of ways to escape from my environment I no longer felt the inner restraint that would have made stealing impossible, and this new freedom made me lonely and afraid.

My feelings became divided; in spite of myself I would dream of a locked cupboard in a near-by neighbor's house where a gun was kept. If I stole it, how much would it bring? When the yearning to leave would become strong in me, I could not keep out of my mind the image of a storehouse at a near-by Negro college that held huge cans of preserved fruits. Yet fear kept me from making any move; the idea of stealing floated tentatively in me. My inability to adjust myself to the white world had already shattered a part of the structure of my personality and had broken down the inner barriers to crime; the only thing that now stood in the way was lack of immediate opportunity, a final push of circumstance. And that came.

I was promoted to bellboy, which meant a small increase in income. But I soon learned that the substantial money came from bootlegging liquor to the white prostitutes in the hotel. The other bellboys were taking these risks, and I fell in. I learned how to walk past a white policeman with contraband upon my hip, sauntering, whistling like a nigger ought to whistle when he is innocent. The extra dollars were coming in, but slowly. How, how, how could I get my hands on more money before I was caught and sent to jail for some trivial misdemeanor? If I were going to violate the law, then I ought to get something out of it. My larcenous aims were modest. A hundred dollars would give me, temporarily, more freedom of movement than I had ever known in my life. I watched and waited, living with the thought.

While waiting for my chance to grab and run, I grew used to seeing the white prostitutes naked upon their beds, sitting nude about their rooms, and I learned new modes of behavior, new rules in how to live the Jim Crow life. It was presumed that we black boys took their nakedness for granted, that it startled us no more than a blue vase or a red rug. Our presence awoke in them no sense of shame whatever, for we blacks were not considered human anyway. If they were alone, I would steal sidelong glances at them. But if they were receiving men, not a flicker of my eyelids would show.

A huge, snowy-skinned blonde took a room on my floor. One night she rang for service and I went to wait upon her. She was in bed with a thickset man; both were nude and uncovered. She said that she wanted some liquor, and slid out of bed and waddled across the floor to get her money from the dresser drawer. Without realizing it, I watched her.

"Nigger, what in hell are you looking at?" the white man asked, raising himself upon his elbows.

"Nothing, sir," I answered, looking suddenly miles deep into the blank wall of the room.

"Keep your eyes where they belong if you want to be healthy!"

"Yes, sir."

I would have continued at the hotel until I left had not a short-cut presented itself. One of the boys at the hotel whispered to me one night that the only local Negro movie house wanted a boy to take tickets at the door.

"You ain't never been in jail, is you?" he asked me.

"Not yet," I answered.

"Then you can get the job," he said. "I'd take it, but I done six months and they know me."

"What's the catch?"

"The girl who sells tickets is using a system," he explained. "If you get the job, you can make some good gravy."

If I stole, I would have a chance to head northward quickly; if I remained barely honest, piddling with pints of bootleg liquor, I merely prolonged my stay, increased my chances of being caught, exposed myself to the possibility of saying the wrong word or doing the wrong thing and paying a penalty that I dared not think of. The temptation to venture into crime was too strong, and I decided to work quickly, taking whatever was in sight, amass a wad of money, and flee. I knew that others had tried it before me and had failed, but I was hoping to be lucky.

My chances for getting the job were good; I had no past record of stealing or violating the laws. When I presented myself to the Jewish proprietor of the movie house I was immediately accepted. The next day I reported for duty and began taking tickets. The boss man warned me:

"Now, look, I'll be honest with you if you'll be honest with me. I don't know who's honest around this joint and who isn't. But if *you* are honest, then the rest are bound to be. All tickets will pass through your hands. There can be no stealing unless you steal."

I gave him a pledge of my honesty, feeling absolutely no qualms about what I intended to do. He was white, and I could never do to him what he and his kind had done to me. Therefore, I reasoned, stealing was not a violation of my ethics, but of his; I felt that things were rigged in his favor and any action I took to circumvent his scheme of life was justified. Yet I had not convinced myself.

During the first afternoon the Negro girl in the ticket office watched me closely and I knew that she was sizing me up, trying to determine when it would be safe to break me into her graft. I waited, leaving it to her to make the first move.

I was supposed to drop each ticket that I took from a customer into a metal receptacle. Occasionally the boss would go to the ticket window and look at the serial number on the roll of unsold tickets and then compare that number with the number on the last ticket I had dropped into the receptacle. The boss continued his watchfulness for a few days, then began to observe me from across the street; finally he absented himself for long intervals.

A tension as high as that I had known when the white men had driven me from the job at the optician's returned to live in me. But I had learned to master a great deal of tension now; I had developed, slowly and painfully, a capacity to contain it within myself without betraying it in any way. Had this not been true, the mere thought of stealing, the risks involved, the inner distress would have so upset me that I would have been in no state of mind to calculate coldly, would have made me so panicky that I would have been afraid to steal at all. But my inner resistance had been blasted. I felt that I had been emotionally cast out of the world, had been made to live outside the normal processes of life, had been conditioned in feeling *against* something daily, had become accustomed to living on the side of those who watched and waited.

While I was eating supper in a near-by café one

night, a strange Negro man walked in and sat beside me.

"Hello, Richard," he said.

"Hello," I said. "I don't think I know you."

"But I know *you*," he said, smiling.

Was he one of the boss's spies?

"How do you know me?" I asked.

"I'm Tel's friend," he said, naming the girl who sold the tickets at the movie.

I looked at him searchingly. Was he telling me the truth? Or was he trying to trap me for the boss? I was already thinking and feeling like a criminal, distrusting everybody.

"We start tonight," he said.

"What?" I asked, still not admitting that I knew what he was talking about.

"Don't be scared. The boss trusts you. He's gone to see some friends. Somebody's watching him and if he starts back to the movie, they'll phone us," he said.

I could not eat my food. It lay cold upon the plate and sweat ran down from my armpits.

"It'll work this way," he explained in a low, smooth tone. "A guy'll come to you and ask for a match. You give him five tickets that you'll hold out of the box, see? We'll give you the signal when to start holding out. The guy'll give the tickets to Tel; she'll resell them all at once, when a crowd is buying at the rush hour. You get it?"

I did not answer. I knew that if I were caught I would go to the chain gang. But was not my life already a kind of chain gang? What, really, did I have to lose?

"Are you with us?" he asked.

I still did not answer. He rose and clapped me on the shoulder and left. I trembled as I went back to the theater. Anything might happen, but I was used to that. Had I not felt that same sensation when I lay on the ground and the white men towered over me, telling me that I was a lucky nigger? Had I not felt it when I walked home from the optical company that morning with my job gone? Had I not felt it when I walked down the hallway of the hotel with the night watchman pointing a gun at my back? Had I not felt it all a million times before? I took the tickets with sweaty fingers. I waited. I was gambling: freedom or the chain gang. There were times when I felt that I could not breathe. I looked up and down the street; the boss was not in sight. Was this a trap? If it were, I would disgrace my family. Would not all of them say that my attitude had been leading to this all along? Would they not rake up the past and find clues that had led to my fate?

The man I had met in the café came through the door and put a ticket in my hand.

"There's a crowd at the box office," he whispered. "Save ten, not five. Start with this one."

Well, here goes, I thought. He gave me the ticket and sat looking at the moving shadows upon the screen. I held on to the ticket and my body grew tense, hot as fire; but I was used to that too. Time crawled through the cells of my brain. My muscles ached. I discovered that crime means suffering. The crowd came in and gave me more tickets. I kept ten of them tucked into my moist palm. No sooner had the crowd thinned than a black boy with a cigarette jutting from his mouth came up to me.

"Gotta match?"

With a slow movement I gave him the tickets. He went out and I kept the door cracked and watched. He went to the ticket office and laid down a coin and I saw him slip the tickets to the girl. Yes, the boy was honest. The girl shot me a quick smile and I went back inside. A few moments later the same tickets were handed to me by other customers.

We worked it for a week and after the money was split four ways, I had fifty dollars. Freedom was almost within my grasp. Ought I risk any more? I dropped the hint to Tel's friend that maybe I would quit; it was a casual hint to test him out. He grew violently angry and I quickly consented to stay, fearing that someone might turn me in for revenge, or to get me out of the way so that another and more pliable boy could have my place. I was dealing with cagey people and I would be cagey.

I went through another week. Late one night I resolved to make that week the last. The gun in the neighbor's house came to my mind, and the cans of fruit preserves in the storehouse of the college. If I stole them and sold them, I would have enough to tide me over in Memphis until I could get a job, work, save, and go north. I crept from bed and found the neighbor's house empty. I looked about; all was quiet. My heart beat so fast that it ached. I forced a window with a screwdriver and entered and took the gun; I slipped it in my shirt and returned home. When I took it out to look at it, it was wet with sweat. I pawned it under an assumed name.

The following night I rounded up two boys whom I knew to be ready for adventure. We broke into the college storehouse and lugged out cans of fruit preserves and sold them to restaurants.

Meanwhile I bought clothes, shoes, a cardboard suitcase, all of which I hid at home. Saturday night came and I sent word to the boss that I was sick. Uncle Tom was upstairs. Granny and Aunt Addie were at church. My brother was sleeping. My mother sat in her rocking chair, humming to herself. I packed my suitcase and went to her.

"Mama, I'm going away," I whispered.

"Oh, no," she protested.

"I've got to, mama. I can't live this way."

"You're not running away from something you've done?"

"I'll send for you, mama. I'll be all right."

"Take care of yourself. And send for me quickly. I'm not happy here," she said.

"I'm sorry for all these long years, mama. But I could not have helped it."

I kissed her and she cried.

"Be quiet, mama. I'm all right."

I went out the back way and walked a quarter of a mile to the railroad tracks. It began to rain as I tramped down the crossties toward town. I reached the station soaked to the skin. I bought my ticket, then went hurriedly to the corner of the block in which the movie house stood. Yes, the boss was there, taking the tickets himself. I returned to the station and waited for my train, my eyes watching the crowd.

An hour later I was sitting in a Jim Crow coach, speeding northward, making the first lap of my journey to a land where I could live with a little less fear. Slowly the burden I had carried for many months lifted somewhat. My cheeks itched and when I scratched them I found tears. In that moment I understood the pain that accompanied crime and I hoped that I would never have to feel it again. I never did feel it again, for I never stole again; and what kept me from it was the knowledge that, for me, crime carried its own punishment.

Well, it's my life, I told myself. I'll see now what I can make of it . . .

Chapter Eleven

I ARRIVED in Memphis on a cold November Sunday morning, in 1925, and lugged my suitcase down quiet, empty sidewalks through winter sunshine. I found Beale Street, the street that I had been told was filled with danger: pickpockets, prostitutes, cutthroats, and black confidence men. After walking several blocks, I saw a big frame house with a sign in the window: ROOMS. I slowed, wondering if it was a rooming house or a whorehouse. I had heard of the foolish blunders that small-town boys made when they went to big cities and I wanted to be very cautious. I walked past the house to the end of the block, then turned and walked slowly past it again. Well, whatever it was, I would stay in it for a day or two, until I found something I was certain of. I had nothing valuable in my suitcase. My money was strapped to my body; in order for anyone to get it, they would have to kill me.

I walked up the steps and was about to ring the bell when I saw a big mulatto woman staring at me through the window. Oh, hell, I thought. This *is* a whorehouse . . . I stopped. The woman smiled. I turned around and went back down the walk. As I neared the street, I looked back in time to see the woman's face leave the window. A moment later she appeared in the doorway.

"Come here, boy!" she called to me.

I hesitated. Goddamn, I've run into a whore right off . . .

"Come here, boy," she commanded loudly. "I'm not going to hurt you."

I turned and walked slowly toward her.

"Come inside," she said.

I stared at her a moment, then stepped into a warm hallway. The woman smiled, turned on a light, and looked at me from my head to my feet.

"How come you was walking past this house so many times?" she asked.

"I was looking for a room," I said.

"Didn't you see the sign?"

"Yes, ma'am."

"Then how come you didn't come in?"

"Well, I don't know. You see, I'm a stranger here . . ."

"Lord, and don't I know it!" She dropped heavily into a chair and went into a gale of laughter that made her big bosom shake as though it were going to fly off. "Anybody could tell that." She gasped, giggled, and grew quiet. She said: "I'm Mrs. Moss."

I told her my name.

"That's a real nice name," she said after a moment's serious thought.

I blinked. What the hell kind of place was this? And who was this woman? I stood with my suitcase in my hand, poised to leave.

"Boy, Lord, this ain't no whorehouse," she said at last. "Folks get the craziest notions about Beale Street. I own this place; this is my home. I'm a church member. I got a daughter seventeen years old, and, by God, I sure make her walk a straight chalk line. Sit down, son. You in safe hands here."

I laughed and sat.

"Where might you be from?" she asked.

"Jackson, Mississippi."

"You act mighty bright to be from there," she commented.

"There are bright people in Jackson," I said.

"If there is, I got yet to see some of 'em. Most of 'em can't talk. They just stand with their heads down, with one foot on top of the other and you have to guess at what they're trying to say."

I was at ease now. I liked her.

"My husband works in a bakery," she rattled on pleasantly, openly, as though she had known me for years. "We take in roomers to help out. We just simple people here. You can call this home, if you got a mind to. The rent's three dollars."

"That's a little high," I said.

"Then give me two dollars and a half till you get yourself a job," she said.

I accepted and she showed me my room. I set my suitcase down.

"You run off, didn't you?" she asked.

I jerked in surprise.

"How did you know?"

"Boy, your heart's like an open book," she said. "I know things. Lotta boys run off to Memphis from little towns. They think they gonna find it easy here, but they don't." She looked at me searchingly. "You drink?"

"Oh, no, ma'am."

"Didn't mean no harm, son," she said. "Just wanted to know. You can drink here, if you like. Just don't make a fool of yourself. You can bring your girl here too. Do anything you want, but be decent."

I sat on the edge of the bed and stared at her in amazement. It was on reputedly disreputable Beale Street in Memphis that I had met the warmest, friendliest person I had ever known, that I discovered that all human beings were not mean and driving, were not bigots like the members of my family.

"You can eat dinner with us when we come from church," she said.

"Thank you. I'd like to."

"Maybe you want to come to church with us?"

"Well . . ." I hedged.

"Naw, you're tired," she said, closing the door.

I lay on the bed and reveled in the delightful sensation of living out a long-sought dream. I had always flinched inwardly from the lonely terror that I had thought I would feel in a strange city, and now I had found a home with friendly people. I relaxed completely and dozed off to sleep, for I had not slept much for many nights. Later I came awake with a sudden start, remembering the fright and tension that had accompanied my foray into crime. Well, all that was gone now. I could start anew. I did not like to feel tension and fear. I wanted something else, to be human, to be caught up in something meaningful. But I must first get a job.

Late that afternoon Mrs. Moss called me for dinner and introduced me to her daughter, Bess, whom I liked at once. She was young, simple, sweet, and brown. Mrs. Moss apologized for her husband, who was still at work. Why was she treating me so kindly? It made me self-conscious. We were eating dessert when Bess spoke.

"Mama's done told me all about you," she said.

"I'm afraid that there isn't much to tell," I said.

"She said you was walking up and down in the street in front of the house, and didn't know whether to come in," Bess said, giggling. "What kind of place did you think this was?"

I hung my head and smiled. Mrs. Moss went into a storm of laughter and left the room.

"Mama says she said to herself soon's she saw you out there on that street with your suitcase, 'That boy's looking for a clean home to live in,'" Bess said. "Mama's good about knowing what folks feel."

"She seems to be," I said, helping Bess to wash the dishes.

"You can eat with us any time you like," Bess said.

"Thanks," I said. "But I couldn't do that."

"How come?" Bess asked. "We got a plenty."

"I know. But a man ought to pay his own way."

"Mama said you'd be like that," Bess said with satisfaction.

Mrs. Moss returned to the kitchen.

"Bess's going to be married soon," she announced.

"Congratulations!" I said. "Who's the lucky man?"

"Oh, I ain't got nobody yet," Bess said.

I was puzzled. Mrs. Moss laughed and nudged me.

"I say gals oughta marry young," she said. "Now, if Bess found a nice young man like *you*, Richard . . ."

"Mama!" Bess wailed, hiding her face in the dish-cloth.

"I mean it," Mrs. Moss said. "Richard's a heap better'n them old ignorant nigger boys you been running after at school."

I gaped at one and then the other. What was happening here? They barely knew me; I had been in the house but a few hours.

"The minute I laid eyes on that boy in the street this morning," Mrs. Moss said, "I said to myself, 'That's the kind of boy for Bess.' "

Bess came to me and leaned her head on my shoulder. I was stunned. How on earth could she act like this?

"Mama, don't," Bess pleaded teasingly.

"I mean it," Mrs. Moss said. "Richard, I'm worried about whose hands this house is going to fall into. I ain't too long for this old world."

"Bess'll find a boy who'll love her," I said uneasily.

"I ain't so sure," Mrs. Moss said, shaking her head.

"I'm going up front," Bess said, giggling, burying her face in her hands, and running out.

Mrs. Moss came close to me and spoke confidently.

"A gal's a funny thing," she said, laughing. "They has to be tamed. Just like wild animals."

"She's all right," I said, wiping the table, thinking furiously, not wanting to become involved too deeply with the family.

"You like Bess, Richard?" Mrs. Moss asked me suddenly.

I stared at her, doubting my ears.

"I've been in the house only a couple of hours," I said hesitantly. "She's a fine girl."

"Now. I mean do you *like* her? Could you *love* her?" she asked insistently.

I stared at Mrs. Moss, wondering if something was wrong with Bess. What kind of people were these?

"You people don't know me. I didn't exist for you five hours ago," I said seriously. Then I shot at her: "I could be a robber or a burglar for all you know."

"Son, I know you," she said emphatically.

Oh, Christ, I thought. I'll have to leave this place.

"You go on up front with Bess," Mrs. Moss said.

"Look, Mrs. Moss, I'm just a poor nobody," I said.

"You got something in you I like," she said. "Money ain't everything. You got a good Christian heart and everybody ain't got that."

I winced and turned my head away. Her naïve simplicity was overwhelming. I felt as though I had been accused of something.

"I worked twenty years and bought this house myself," she went on. "I'd be happy when I died if I thought Bess had a husband like you."

"Oh, mama!" Bess shrieked with protesting laughter from the front room.

I went into a warm, cozy front room and sat on the sofa. Bess was sitting on a little bench, looking out the window. How must I act toward this girl? I did not want to be drawn into something I did not want, and neither did I wish to wound anybody's feelings.

"Don't you wanna set here with me?" Bess said.

I rose and sat with her. Neither of us spoke for a long time.

"I'm the same age as you," Bess said. "I'm seventeen."

"Do you go to school?" I asked to make conversation.

"Yes," she said. "Wanna see my books?"

"I'd like to."

She rose and brought her schoolbooks to me. I saw that she was in the fifth grade.

"I ain't so good in school," she said, tossing her head. "But I don't care."

"Well, school's kind of important, you know," I said cautiously.

"Love is the important thing," she countered strongly.

I wondered if she were demented. The behavior of the mother and the daughter ran counter to all I had ever seen or known. Mrs. Moss came into the room.

"I think I'll go out and look for a job," I said, wanting to escape them.

"On a Sunday!" Mrs. Moss exclaimed. "Wait till in the morning."

"But I can learn the streets tonight anyway," I said.

"That's really a good thought," Mrs. Moss said after a moment's reflection. "You see, Bess? That boy thinks."

I felt awkard, embarrassed, called upon to say something.

"I'll be glad to help you with your lessons, Bess," I said.

"You think you can?" she asked, doubting.

"Well, I used to take charge of classes at school last year," I said.

"Now ain't that nice?" Mrs. Moss said in a honeyed tone.

I went to my room and lay on the bed and tried to fathom out the kind of home I had come to. That they were serious, I had no doubt. Would they be angry with me when they learned that my life was a million miles from theirs? How could I avoid that? Was it wise to remain here with a seventeen-year-old girl eager for marriage and a mother equally anxious to have her marry me? What on earth had they seen in me to have made them act toward me as they had? My clothes were not good. True, I had manners, manners that had been drilled into me at home, at school, manners that had been kicked into me on jobs; but anybody could have manners. I had learned to know these people better in five hours than I had learned to know my own family in five years.

Later, after I had grown to understand the peasant mentality of Bess and her mother, I learned the full degree to which my life at home had cut me off, not only from white people but from Negroes as well. To Bess and her mother, money was important, but they did not strive for it too hard. They had no tensions, unappeasable longings, no desire to do something to redeem themselves. The main value in their lives was simple, clean, good living and when they thought they had found those same qualities in one of their race, they instinctively embraced him, liked him, and asked no questions. But such simple unaffected trust flabbergasted me. It was impossible.

I walked down Beale Street and into the heart of Memphis. My body was thin, my overcoat shabby, and each gust of wind chilled my blood. On Main Street I saw a sign in a café window:

DISH WASHER WANTED

I went in and spoke to the manager and was hired to come to work the following night. The salary was ten dollars for the first week and twelve thereafter.

"Don't hire anyone else," I told him. "I'll be here."

I would get two meals at the café. But how would I eat in the daytime? I went into a store and bought a can of pork and beans and a can opener. Well, that problem was solved. I would pay two dollars and a half a week for my room and I would save the balance for my trip to Chicago. All my thoughts and movements were dictated by distant hopes.

Mrs. Moss was astonished when I told her that I had a job.

"You see, Bess," she said. "That boy's got a job his first day here. That's get-up for you. He's going somewhere. He just don't sit and gab. He moves."

Bess smiled at me. It seemed that every move I

made captivated her. Mrs. Moss went upstairs to bed. I was uneasy.

"Lemme rest your coat," Bess said.

She took my coat and felt the can in the pocket. "What you got in there?" she asked.

"Oh, nothing," I mumbled, trying to take the coat from her.

She pulled out the beans and the can opener. Her eyes widened with pity.

"Richard, you hungry, ain't you?" she asked me.

"Naw," I mumbled.

"Then let's eat some chicken," she said.

"Oh, all right," I said.

Bess ran to the stairway.

"Mama!" she called.

"Don't disturb her," I said, knowing that she was going to tell Mrs. Moss about my wanting to eat out of a can and feeling my heart fill with shame. My muscles flexed to hit her.

Mrs. Moss came down in her house robe.

"Mama, look what Richard was gonna do," Bess said, showing the can. "He was gonna eat this in his room."

"Lord, boy," Mrs. Moss said. "You don't have to do that."

"I'm used to it," I said. "I've got to save money."

"I just won't let you eat out of a can in my house," she said. "You don't have to pay me to eat. Go in the kitchen and eat. That's all."

"But I wouldn't dirty your room with the can," I said.

"It ain't that, son," Mrs. Moss said. "Why do you want to eat out of a can when you can set at the table with us?"

"I don't want to be a burden to anybody," I said.

Mrs. Moss stared at me, then hung her head and cried. I was stunned. It was incredible that what I did or the way I lived could evoke tears from anyone. Then my shame made me angry.

"You just ain't never had no home life," she said. "I'm sorry for you."

I stiffened. I did not like that. She was reaching into my inner life, where it was sore, and I did not want anyone there.

"I'm all right," I mumbled.

Mrs. Moss shook her head and went upstairs. I sighed. I was afraid that the family was getting too good a hold on me. Bess and I ate chicken, but I did not have much appetite. Bess was looking at me with melting eyes. We went back to the front room.

"I wanna get married," she whispered to me.

"You have a lot of time yet for that," I said, tense and uneasy.

"I wanna get married now. I wanna love," she said.

I had never met anyone like her, so direct, so easy in the expression of her feelings.

"Do you know what this means?" she asked me as she rose and went to a table and picked up a comb and came and stood before me.

I stared at the comb, then at her.

"What're you talking about?" I asked.

She did not answer. She smiled, then came close to me and reached out with the comb and touched my head. I drew back.

"What're you doing?"

She laughed and drew the comb through my hair. I stared at her, completely baffled.

"But my hair doesn't need combing," I said.

"I know it," she said, still combing.

"But why are you doing this?"

"Because I want to."

"What does it mean?"

She laughed again. I tried to get up and she caught hold of my arm and held me in the chair.

"You have nice hair," she said.

"It's just common nigger hair," I said.

"It's nice hair," she repeated.

"But why are you combing my hair?" I asked again.

"You know," she said.

"I don't."

" 'Cause I like you," she purred.

"Is this your way of telling me that?"

"It's a custom," she said. "You just fooling me. You know that. Everybody knows that. When a girl likes a man, she combs his hair."

"You're young. Give yourself a chance," I said.

"Don't you like me?" she asked.

"I do," I said. "We're friends."

"But I want more'n a friend," she sighed.

Her simplicity frightened me. The girls I had known had been hard and calculating, those who had worked at the hotel and those whom I had met at school. We were silent for a while.

"Say, what's them books in your room?" she asked.

"Were you in my room?" I asked with soft pointedness.

"Sure," she said without batting an eye. "I looked through your suitcase."

What could I do with a girl like this? Was I dumb or was she dumb? I felt that it would be easy to have sex relations with her and I was tempted. But what would happen? Love simply did not come to me that quickly and easily. And she was talking of marriage. Could I ever talk to her about what I felt, hoped? Could she ever understand my life? What had I above sex to share with her, and what had she? But I knew that such questions did not bother her. I did not love her and did not want to marry her. The prize of the house did not tempt me. Yet I sat beside her, feeling the attraction of her body increasing and deepening for me. What if I made her pregnant? I was sure that the fear of becoming pregnant did not bother her. Perhaps she would have liked it. I had come from a home where feelings were never expressed, except in rage or religious dread, where each member of the household lived locked in his own dark world, and the light that shone out of this child's heart—for she was a child—blinded me.

She leaned over and kissed me. What the hell, I

thought. Have it out with her, and if anything happens, leave . . . I kissed and petted her. She was warm, eager, childish, pliable. She threw her arms and legs about me and hugged me fiercely. I began to wonder how old she was.

"What would your mother say?" I asked in a whisper.

"She's sleeping."

"But what if she saw us?"

"I don't care."

She was crazy. Plainly she would have married me that instant, knowing no more about me than she did.

"Let's go to my room," I said.

"Naw. Mama wouldn't like that," she said.

She would let me do anything to her in her own front room, but she did not want me to do it to her in my room. It was crazy, utterly crazy.

"Mama's sleeping," she observed.

I began to suspect that she had had every boy in the block.

"You love me?" she asked in a whisper.

I stared at her, becoming more aware each minute of the terrible simplicity of her life. That was life for her, simple, direct. She just did not attach to words the same meanings I did. She caught my hands in a vise-like grip. I looked at her and could not believe in her existence.

"I love you," she said.

"Don't say that," I said, then was sorry that I had said it.

"But I do love you," she said again.

Her voice had come so clearly that I could no longer doubt her. For Christ's sake, I said to myself. The girl was astoundingly simple, yet vital in a way that I had never known. What kind of life had I lived that made the reality of this girl so strange? I sat thinking of Aunt Addie, her stern face, her forbidding nature, her caution, her restraint, her keen struggle to be good and holy.

"I'd make a good wife," she said.

I disengaged my hand from hers. I looked at her and wanted either to laugh or to slap her. I was about to hurt her and I did not want to. I rose. Oh, hell . . . This girl's crazy . . . I heard her crying and I bent to her.

"Look," I whispered. "You don't know me. Let's get to know each other better."

Her eyes were beaten, baffled. Love was that simple to her; it could be turned on or off in a moment.

"You just think I'm nothing," she whimpered.

I reached out my hand to touch her, to speak to her, to try to tell her of my life, my feelings, my doubts; and she leaped to her feet.

"I hate you," she burst out in a passionate whisper and ran out of the room.

I lit a cigarette and sat for a long time. I had never dreamed that anyone would accept me so simply, so completely, without question or the least hint of personal aggrandizement. The truth was that I had— even though I had fought against it—grown to accept the value of myself that my old environment had created in me, and I had thought that no other kind of environment was possible. My life had changed too suddenly. Had I met Bess upon a Mississippi plantation, I would have expected her to act as she had. But in Memphis, on Beale Street, how could there be such hope, belief, faith in others? I wanted to go to Bess and talk to her, but I knew no words to say to her.

When I awakened the next morning and recalled Bess's naïve hopes, I was glad that I had the can of pork and beans. I did not want to face her across the breakfast table. I dressed to go out; then, with my coat and hat on, I sat on the edge of the bed and propped my feet on a chair. Taking puffs from a cigarette, I scooped the beans out of the can with my fingers and ate them. I slipped out of the house and went to the water front and sat on a knoll of earth in the cold wind and sun, looking at the boats on the Mississippi River. Tonight I would begin my new job. I knew how to save money, thanks to my long starvation in Mississippi. My heart was at peace. I was freer than I had ever been.

A black boy came up to me.

"Hy," he said.

"Hy," I said.

"What you doing these days?" he asked.

"Nothing. Waiting for night. I got a job in a café," I said.

"Shucks," he said. "I'm looking for a buddy." He was trying to act tough, but I thought that he was lonely. "I wanna hop a freight and go north."

"Why not hop one alone?" I asked.

He grinned nervously.

"Did you run off from home?" I asked.

"Yeah. Four years ago," he said.

"What have you been doing?"

"Nothing."

That should have warned me, but I was not yet wise in the ways of the world or the road.

We talked a while longer, then walked down a path toward the river's edge, skirting high weeds. The boy stopped suddenly and pointed.

"What's that?"

"Looks like a can of some sort," I said.

I saw a huge can partially screened by high weeds. We went to it and found that it was full of something heavy. I pulled out the stopper and smelt it.

"This stuff is liquor," I said.

The boy smelt it and his eyes widened.

"Reckon we can sell it?" he asked.

"But whose is it?" I asked.

"Gee, I wish I could sell this stuff," he said.

"Maybe somebody's watching," I suggested.

We looked about, but no one was in sight.

"This belongs to a bootlegger," I said.

"Let's see if we can sell it," he said.

"I wouldn't take that can out of here," I said. "The cops might see us."

"I need money," the boy said. "This'll help me on the road."

We agreed to look for a white buyer. We went into the streets and looked over the white men who passed. Finally we spotted one sitting alone in his car. We went up to him.

"Mister," the boy said, "we found a big can of liquor over there in the weeds. You want to buy it?"

The man screwed up his eyes and studied us.

"Is it good liquor?" he asked.

"I don't know," I said. "Go and see it."

"You niggers ain't lying to me, are you?" he asked suspiciously.

"Come on. I'll show it to you," I said.

We led the white man to the liquor; he unstoppered it and smelt it, then tasted the wetness on the cork.

"Holy cats," he said. He looked at us. "Did you really find this here?"

"Oh, yes, sir," we said.

"If you two niggers are lying, I'll kill both of you," he breathed.

"We're telling the truth," I said.

The other boy stood awkwardly and looked on. I wondered why he did not say anything. Some vague thought was trying to worm its way into my dense, naïve, childlike mind. But it did not come clear and I brushed it away.

"You boys bring this can to my car," the white man said.

I was afraid. But the other boy was eager and willing. With the white man encouraging us, we lugged the can to his car and put it into the back upon the floor.

"Here," the white man said, extending a five-dollar bill to the boy. The car drove off and I could see the white man looking about anxiously, fearing a trap; or so it seemed to me.

"Gee, let's get this changed," the boy said.

"All right," I said. "We'll split it."

The boy pointed across the street.

"There's a store over there," he said. "I'll run over and get change."

"O.K.," I said, angel-like.

I sat on a sloping embankment and waited. He ran off in the direction of the store, but I was so confident that I did not even watch him. I felt amused. I was going to get two and one-half dollars for finding a cache of liquor. I was a hijacker already. Last night a girl had thrown herself at me. And all this had happened within forty-eight hours of my leaving home. I wanted to laugh out loud. Things could happen to one when one was not at home. I looked up, waiting for the boy to return. But I did not see him. He's sure taking his time, I thought, pushing down other ideas that were trying to bubble into my mind. I waited longer, then rose and went quickly to the store and peered through the window. The boy was not inside. I went in and asked the proprietor if a boy had been in.

"Yeah," he said. "A nigger boy came in here, looked around, then went out of the back door. He went like a light. Did he have something of yours?"

"Yes," I said.

"Well, you'll never see that nigger again," the man said.

I walked along the streets in the winter sun, thinking: Well, that's good enough for you, you fool. You had no business monkeying in that liquor business anyway. Then I stopped in my tracks. *They had been together!* The white man and the black boy had seen me loitering in the vicinity of their liquor and had thought I was a hijacker; and they had used me in disposing of their liquor.

Last night I had found a naïve girl. This morning I had been a naïve boy.

Chapter Twelve

WHILE wandering aimlessly about the streets of Memphis, gaping at the tall buildings and the crowds, killing time, eating bags of popcorn, I was struck by an odd and sudden idea. If I had attempted to work for an optical company in Jackson and had failed, why should I not try to work for an optical company in Memphis? Memphis was not a small town like Jackson; it was urban and I felt that no one would hold the trivial trouble I had had in Jackson against me.

I looked for the address of a company in a directory and walked boldly into the building, rode up in the elevator with a fat, round, yellow Negro of about five feet in height. At the fifth floor I stepped into an office. A white man rose to meet me.

"Pull off your hat," he said.

"Oh, yes, sir," I said, jerking off my hat.

"What do you want?"

"I was wondering if you needed a boy," I said. "I worked for an optical company for a short while in Jackson."

"Why did you leave?" he asked.

"I had a little trouble there," I said honestly.

"Did you steal something?"

"No, sir," I said. "A white boy there didn't want me to learn the optical trade and ran me off the job."

"Come and sit down."

I sat and recounted the story from beginning to end.

"I'll write Mr. Crane," he said. "But you won't get a

chance to learn the optical trade here. That's not our policy."

I told him that I understood and accepted his policy. I was hired at eight dollars per week and promised a raise of a dollar a week until my wages reached ten. Though this was less than I had been offered for the café job, I accepted it. I liked the open, honest way in which the man talked to me; and, too, the place seemed clean, brisk, businesslike.

I was assigned to run errands and wash eyeglasses after they had come from the rouge-smeared machines. Each evening I had to take sacks of packages to the post office for mailing. It was light work and I was fast on my feet. At noon I would forgo my lunch hour and run errands for the white men who were employed in the shop. I would buy their lunches, take their suits out to have them pressed, pay their light, telephone, and gas bills, and deliver notes for them to their stenographer girl friends in near-by office buildings. The first day I made a dollar and a half in tips. I deposited the money I had left from my trip and resolved to live off my tips.

I was now rapidly learning to contain the tension I felt in my relations with whites, and the people in Memphis had an air of relative urbanity that took some of the sharpness off the attitude of whites toward Negroes. There were about a dozen white men in the sixth-floor shop where I spent most of my time; they varied from Ku Klux Klanners to Jews, from theosophists to just plain poor whites. Although I could detect disdain and hatred in their attitudes, they never shouted at me or abused me. It was fairly easy to contemplate the race issue in the shop without reaching those heights of fear that devastated me. A measure of objectivity entered into my observations of white men and women. Either I could stand more mental strain than formerly or I had discovered deep within me ways of handling it.

When I returned to Mrs. Moss's that Monday night, she was surprised that I had changed my plans and had taken a new job. I showed her my bankbook and told her my plan for saving money and bringing my mother to Memphis. As I talked to her I tried to tell from her manner if Bess had said anything about what had happened between us, but Mrs. Moss was bland and motherly as always.

Bess avoided me, refusing to speak when we were alone together; but when her mother was present, she was polite. A few days later Mrs. Moss came to me with a baffled look in her eyes.

"What's happened between you and Bess?" she asked.

"Nothing," I lied, burning with shame.

"She don't seem to like you no more," she said. "I wanted you-all to kinda hit it off." She looked at me searchingly. "Don't you like her none?"

I could not answer or look at her; I wondered if she had told Bess to give herself to me.

"Well," she drawled, sighing, "I guess folks just have to love each other naturally. You can't make 'em." Tears rolled down her cheeks. "Bess'll find somebody."

I felt sick, filled with a consciousness of the woman's helplessness, of her naïve hope. Time and again she told me that Bess loved me, wanted me. She even suggested that I "try Bess and see if you like her. Ain't no harm in that." And her words evoked in me a pity for her that had no name.

Finally it became unbearable. One night I returned home from work and found Mrs. Moss sitting by the stove in the hall, nodding. She blinked her eyes and smiled.

"How're you, son?" she asked.

"Pretty good," I said.

"Ain't you and Bess got to be friends or something yet?"

"No ma'am," I said softly.

"How come you don't like Bess?" she demanded.

"Oh, I don't know." I was becoming angry.

"It's 'cause she ain't so bright?"

"No, ma'am. Bess's bright," I lied.

"Then how come?"

I still could not tell her.

"You and Bess could have this house for your home," she went on. "You-all could bring up your children here."

"But people have to find their own way to each other," I said.

"Young folks ain't got no sense these days," she said at last. "If somebody had fixed things for me when I was a gal, I sure would've taken it."

"Mrs. Moss," I said, "I think I'd better move."

"Move then!" she exploded. "You ain't got no sense!"

I went to my room and began to pack. A knock came at the door. I opened it. Mrs. Moss stood in the doorway, weeping.

"Son, forgive me," she said. "I didn't mean it. I wouldn't hurt you for nothing. You just like a son to me."

"That's all right," I said. "But I'd better move."

"No!" she wailed. "Then you ain't forgive me! When a body asks forgiveness, they means it!"

I stared. Bess appeared in the doorway.

"Don't leave, Richard," she said.

"We won't bother you no more," Mrs. Moss said.

I wilted, baffled, sorry, ashamed. Mrs. Moss took Bess's hand and led her away.

I centered my attention now upon making enough money to send for my mother and brother. I saved each penny I came by, stinting myself on food, walking to work, eating out of paper bags, living on a pint of milk and two sweet rolls for breakfast, a hamburger and peanuts for lunch, and a can of beans which I would eat at night in my room. I was used to hunger and I did not need much food to keep me alive.

I now had more money than I had ever had before, and I began patronizing secondhand bookstores, buying magazines and books. In this way I became acquainted with periodicals like *Harper's Magazine*, the *Atlantic Monthly*, and the *American Mercury*. I would buy them for a few cents, read them, then resell them to the bookdealer.

Once Mrs. Moss questioned me about my reading.

"What you reading all them books for, boy?"

"I just like to."

"You studying for law?"

"No, ma'am."

"Well, I reckon you know what you doing," she said.

Though I did not have to report for work until nine o'clock each morning, I would arrive at eight and go into the lobby of the downstairs bank—where I knew the Negro porter—and read the early edition of the Memphis *Commercial Appeal,* thereby saving myself five cents each day, which I spent for lunch. After reading, I would watch the black porter perform his morning ritual: he would get a mop, bucket, soap flakes, water, then would pause dramatically, roll his eyes to the ceiling and sing out:

"Lawd, today! Ahm still working for white folks!"

And he would mop until he sweated. He hated his job and talked incessantly of leaving to work in the post office.

The most colorful of the Negro boys on the job was Shorty, the round, yellow, fat elevator operator. He had tiny, beady eyes that looked out between rolls of flesh with a hard but humorous stare. He had the complexion of a Chinese, a short forehead, and three chins. Psychologically he was the most amazing specimen of the southern Negro I had ever met. Hardheaded, sensible, a reader of magazines and books, he was proud of his race and indignant about its wrongs. But in the presence of whites he would play the role of a clown of the most debased and degraded type.

One day he needed twenty-five cents to buy his lunch.

"Just watch me get a quarter from the first white man I see," he told me as I stood in the elevator that morning.

A white man who worked in the building stepped

into the elevator and waited to be lifted to his floor. Shorty sang in a low mumble, smiling, rolling his eyes, looking at the white man roguishly.

"I'm hungry, Mister White Man. I need a quarter for lunch."

The white man ignored him. Shorty, his hands on the controls of the elevator, sang again:

"I ain't gonna move this damned old elevator till I get a quarter, Mister White Man."

"The hell with you, Shorty," the white man said, ignoring him and chewing on his black cigar.

"I'm hungry, Mister White Man. I'm dying for a quarter," Shorty sang, drooling, drawling, humming his words.

"If you don't take me to my floor, you will die," the white man said, smiling a little for the first time.

"But this black sonofabitch sure needs a quarter," Shorty sang, grimacing, clowning, ignoring the white man's threat.

"Come on, you black bastard, I got to work," the white man said, intrigued by the element of sadism involved, enjoying it.

"It'll cost you twenty-five cents, Mister White Man; just a quarter, just two bits," Shorty moaned.

There was silence. Shorty threw the lever and the elevator went up and stopped about five feet ·shy of the floor upon which the white man worked.

"Can't go no more, Mister White Man, unless I get my quarter," he said in a tone that sounded like crying.

"What would you do for a quarter?" the white man asked, still gazing off.

"I'll do anything for a quarter," Shorty sang.

"What, for example?" the white man asked.

Shorty giggled, swung around, bent over, and poked out his broad, fleshy ass.

"You can kick me for a quarter," he sang, looking impishly at the white man out of the corners of his eyes.

The white man laughed softly, jingled some coins

in his pocket, took out one and thumped it to the floor. Shorty stooped to pick it up and the white man bared his teeth and swung his foot into Shorty's rump with all the strength of his body. Shorty let out a howling laugh that echoed up and down the elevator shaft.

"Now, open this door, you goddamn black sonofabitch," the white man said, smiling with tight lips.

"Yeeeess, siiiiir," Shorty sang; but first he picked up the quarter and put it into his mouth. "This monkey's got the peanuts," he chortled.

He opened the door and the white man stepped out and looked back at Shorty as he went toward his office.

"You're all right, Shorty, you sonofabitch," he said.

"I know it!" Shorty screamed, then let his voice trail off in a gale of wild laughter.

I witnessed this scene or its variant at least a score of times and I felt no anger or hatred, only disgust and loathing. Once I asked him:

"How in God's name can you do that?"

"I needed a quarter and I got it," he said soberly, proudly.

"But a quarter can't pay you for what he did to you," I said.

"Listen, nigger," he said to me, "my ass is tough and quarters is scarce."

I never discussed the subject with him after that.

Other Negroes worked in the building: an old man whom we called Edison; his son, John; and a night janitor who answered to the name of Dave. At noon, when I was not running errands, I would join the rest of the Negroes in a little room at the front of the building overlooking the street. Here, in this underworld pocket of the building, we munched our lunches and discussed the ways of white folks toward Negroes. When two or more of us were talking, it was impossible for this subject not to come up. Each of us hated and feared the whites, yet had a white man put in a sudden appearance we would have assumed silent, obedient smiles.

To our minds the white folks formed a kind of super-world: what was said by them during working hours was rehashed and weighed here; how they looked; what they wore; what moods they were in; who had outdistanced whom in business; who was replacing whom on the job; who was getting fired and who was getting hired. But never once did we openly say that we occupied none but subordinate positions in the building. Our talk was restricted to the petty relations which formed the core of life for us.

But under all our talk floated a latent sense of violence; the whites had drawn a line over which we dared not step and we accepted that line because our bread was at stake. But within our boundaries we, too, drew a line that included our right to bread regardless of the indignities or degradations involved in getting it. If a white man had sought to keep us from obtaining a job, or enjoying the rights of citizenship, we would have bowed silently to his power. But if he had sought to deprive us of a dime, blood might have been spilt. Hence, our daily lives were so bound up with trivial objectives that to capitulate when challenged was tantamount to surrendering the right to life itself. Our anger was like the anger of children, passing quickly from one petty grievance to another, from the memory of one slight wrong to another.

"You know what the bastard Olin said to me this morning?" John would ask, biting into a juicy hamburger.

"What?" Shorty would ask.

"Well, I brought him his change from paying his gas bill and he said: 'Put it here in my pocket; my hands are dirty,'" John said. "Hunh . . . I just laid the money on the bench besides him. I ain't no personal slave to him and I'll be damned if I'll put his *own* money in his *own* pocket."

"Hell, you're right," Shorty would say.

"White folks just don't think," old man Edison would say.

"You sure got to watch 'em," Dave, the night janitor, would say. (He would have slept in the room on a cot after his night's cleaning; he would be ready now to keep a date with some girl friend.)

"Falk sent me to have his suit pressed," I would say. "He didn't give me a penny. Told me he would remember it on payday."

"Ain't that some nerve?" John would say.

"You can't eat his memories," Shorty would say.

"But you got to keep on doing them favors," old man Edison would say. "If you don't, they won't like you."

"I'm going north one of these days," Shorty would say.

We would all laugh, knowing that Shorty would never leave, that he depended too much upon the whites for the food he ate.

"What would you do up north?" I would ask Shorty.

"I'd pass for Chinese," Shorty would say.

And we would laugh again. The lunch hour would pass and we would go back to work, but there would be in our faces not one whit of the sentiment we had felt during the hour of discussion.

One day I went to the optical counter of a department store to deliver a pair of eyeglasses. The counter was empty of customers and a tall, florid-faced white man looked at me curiously. He was unmistakably a Yankee, for his physical build differed sharply from that of the lanky Southerner.

"Will you please sign for this, sir?" I asked, presenting the account book and the eyeglasses.

He picked up the book and the glasses, but his eyes were still upon me.

"Say, boy, I'm from the North," he said quietly.

I held very still. Was this a trap? He had mentioned a tabooed subject and I wanted to wait until I knew what he meant. Among the topics that southern white men did not like to discuss with Negroes were the following: American white women; the Ku Klux Klan; France, and how Negro soldiers fared while there; Frenchwomen; Jack Johnson; the entire northern part of the United States; the Civil War; Abraham Lincoln; U. S. Grant; General Sherman; Catholics; the Pope; Jews; the Republican party; slavery; social equality; Communism; Socialism; the 13th, 14th, and 15th Amendments to the Constitution; or any topic calling for positive knowledge or manly self-assertion on the part of the Negro. The most accepted topics were sex and religion. I did not look at the man or answer. With one sentence he had lifted out of the silent dark the race question and I stood on the edge of a precipice.

"Don't be afraid of me," he went on. "I just want to ask you one question."

"Yes, sir," I said in a waiting, neutral tone.

"Tell me, boy, are you hungry?" he asked seriously.

I stared at him. He had spoken one word that touched the very soul of me, but I could not talk to him, could not let him know that I was starving myself to save money to go north. I did not trust him. But my face did not change its expression.

"Oh, no, sir," I said, managing a smile.

I was hungry and he knew it; but he was a white man and I felt that if I told him I was hungry I would have been revealing something shameful.

"Boy, I can see hunger in your face and eyes," he said.

"I get enough to eat," I lied.

"Then why do you keep so thin?" he asked me.

"Well, I suppose I'm just that way, naturally," I lied.

"You're just scared, boy," he said.

"Oh, no, sir," I lied again.

I could not look at him. I wanted to leave the counter, yet he was a white man and I had learned not to walk abruptly away from a white man when he was talking to me. I stood, my eyes looking away. He ran his hand into his pocket and pulled out a dollar bill.

"Here, take this dollar and buy yourself some food," he said.

"No, sir," I said.

"Don't be a fool," he said. "You're ashamed to take it. God, boy, don't let a thing like that stop you from taking a dollar and eating."

The more he talked the more it became impossible for me to take the dollar. I wanted it, but I could not look at it. I wanted to speak, but I could not move my tongue. I wanted him to leave me alone. He frightened me.

"Say something," he said.

All about us in the store were piles of goods; white men and women went from counter to counter. It was summer and from a high ceiling was suspended a huge electric fan that whirred. I stood waiting for the white man to give me the signal that would let me go.

"I don't understand it," he said through his teeth. "How far did you go in school?"

"Through the ninth grade, but it was really the eighth," I told him. "You see, our studies in the ninth grade were more or less a review of what we had in the eighth grade."

Silence. He had not asked me for this long explanation, but I had spoken at length to fill up the yawning, shameful gap that loomed between us; I had spoken to try to drag the unreal nature of the conversation back to safe and sound southern ground. Of course, the conversation was real; it dealt with my welfare, but it had brought to the surface of day all the dark fears I had known all my life. The Yankee white man did not know how dangerous his words were.

(There are some elusive, profound, recondite things that men find hard to say to other men; but with the Negro it is the little things of life that become hard to say, for these tiny items shape his destiny. A man will seek to express his relation to the stars; but when a man's consciousness has been riveted upon obtaining a loaf of bread, that loaf of bread is as important as the stars.)

Another white man walked up to the counter and I sighed with relief.

"Do you want the dollar?" the man asked.

"No, sir," I whispered.

"All right," he said. "Just forget it."

He signed the account book and took the eyeglasses. I stuffed the book into my bag and turned from the counter and walked down the aisle, feeling a physical tingling along my spine, knowing that the white man knew I was really hungry. I avoided him after that. Whenever I saw him I felt in a queer way that he was my enemy, for he knew how I felt and the safety of my life in the South depended upon how well I concealed from all whites what I felt.

One summer morning I stood at a sink in the rear of the factory washing a pair of eyeglasses that had just come from the polishing machines whose throbbing shook the floor upon which I stood. At each machine a white man was bent forward, working intently. To my left sunshine poured through a window, lighting up the rouge smears and making the factory look garish, violent, dangerous. It was nearing noon and my mind was drifting toward my daily lunch of a hamburger and a bag of peanuts. It had been a routine day, a day more or less like the other days I had spent on the job as errand boy and washer of eyeglasses. I was at peace with the world, that is, at peace in the only way in which a black boy in the South can be at peace with a world of white men.

Perhaps it was the mere sameness of the day that soon made it different from the other days; maybe the white men who operated the machines felt bored with their dull, automatic tasks and hankered for some kind of excitement. Anyway, I presently heard footsteps behind me and turned my head. At my elbow stood a young white man, Mr. Olin, the immediate foreman under whom I worked. He was smiling and observing me as I cleaned emery dust from the eyeglasses.

"Boy, how's it going?" he asked.

"Oh, fine, sir!" I answered with false heartiness, falling quickly into that nigger-being-a-good-natured-boy-in-the-presence-of-a-white-man pattern, a pattern into which I could now slide easily; although I was wondering if he had any criticism to make of my work.

He continued to hover wordlessly at my side. What did he want? It was unusual for him to stand there and watch me; I wanted to look at him, but was afraid to.

"Say, Richard, do you believe that I'm your friend?" he asked me.

The question was so loaded with danger that I could not reply at once. I scarcely knew Mr. Olin. My relationship to him had been the typical relationship of Negroes to southern whites. He gave me orders and I said, "Yes, sir," and obeyed them. Now, without warning, he was asking me if I thought that he was my friend; and I knew that all southern white men fancied themselves as friends of niggers. While fishing for an answer that would say nothing, I smiled.

"I mean," he persisted, "do you think I'm your friend?"

"Well," I answered, skirting the vast racial chasm between us, "I hope you are."

"I am," he said emphatically.

I continued to work, wondering what motives were prompting him. Already apprehension was rising in me.

"I want to tell you something," he said.

"Yes, sir," I said.

"We don't want you to get hurt," he explained. "We like you round here. You act like a good boy."

"Yes, sir," I said. "What's wrong?"

"You don't deserve to get into trouble," he went on.

"Have I done something that somebody doesn't like?" I asked, my mind frantically sweeping over all my past actions, weighing them in the light of the way southern white men thought Negroes should act.

"Well, I don't know," he said and paused, letting his words sink meaningfully into my mind. He lit a cigarette. "Do you know Harrison?"

He was referring to a Negro boy of about my own age who worked across the street for a rival optical house. Harrison and I knew each other casually, but there had never been the slightest trouble between us.

"Yes, sir," I said. "I know him."

"Well, be careful," Mr. Olin said. "He's after you."

"After me? For what?"

"He's got a terrific grudge against you," the white man explained. "What have you done to him?"

The eyeglasses I was washing were forgotten. My eyes were upon Mr. Olin's face, trying to make out what he meant. Was this something serious? I did not trust the white man, and neither did I trust Harrison. Negroes who worked on jobs in the South were usually loyal to their white bosses; they felt that that was the best way to ensure their jobs. Had Harrison felt that I had in some way jeopardized his job? Who was my friend: the white man or the black boy?

"I haven't done anything to Harrison," I said.

"Well, you better watch that nigger Harrison," Mr. Olin said in a low, confidential tone. "A little while ago I went down to get a Coca-Cola and Harrison was waiting for you at the door of the building with a knife. He asked me when you were coming down. Said he was going to get you. Said you called him a dirty name. Now, we don't want any fighting or bloodshed on the job."

I still doubted the white man, yet thought that perhaps Harrison had really interpreted something I had said as an insult.

"I've got to see that boy and talk to him," I said, thinking out loud.

"No, you'd better not," Mr. Olin said. "You'd better let some of us white boys talk to him."

"But how did this start?" I asked, still doubting but half believing.

"He just told me that he was going to get even with

you, going to cut you and teach you a lesson," he said. "But don't you worry. Let me handle this."

He patted my shoulder and went back to his machine. He was an important man in the factory and I had always respected his word. He had the authority to order me to do this or that. Now, why would he joke with me? White men did not often joke with Negroes, therefore what he had said was serious. I was upset. We black boys worked long hard hours for what few pennies we earned and we were edgy and tense. Perhaps that crazy Harrison was really after me. My appetite was gone. I had to settle this thing. A white man had walked into my delicately balanced world and had tipped it and I had to right it before I could feel safe. Yes, I would go directly to Harrison and ask what was the matter, what I had said that he resented. Harrison was black and so was I; I would ignore the warning of the white man and talk face to face with a boy of my own color.

At noon I went across the street and found Harrison sitting on a box in the basement. He was eating lunch and reading a pulp magazine. As I approached him, he ran his hand into his pocket and looked at me with cold, watchful eyes.

"Say, Harrison, what's this all about?" I asked, standing cautiously four feet from him.

He looked at me a long time and did not answer.

"I haven't done anything to you," I said.

"And I ain't got nothing against you," he mumbled, still watchful. "I don't bother nobody."

"But Mr. Olin said that you came over to the factory this morning, looking for me with a knife."

"Aw, naw," he said, more at ease now. "I ain't been in your factory all day." He had not looked at me as he spoke.

"Then what did Mr. Olin mean?" I asked. "I'm not angry with you."

"Shucks, I thought *you* was looking for me to cut me," Harrison explained. "Mr. Olin, he came over here this morning and said you was going to kill me with a knife the moment you saw me. He said you was mad at me because I had insulted you. But I ain't said nothing about you." He still had not looked at me. He rose.

"And I haven't said anything about you," I said.

Finally he looked at me and I felt better. We two black boys, each working for ten dollars a week, stood staring at each other, thinking, comparing the motives of the absent white man, each asking himself if he could believe the other.

"But why would Mr. Olin tell me things like that?" I asked.

Harrison dropped his head; he laid his sandwich aside.

"I . . . I . . ." he stammered and pulled from his pocket a long, gleaming knife; it was already open. "I was just waiting to see what you was gonna do to me . . ."

I leaned weakly against a wall, feeling sick, my eyes upon the sharp steel blade of the knife.

"You were going to cut me?" I asked.

"If you had cut me, I was gonna cut you first," he said. "I ain't taking no chances."

"Are you angry with me about something?" I asked.

"Man, I ain't mad at nobody," Harrison said uneasily.

I felt how close I had come to being slashed. Had I come suddenly upon Harrison, he would have thought I was trying to kill him and he would have stabbed me, perhaps killed me. And what did it matter if one nigger killed another?

"Look here," I said. "Don't believe what Mr. Olin says."

"I see now," Harrison said. "He's playing a dirty trick on us."

"He's trying to make us kill each other for nothing."

"How come he wanna do that?" Harrison asked.

I shook my head. Harrison sat, but still played with the open knife. I began to doubt. Was he really angry with me? Was he waiting until I turned my back to stab me? I was in torture.

"I suppose it's fun for white men to see niggers fight," I said, forcing a laugh.

"But you might've killed me," Harrison said.

"To white men we're like dogs or cocks," I said.

"I don't want to cut you," Harrison said.

"And I don't want to cut you," I said.

Standing well out of each other's reach, we discussed the problem and decided that we would keep silent about our conference. We would not let Mr. Olin know that we knew that he was egging us to fight. We agreed to ignore any further provocations. At one o'clock I went back to the factory. Mr. Olin was waiting for me, his manner grave, his face serious.

"Did you see that Harrison nigger?" he asked.

"No, sir," I lied.

"Well, he still has that knife for you," he said.

Hate tightened in me. But I kept a dead face.

"Did you buy a knife yet?" he asked me.

"No, sir," I answered.

"Do you want to use mine?" he asked. "You've got to protect yourself, you know."

"No, sir. I'm not afraid," I said.

"Nigger, you're a fool," he spluttered. "I thought you had some sense! Are you going to just let that nigger cut your heart out? His boss gave *him* a knife to use against *you!*" Take this knife, nigger, and stop acting crazy!"

I was afraid to look at him; if I had looked at him I would have had to tell him to leave me alone, that I knew he was lying, that I knew he was no friend of mine, that I knew if anyone had thrust a knife through my heart he would simply have laughed. But I said nothing. He was the boss and he could fire me if he did not like me. He laid an open knife on the edge of his workbench, about a foot from my hand. I had a fleeting urge to pick it up and give it to him, point first into his chest. But I did nothing of the kind. I picked up the knife and put it into my pocket.

"Now, you're acting like a nigger with some sense," he said.

As I worked Mr. Olin watched me from his machine. Later when I passed him he called me.

"Now, look here, boy," he began. "We told that Harrison nigger to stay out of this building and leave you alone, see? But I can't protect you when you go home. If that nigger starts at you when you are on your way home, you stab him before he gets a chance to stab you, see?"

I avoided looking at him and remained silent.

"Suit yourself, nigger," Mr. Olin said. "But don't say I didn't warn you."

I had to make my round of errands to deliver eyeglasses and I stole a few minutes to run across the street to talk to Harrison. Harrison was sullen and bashful, wanting to trust me, but afraid. He told me that Mr. Olin had telephoned his boss and had told him to tell Harrison that I had planned to wait for him at the back entrance of the building at six o'clock and stab him. Harrison and I found it difficult to look at each other; we were upset and distrustful. We were not really angry at each other; we knew that the idea of murder had been planted in each of us by the white men who employed us. We told ourselves again and again that we did not agree with the white men; we urged ourselves to keep faith in each other. Yet there lingered deep down in each of us a suspicion that maybe one of us was trying to kill the other.

"I'm not angry with you, Harrison," I said.

"I don't wanna fight nobody," Harrison said bashfully, but he kept his hand in his pocket on his knife.

Each of us felt the same shame, felt how foolish and weak we were in the face of the domination of the whites.

"I wish they'd leave us alone," I said.

"Me too," Harrison said.

"There are a million black boys like us to run errands," I said. "They wouldn't care if we killed each other."

"I know it," Harrison said.

Was he acting? I could not believe in him. We were

toying with the idea of death for no reason that stemmed from our own lives, but because the men who ruled us had thrust the idea into our minds. Each of us depended upon the whites for the bread we ate, and we actually trusted the whites more than we did each other. Yet there existed in us a longing to trust men of our own color. Again Harrison and I parted, vowing not to be influenced by what our white boss men said to us.

The game of egging Harrison and me to fight, to cut each other, kept up for a week. We were afraid to tell the white men that we did not believe them, for that would have been tantamount to calling them liars or risking an argument that might have ended in violence being directed against us.

One morning a few days later Mr. Olin and a group of white men came to me and asked me if I was willing to settle my grudge with Harrison with gloves, according to boxing rules. I told them that, though I was not afraid of Harrison, I did not want to fight him and that I did not know how to box. I could feel now that they knew I no longer believed them.

When I left the factory that evening, Harrison yelled at me from down the block. I waited and he ran toward me. Did he want to cut me? I backed away as he approached. We smiled uneasily and sheepishly at each other. We spoke haltingly, weighing our words.

"Did they ask you to fight me with gloves?" Harrison asked.

"Yes," I told him. "But I didn't agree."

Harrison's face became eager.

"They want us to fight four rounds for five dollars apiece," he said. "Man, if I had five dollars, I could pay down on a suit. Five dollars is almost half a week's wages for me."

"I don't want to," I said.

"We won't hurt each other," he said.

"But why do a thing like that for white men?"

"To get that five dollars."

"I don't need five dollars that much."

"Aw, you're a fool," he said. Then he smiled quickly.

"Now, look here," I said. "Maybe you *are* angry with me . . ."

"Naw, I'm not." He shook his head vigorously.

"I don't want to fight for white men. I'm no dog or rooster."

I was watching Harrison closely and he was watching me closely. Did he really want to fight me for some reason of his own? Or was it the money? Harrison stared at me with puzzled eyes. He stepped toward me and I stepped away. He smiled nervously.

"I need that money," he said.

"Nothing doing," I said.

He walked off wordlessly, with an air of anger. Maybe he will stab me now, I thought. I got to watch that fool . . .

For another week the white men of both factories begged us to fight. They made up stories about what Harrison had said about me; and when they saw Harrison they lied to him in the same way. Harrison and I were wary of each other whenever we met. We smiled and kept out of arm's reach, ashamed of ourselves and of each other.

Again Harrison called to me one evening as I was on my way home.

"Come on and fight," he begged.

"I don't want to and quit asking me," I said in a voice louder and harder than I had intended.

Harrison looked at me and I watched him. Both of us still carried the knives that the white men had given us.

"I wanna make a payment on a suit of clothes with that five dollars," Harrison said.

"But those white men will be looking at us, laughing at us," I said.

"What the hell," Harrison said. "They look at you and laugh at you every day, nigger."

It was true. But I hated him for saying it. I ached to hit him in his mouth, to hurt him.

"What have we got to lose?" Harrison asked.

"I don't suppose we have anything to lose," I said.

"Sure," he said. "Let's get the money. We don't care."

"And now they know that we know what they tried to do to us," I said, hating myself for saying it. "And they hate us for it."

"Sure," Harrison said. "So let's get the money. You can use five dollars, can't you?"

"Yes."

"Then let's fight for 'em."

"I'd feel like a dog."

"To them, both of us are dogs," he said.

"Yes," I admitted. But again I wanted to hit him.

"Look, let's fool them white men," Harrison said. "We won't hurt each other. We'll just pretend, see? We'll show 'em we ain't dumb as they think, see?"

"I don't know."

"It's just exercise. Four rounds for five dollars. You scared?"

"No."

"Then come on and fight."

"All right," I said. "It's just exercise. I'll fight."

Harrison was happy. I felt that it was all very foolish. But what the hell. I would go through with it and that would be the end of it. But I still felt a vague anger that would not leave.

When the white men in the factory heard that we had agreed to fight, their excitement knew no bounds. They offered to teach me new punches. Each morning they would tell me in whispers that Harrison was eating raw onions for strength. And—from Harrison—I heard that they told him I was eating raw meat for strength. They offered to buy me my meals each day, but I refused. I grew ashamed of what I had agreed to do and wanted to back out of the fight, but I was afraid that they would be angry if I tried to. I felt that if white men tried to persuade two black boys to stab each other for no reason save their own pleasure, then it would not be difficult for them to aim a wanton blow at a black boy in a fit of anger, in a passing mood of frustration.

The fight took place one Saturday afternoon in the basement of a Main Street building. Each white man who attended the fight dropped his share of the pot into a hat that sat on the concrete floor. Only white men were allowed in the basement; no women or Negroes were admitted. Harrison and I were stripped to the waist. A bright electric bulb glowed above our heads. As the gloves were tied on my hands, I looked at Harrison and saw his eyes watching me. Would he keep his promise? Doubt made me nervous.

We squared off and at once I knew that I had not thought sufficiently about what I had bargained for. I could not pretend to fight. Neither Harrison nor I knew enough about boxing to deceive even a child for a moment. Now shame filled me. The white men were smoking and yelling obscenities at us.

"Crush that nigger's nuts, nigger!"

"Hit that nigger!"

"Aw, fight, you goddamn niggers!"

"Sock 'im in his f--k--g piece!"

"Make 'im bleed!"

I lashed out with a timid left. Harrison landed high on my head and, before I knew it, I had landed a hard right on Harrison's mouth and blood came. Harrison shot a blow to my nose. The fight was on, was on against our will. I felt trapped and ashamed. I lashed out even harder, and the harder I fought the harder Harrison fought. Our plans and promises now meant nothing. We fought four hard rounds, stabbing, slugging, grunting, spitting, cursing, crying, bleeding. The shame and anger we felt for having allowed ourselves to be duped crept into our blows and blood ran into our eyes, half blinding us. The hate we felt for the men whom we had tried to cheat went into the blows we threw at each other. The white men made the rounds last as long as five minutes and each of us was afraid to stop and ask for time for fear of receiving a blow that would knock us out. When we were on the point of collapsing from exhaustion, they pulled us apart.

I could not look at Harrison. I hated him and I hated

myself. I clutched my five dollars in my fist and walked home. Harrison and I avoided each other after that and we rarely spoke. The white men attempted to arrange other fights for us, but we had sense enough to refuse. I heard of other fights being staged between other black boys, and each time I heard those plans falling from the lips of the white men in the factory I eased out of earshot. I felt that I had done something unclean, something for which I could never properly atone.

Chapter Thirteen

ONE morning I arrived early at work and went into the bank lobby where the Negro porter was mopping. I stood at a counter and picked up the Memphis *Commercial Appeal* and began my free reading of the press. I came finally to the editorial page and saw an article dealing with one H. L. Mencken. I knew by hearsay that he was the editor of the *American Mercury*, but aside from that I knew nothing about him. The article was a furious denunciation of Mencken, concluding with one, hot, short sentence: Mencken is a fool.

I wondered what on earth this Mencken had done to call down upon him the scorn of the South. The only people I had ever heard denounced in the South were Negroes, and this man was not a Negro. Then what ideas did Mencken hold that made a newspaper like the *Commercial Appeal* castigate him publicly? Undoubtedly he must be advocating ideas that the South did not like. Were there, then, people other than Negroes who criticized the South? I knew that during the Civil War the South had hated northern whites, but I had not encountered such hate during my life. Knowing no more of Mencken than I did at that moment, I felt a vague sympathy for him. Had not the South, which had assigned me the role of a non-man, cast at him its hardest words?

Now, how could I find out about this Mencken? There was a huge library near the riverfront, but I knew that Negroes were not allowed to patronize its shelves any more than they were the parks and playgrounds of the city. I had gone into the library several times to get books for the white men on the job. Which of them would now help me to get books? And how could I read them without causing concern to the white men with whom I worked? I had so far been successful in hiding my thoughts and feelings from them, but I knew that I would create hostility if I went about this business of reading in a clumsy way.

I weighed the personalities of the men on the job. There was Don, a Jew; but I distrusted him. His position was not much better than mine and I knew that he was uneasy and insecure; he had always treated me in an offhand, bantering way that barely concealed his contempt. I was afraid to ask him to help me to get books; his frantic desire to demonstrate a racial solidarity with the whites against Negroes might make him betray me.

Then how about the boss? No, he was a Baptist and I had the suspicion that he would not be quite able to comprehend why a black boy would want to read Mencken. There were other white men on the job whose attitudes showed clearly that they were Kluxers or sympathizers, and they were out of the question.

There remained only one man whose attitude did not fit into an anti-Negro category, for I had heard the white men refer to him as a "Pope lover." He was an Irish Catholic and was hated by the white Southerners. I knew that he read books, because I had got him volumes from the library several times. Since he, too, was an object of hatred, I felt that he might refuse me but would hardly betray me. I hesitated, weighing and balancing the imponderable realities.

One morning I paused before the Catholic fellow's desk.

"I want to ask you a favor," I whispered to him. "What is it?"

"I want to read. I can't get books from the library. I wonder if you'd let me use your card?"

He looked at me suspiciously.

"My card is full most of the time," he said.

"I see," I said and waited, posing my question silently.

"You're not trying to get me into trouble, are you, boy?" he asked, staring at me.

"Oh, no, sir."

"What book do you want?"

"A book by H. L. Mencken."

"Which one?"

"I don't know. Has he written more than one?"

"He has written several."

"I didn't know that."

"What makes you want to read Mencken?"

"Oh, I just saw his name in the newspaper," I said.

"It's good of you to want to read," he said. "But you ought to read the right things."

I said nothing. Would he want to supervise my reading?

"Let me think," he said. "I'll figure out something."

I turned from him and he called me back. He stared at me quizzically.

"Richard, don't mention this to the other white men," he said.

"I understand," I said. "I won't say a word."

A few days later he called me to him.

"I've got a card in my wife's name," he said. "Here's mine."

"Thank you, sir."

"Do you think you can manage it?"

"I'll manage fine," I said.

"If they suspect you, you'll get in trouble," he said.

"I'll write the same kind of notes to the library that you wrote when you sent me for books," I told him. "I'll sign your name."

He laughed.

"Go ahead. Let me see what you get," he said.

That afternoon I addressed myself to forging a note.

Now, what were the names of books written by H. L. Mencken? I did not know any of them. I finally wrote what I thought would be a foolproof note: *Dear Madam: Will you please let this nigger boy*—I used the word "nigger" to make the librarian feel that I could not possibly be the author of the note—*have some books by H. L. Mencken?* I forged the white man's name.

I entered the library as I had always done when on errands for whites, but I felt that I would somehow slip up and betray myself. I doffed my hat, stood a respectful distance from the desk, looked as unbookish as possible, and waited for the white patrons to be taken care of. When the desk was clear of people, I still waited. The white librarian looked at me.

"What do you want, boy?"

As though I did not possess the power of speech, I stepped forward and simply handed her the forged note, not parting my lips.

"What books by Mencken does he want?" she asked.

"I don't know, ma'am," I said, avoiding her eyes.

"Who gave you this card?"

"Mr. Falk," I said.

"Where is he?"

"He's at work, at the M—— Optical Company," I said. "I've been in here for him before."

"I remember," the woman said. "But he never wrote notes like this."

Oh, God, she's suspicious. Perhaps she would not let me have the books? If she had turned her back at that moment, I would have ducked out the door and never gone back. Then I thought of a bold idea.

"You can call him up, ma'am," I said, my heart pounding.

"You're not using these books, are you?" she asked pointedly.

"Oh, no, ma'am. I can't read."

"I don't know what he wants by Mencken," she said under her breath.

I knew now that I had won; she was thinking of

other things and the race question had gone out of her mind. She went to the shelves. Once or twice she looked over her shoulder at me, as though she was still doubtful. Finally she came forward with two books in her hand.

"I'm sending him two books," she said. "But tell Mr. Falk to come in next time, or send me the names of the books he wants. I don't know what he wants to read."

I said nothing. She stamped the card and handed me the books. Not daring to glance at them, I went out of the library, fearing that the woman would call me back for further questioning. A block away from the library I opened one of the books and read a title: *A Book of Prefaces.* I was nearing my nineteenth birthday and I did not know how to pronounce the word "preface." I thumbed the pages and saw strange words and strange names. I shook my head, disappointed. I looked at the other book; it was called *Prejudices.* I knew what that word meant; I had heard it all my life. And right off I was on guard against Mencken's books. Why would a man want to call a book *Prejudices*? The word was so stained with all my memories of racial hate that I could not conceive of anybody using it for a title. Perhaps I had made a mistake about Mencken? A man who had prejudices must be wrong.

When I showed the books to Mr. Falk, he looked at me and frowned.

"That librarian might telephone you," I warned him.

"That's all right," he said. "But when you're through reading those books, I want you to tell me what you get out of them."

That night in my rented room, while letting the hot water run over my can of pork and beans in the sink, I opened *A Book of Prefaces* and began to read. I was jarred and shocked by the style, the clear, clean, sweeping sentences. Why did he write like that? And how did one write like that? I pictured the man as a raging demon, slashing with his pen, consumed with

hate, denouncing everything American, extolling everything European or German, laughing at the weaknesses
of people, mocking God, authority. What was this?
I stood up, trying to realize what reality lay behind
the meaning of the words . . . Yes, this man was
fighting, fighting with words. He was using words as
a weapon, using them as one would use a club. Could
words be weapons? Well, yes, for here they were.
Then, maybe, perhaps, I could use them as a weapon?
No. It frightened me. I read on and what amazed
me was not what he said, but how on earth anybody
had the courage to say it.

Occasionally I glanced up to reassure myself that
I was alone in the room. Who were these men about
whom Mencken was talking so passionately? Who was
Anatole France? Joseph Conrad? Sinclair Lewis, Sher-
wood Anderson, Dostoevski, George Moore, Gustave
Flaubert, Maupassant, Tolstoy, Frank Harris, Mark
Twain, Thomas Hardy, Arnold Bennett, Stephen
Crane, Zola, Norris, Gorky, Bergson, Ibsen, Balzac,
Bernard Shaw, Dumas, Poe, Thomas Mann, O. Henry,
Dreiser, H. G. Wells, Gogol, T. S. Eliot, Gide,
Baudelaire, Edgar Lee Masters, Stendhal, Turgenev,
Huneker, Nietzsche, and scores of others? Were these
men real? Did they exist or had they existed? And
how did one pronounce their names?

I ran across many words whose meanings I did not
know, and I either looked them up in a dictionary
or, before I had a chance to do that, encountered
the word in a context that made its meaning clear.
But what strange world was this? I concluded the
book with the conviction that I had somehow over-
looked something terribly important in life. I had once
tried to write, had once reveled in feeling, had let my
crude imagination roam, but the impulse to dream had
been slowly beaten out of me by experience. Now it
surged up again and I hungered for books, new ways
of looking and seeing. It was not a matter of believing
or disbelieving what I read, but of feeling something

new, of being affected by something that made the look of the world different.

As dawn broke I ate my pork and beans, feeling dopey, sleepy. I went to work, but the mood of the book would not die; it lingered, coloring everything I saw, heard, did. I now felt that I knew what the white men were feeling. Merely because I had read a book that had spoken of how they lived and thought, I identified myself with that book. I felt vaguely guilty. Would I, filled with bookish notions, act in a manner that would make the whites dislike me?

I forged more notes and my trips to the library became frequent. Reading grew into a passion. My first serious novel was Sinclair Lewis's *Main Street*. It made me see my boss, Mr. Gerald, and identify him as an American type. I would smile when I saw him lugging his golf bags into the office. I had always felt a vast distance separating me from the boss, and now I felt closer to him, though still distant. I felt now that I knew him, that I could feel the very limits of his narrow life. And this had happened because I had read a novel about a mythical man called George F. Babbitt.

The plots and stories in the novels did not interest me so much as the point of view revealed. I gave myself over to each novel without reserve, without trying to criticize it; it was enough for me to see and feel something different. And for me, everything was something different. Reading was like a drug, a dope. The novels created moods in which I lived for days. But I could not conquer my sense of guilt, my feeling that the white men around me knew that I was changing, that I had begun to regard them differently.

Whenever I brought a book to the job, I wrapped it in newspaper—a habit that was to persist for years in other cities and under other circumstances. But some of the white men pried into my packages when I was absent and they questioned me.

"Boy, what are you reading those books for?"

"Oh, I don't know, sir."

"That's deep stuff you're reading, boy."

"I'm just killing time, sir."

"You'll addle your brains if you don't watch out."

I read Dreiser's *Jennie Gerhardt* and *Sister Carrie* and they revived in me a vivid sense of my mother's suffering; I was overwhelmed. I grew silent, wondering about the life around me. It would have been impossible for me to have told anyone what I derived from these novels, for it was nothing less than a sense of life itself. All my life had shaped me for the realism, the naturalism of the modern novel, and I could not read enough of them.

Steeped in new moods and ideas, I bought a ream of paper and tried to write; but nothing would come, or what did come was flat beyond telling. I discovered that more than desire and feeling were necessary to write and I dropped the idea. Yet I still wondered how it was possible to know people sufficiently to write about them? Could I ever learn about life and people? To me, with my vast ignorance, my Jim Crow station in life, it seemed a task impossible of achievement. I now knew what being a Negro meant. I could endure the hunger. I had learned to live with hate. But to feel that there were feelings denied me, that the very breath of life itself was byeond my reach, that more than anything else hurt, wounded me. I had a new hunger.

In buoying me up, reading also cast me down, made me see what was possible, what I had missed. My tension returned, new, terrible, bitter, surging, almost too great to be contained. I no longer *felt* that the world about me was hostile, killing; I *knew* it. A million times I asked myself what I could do to save myself, and there were no answers. I seemed forever condemned, ringed by walls.

I did not discuss my reading with Mr. Falk, who had lent me his library card; it would have meant talking about myself and that would have been too painful. I smiled each day, fighting desperately to maintain my old behavior, to keep my disposition seemingly sunny. But some of the white men discerned that I had begun to brood.

"Wake up there, boy!" Mr. Olin said one day.

"Sir!" I answered for the lack of a better word.

"You act like you've stolen something," he said.

I laughed in the way I knew he expected me to laugh, but I resolved to be more conscious of myself, to watch my every act, to guard and hide the new knowledge that was dawning within me.

If I went north, would it be possible for me to build a new life then? But how could a man build a life upon vague, unformed yearnings? I wanted to write and I did not even know the English language. I bought English grammars and found them dull. I felt that I was getting a better sense of the language from novels than from grammars. I read hard, discarding a writer as soon as I felt that I had grasped his point of view. At night the printed page stood before my eyes in sleep.

Mrs. Moss, my landlady, asked me one Sunday morning:

"Son, what is this you keep on reading?"

"Oh, nothing. Just novels."

"What you get out of 'em?"

"I'm just killing time," I said.

"I hope you know your own mind," she said in a tone which implied that she doubted if I had a mind.

I knew of no Negroes who read the books I liked and I wondered if any Negroes ever thought of them. I knew that there were Negro doctors, lawyers, newspapermen, but I never saw any of them. When I read a Negro newspaper I never caught the faintest echo of my preoccupation in its pages. I felt trapped and occasionally, for a few days, I would stop reading. But a vague hunger would come over me for books, books that opened up new avenues of feeling and seeing, and again I would forge another note to the white librarian. Again I would read and wonder as only the naïve and unlettered can read and wonder, feeling that I carried a secret, criminal burden about with me each day.

That winter my mother and brother came and we set up housekeeping, buying furniture on the installment plan, being cheated and yet knowing no way to avoid it. I began to eat warm food and to my surprise found that regular meals enabled me to read faster. I may have lived through many illnesses and survived them, never suspecting that I was ill. My brother obtained a job and we began to save toward the trip north, plotting our time, setting tentative dates for departure. I told none of the white men on the job that I was planning to go north; I knew that the moment they felt I was thinking of the North they would change toward me. It would have made them feel that I did not like the life I was living, and because my life was completely conditioned by what they said or did, it would have been tantamount to challenging them.

I could calculate my chances for life in the South as a Negro fairly clearly now.

I could fight the southern whites by organizing with other Negroes, as my grandfather had done. But I knew that I could never win that way; there were many whites and there were but few blacks. They were strong and we were weak. Outright black rebellion could never win. If I fought openly I would die and I did not want to die. News of lynchings were frequent.

I could submit and live the life of a genial slave, but that was impossible. All of my life had shaped me to live by my own feelings and thoughts. I could make up to Bess and marry her and inherit the house. But that, too, would be the life of a slave; if I did that, I would crush to death something within me, and I would hate myself as much as I knew the whites already hated those who had submitted. Neither could I ever willingly present myself to be kicked, as Shorty had done. I would rather have died than do that.

I could drain off my restlessness by fighting with Shorty and Harrison. I had seen many Negroes solve the problem of being black by transferring their hatred of themselves to others with a black skin and fighting them. I would have to be cold to do that, and I was not cold and I could never be.

I could, of course, forget what I had read, thrust the whites out of my mind, forget them; and find release from anxiety and longing in sex and alcohol. But the memory of how my father had conducted himself made that course repugnant. If I did not want others to violate my life, how could I voluntarily violate it myself?

I had no hope whatever of being a professional man. Not only had I been so conditioned that I did not desire it, but the fulfillment of such an ambition was beyond my capabilities. Well-to-do Negroes lived in a world that was almost as alien to me as the world inhabited by whites.

What, then, was there? I held my life in my mind, in my consciousness each day, feeling at times that I would stumble and drop it, spill it forever. My reading had created a vast sense of distance between me and the world in which I lived and tried to make a living, and that sense of distance was increasing each day. My days and nights were one long, quiet, continuously contained dream of terror, tension, and anxiety. I wondered how long I could bear it.

Chapter Fourteen

THE accidental visit of Aunt Maggie to Memphis formed a practical basis for my planning to go north. Aunt Maggie's husband, the "uncle" who had fled from Arkansas in the dead of night, had deserted her; and now she was casting about for a living. My mother, Aunt Maggie, my brother, and I held long conferences, speculating on the prospects of jobs and the cost of apartments in Chicago. And every time we conferred, we defeated ourselves. It was impossible for all four of us to go at once; we did not have enough money.

Finally sheer wish and hope prevailed over common sense and facts. We discovered that if we waited until we were prepared to go, we would never leave, we would never amass enough money to see us through. We would have to gamble. We finally decided that Aunt Maggie and I would go first, even though it was winter, and prepare a place for my mother and brother. Why wait until next week or next month? If we were going, why not go at once?

Next loomed the problem of leaving my job cleanly, smoothly, without arguments or scenes. How could I present the fact of leaving to my boss? Yes, I would pose as an innocent boy; I would tell him that my aunt was taking me and my paralyzed mother to Chicago. That would create in his mind the impression that I was not asserting my will; it would block any expression of dislike on his part for my act. I knew that southern whites hated the idea of Negroes leaving to live in places where the racial atmosphere was different.

It worked as I had planned. When I broke the news of my leaving two days before I left—I was afraid to tell it sooner for fear that I would create hostility on the part of the whites with whom I worked—the boss leaned back in his swivel chair and gave me the longest and most considerate look he had ever given me.

"Chicago?" he repeated softly.

"Yes, sir."

"Boy, you won't like it up there," he said.

"Well, I have to go where my family is, sir," I said.

The other white office workers paused in their tasks and listened. I grew self-conscious, tense.

"It's cold up there," he said.

"Yes, sir. They say it is," I said, keeping my voice in a neutral tone.

He became conscious that I was watching him and he looked away, laughing uneasily to cover his concern and dislike.

"Now, boy," he said banteringly, "don't you go up there and fall into that lake."

"Oh, no, sir," I said, smiling as though there existed the possibility of my falling accidentally into Lake Michigan.

He was serious again, staring at me. I looked at the floor.

"You think you'll do any better up there?" he asked.

"I don't know, sir."

"You seem to've been getting along all right down here," he said.

"Oh, yes, sir. If it wasn't for my mother's going, I'd stay right here and work," I lied as earnestly as possible.

"Well, why not stay? You can send her money," he suggested.

He had trapped me. I knew that staying now would never do. I could not have controlled my relations with the whites if I had remained after having told them that I wanted to go north.

"Well, I want to be with my mother," I said.

"You want to be with your mother," he repeated idly. "Well, Richard, we enjoyed having you with us."

"And I enjoyed working here," I lied.

There was silence; I stood awkwardly, then moved to the door. There was still silence; white faces were looking strangely at me. I went upstairs, feeling like a criminal. The word soon spread through the factory and the white men looked at me with new eyes. They came to me.

"So you're going north, hunh?"

"Yes, sir. My family's taking me with 'em."

"The North's no good for your people, boy."

"I'll try to get along, sir."

"Don't believe all the stories you hear about the North."

"No, sir. I don't."

"You'll come back here where your friends are."

"Well, sir. I don't know."

"How're you going to act up there?"

"Just like I act down here, sir."

"Would you speak to a white girl up there?"

"Oh, no, sir. I'll act there just like I act here."

"Aw, no, you won't. You'll change. Niggers change when they go north."

I wanted to tell him that I was going north precisely to change, but I did not.

"I'll be the same," I said, trying to indicate that I had no imagination whatever.

As I talked I felt that I was acting out a dream. I did not want to lie, yet I had to lie to conceal what I felt. A white censor was standing over me and, like dreams forming a curtain for the safety of sleep, so did my lies form a screen of safety for my living moments.

"Boy, I bet you've been reading too many of them damn books."

"Oh, no, sir."

I made my last errand to the post office, put my bag away, washed my hands, and pulled on my cap. I shot a quick glance about the factory; most of the men were working late. One or two looked up. Mr. Falk, to whom I had returned my library card, gave me a quick, secret smile. I walked to the elevator and rode down with Shorty.

"You lucky bastard," he said bitterly.

"Why do you say that?"

"You saved your goddamn money and now you're gone."

"My problems are just starting," I said.

"You'll never have any problems as hard as the ones you had here," he said.

"I hope not," I said. "But life is tricky."

"Sometimes I get so goddamn mad I want to kill everybody," he spat in a rage.

"You can leave," I said.

"I'll never leave this goddamn South," he railed. "I'm always saying I am, but I won't . . . I'm lazy. I like to sleep too goddamn much. I'll die here. Or maybe they'll kill me."

I stepped from the elevator into the street, half expecting someone to call me back and tell me that it was all a dream, that I was not leaving.

This was the culture from which I sprang. This was the terror from which I fled.

The next day when I was already in full flight— aboard a northward bound train—I could not have accounted, if it had been demanded of me, for all the varied forces that were making me reject the culture that had molded and shaped me. I was leaving without a qualm, without a single backward glance. The face of the South that I had known was hostile and forbidding, and yet out of all the conflicts and the curses, the blows and the anger, the tension and the terror, I had somehow gotten the idea that life could be different, could be lived in a fuller and richer manner. As had happened when I had fled the orphan home, I was now running more away from something than toward something. But that did not matter to me. My mood was: I've got to get away; I can't stay here.

But what was it that always made me feel that way? What was it that made me conscious of possibilities? From where in this southern darkness had I caught a sense of freedom? Why was it that I was able to act upon vaguely felt notions? What was it that made me feel things deeply enough for me to try to order my life by my feelings? The external world of whites and blacks, which was the only world that I had ever known, surely had not evoked in me any belief in myself. The people I had met had advised and demanded submission. What, then, was I after? How dare I consider my feelings superior to the gross environment that sought to claim me?

It had been only through books—at best, no more than vicarious cultural transfusions—that I had managed to keep myself alive in a negatively vital way. Whenever my environment had failed to support or nourish me, I had clutched at books; consequently, my belief in books had risen more out of a sense of desperation than from any abiding conviction of their ultimate value. In a peculiar sense, life had trapped me in a realm of emotional rejection; I had not embraced insurgency through open choice. Existing emotionally on the sheer, thin margin of southern culture, I had felt that nothing short of life itself hung upon each of my actions and decisions; and I had grown used to change, to movement, to making many adjustments.

In the main, my hope was merely a kind of self-defence, a conviction that if I did not leave I would perish, either because of possible violence of others against me, or because of my possible violence against them. The substance of my hope was formless and devoid of any real sense of direction, for in my southern living I had seen no looming landmark by which I could, in a positive sense, guide my daily actions. The shocks of southern living had rendered my personality tender and swollen, tense and volatile, and my flight was more a shunning of external and internal dangers than an attempt to embrace what I felt I wanted.

It had been my accidental reading of fiction and literary criticism that had evoked in me vague glimpses of life's possibilities. Of course, I had never seen or met the men who wrote the books I read, and the kind of world in which they lived was as alien to me as the moon. But what enabled me to overcome my chronic distrust was that these books—written by men like Dreiser, Masters, Mencken, Anderson, and Lewis —seemed defensively critical of the straitened American environment. These writers seemed to feel that America could be shaped nearer to the hearts of those who lived in it. And it was out of these novels and stories and articles, out of the emotional impact of imaginative constructions of heroic or tragic deeds, that I felt touching my face a tinge of warmth from an unseen light; and in my leaving I was groping toward that invisible light, always trying to keep my face so set and turned that I would not lose the hope of its faint promise, using it as my justification for action.

The white South said that it knew "niggers," and I was what the white South called a "nigger." Well, the white South had never known me—never known what I thought, what I felt. The white South said that I had a "place" in life. Well, I had never felt my "place"; or, rather, my deepest instincts had always made me reject the "place" to which the white South had assigned me. It had never occurred to me that I was in any way an inferior being. And no word that I had ever heard fall from the lips of southern white men had ever made me really doubt the worth of my own humanity. True, I had lied. I had stolen. I had struggled to contain my seething anger. I had fought. And it was perhaps a mere accident that I had never killed . . . But in what other ways had the South allowed me to be natural, to be real, to be myself, except in rejection, rebellion, and aggression?

Not only had the southern whites not known me, but, more important still, as I had lived in the South I had not had the chance to learn who I was. The pressure of southern living kept me from being the kind of person that I might have been. I had been what my surroundings had demanded, what my family—conforming to the dictates of the whites above them—had exacted of me, and what the whites had said that I must be. Never being fully able to be myself, I had slowly learned that the South could recognize but a part of a man, could accept but a fragment of his personality, and all the rest—the best and deepest things of heart and mind—were tossed away in blind ignorance and hate.

I was leaving the South to fling myself into the unknown, to meet other situations that would perhaps elicit from me other responses. And if I could meet enough of a different life, then, perhaps, gradually and slowly I might learn who I was, what I might be. I was not leaving the South to forget the South, but so that some day I might understand it, might come to know what its rigors had done to me, to its children. I fled so that the numbness of my defensive living might thaw out and let me feel the pain—years later and far away—of what living in the South had meant.

Yet, deep down, I knew that I could never really leave the South, for my feelings had already been formed by the South, for there had been slowly instilled into my personality and consciousness, black though I was, the culture of the South. So, in leaving, I was taking a part of the South to transplant in alien soil, to see if it could grow differently, if it could drink of new and cool rains, bend in strange winds, respond to the warmth of other suns, and, perhaps, to bloom . . . And if that miracle ever happened, then I would know that there was yet hope in that southern swamp of despair and violence, that light could emerge even out of the blackest of the southern night. I would know that the South too could overcome its fear, its hate, its cowardice, its heritage of guilt and blood, its burden of anxiety and compulsive cruelty.

With ever watchful eyes and bearing scars, visible and invisible, I headed North, full of a hazy notion that life could be lived with dignity, that the personalities of others should not be violated, that men should be able to confront other men without fear or shame, and that if men were lucky in their living on earth they might win some redeeming meaning for their having struggled and suffered here beneath the stars.

AFTERWORD

A CHILDHOOD fraught with humiliation and beating; a home devoid of understanding or affection: such was Richard Wright's preparation for existence in a white man's world. With physical threats and psychological assault, Richard's parents, grandparents, uncles, and aunts created a bleak and authoritarian environment. And when he refused to fall into this miserable mould, they cut him off, isolated him. What was the purpose of such treatment? What forced these adults to bring up a child in such a manner?

They were educating their child for a world which would recognize him only as a *black boy*, a world which could murder a Negro businessman, as Uncle Hoskins was murdered, simply for being successful, and which could run a boy off a job, as would happen to Richard himself, merely for wanting to learn a trade.

In the method of this Southern Negro education we see the awful degradation of the Afro-American experience. Given the Jim Crow way of life, Negroes must, in order to acculturate themselves, deny their own honesty and passion and brutalize their children. In order to live in a society built on the white man's belief that they are less than human, Negroes must behave inhumanly.

But if *Black Boy* is the story of the Negro folk system of education, it is the story of its failure. Richard Wright could not learn his role. Nor could he learn to be secure in the traditional consolation of the oppressed— the hope of a better world hereafter. *Black Boy* is the story of self-education achieved in rebellion against the conventions of Negro society.

Richard's knowledge began in intuition. After his uncle's murder, his mother and aunt returned to their mother's house to make a new plan of life, for they were without spiritual or financial resources. When Richard asked for explanations he was given a silencing slap; and he began to feel the extent to which their lives were ruled by white terror. His mother's paralysis became a symbol of the troubles he saw and experienced as a boy. His mother's pain and helplessness and the family's poverty and futility in the face of illness embodied a fateful significance for twelve-year-old Richard Wright. They convinced him that the meaning of living is to be *found* in meaningless suffering, not that living *is* meaningless suffering, as those around him believed.

As intuition developed and ripened into resolution, Wright saw his entire culture acting to discourage him from understanding. The schools gave him no knowledge about Negroes, and his classmates laughed off his efforts to get "the whole picture" of their lives. Only a deadening of his consciousness of reality would make him acceptable within a racist society. In recoiling from this possibility, Richard Wright discovered the complex relationship between individuals and their social context. From his earliest years he had felt a strange lack of warmth and tenderness in the life of his home. As he grew older he saw that the emotional lives of other Negroes also consisted of feelings of fear, insecurity, and self-deprecation. Too often there was a void where joy might have been. His intellectual majority was reached when he understood that the personality of man is the meetingplace of society and the individual and realized that his personal troubles—all that the symbol of his mother's paralysis represented—derived largely from social experience. It was perfectly obvious that his membership in the Negro race prevented the individual Richard Wright from using the public library; and it became equally clear to him that the derisive laughter of his schoolmates at his questions about the Negro condition and his uncle's craven advice about his valedictory speech were examples of behavior conditioned by social oppression.

It is precisely Wright's insight into the dynamics of man in society that is his strength as a writer. *Black Boy*, recording the growth and development of this insight, is thus the story of a writer's education. Realistic fiction functions by creating characters who are simultaneously individuals seeking autonomy and representatives of a society larger than themselves. This is the way in which Wright came to see his own experience; literature authenticated this experience and became the outlet for it. Though *Black Boy* ends as the author heads North in defense of the right to his own mind, it is already obvious that his resistance to the effort made to mould him has been the means of his education.

JOHN REILLY
State University of New York at Albany